THE JAZZ BARN

THE JAZZ BARN

Music Inn, the Berkshires, and the Place of Jazz in American Life

JOHN GENNARI

Brandeis University Press
Waltham, Massachusetts

Brandeis University Press
© 2025 by John Gennari
All rights reserved

Manufactured in the United States of America
Book design by Endpaper Studio
Typeset in Dante Pro and Resolve Sans

For permission to reproduce any of the material in this book, contact
Brandeis University Press, 415 South Street, Waltham MA 02453, or visit
brandeisuniversitypress.com

Library of Congress Cataloging-in-publishing Data available at
https://catalog.loc.gov/
LCCN 2025019260 (print)
cloth ISBN 978-1-68458-285-3
e-book ISBN 978-1-68458-286-0

5 4 3 2 1

For my beloved siblings Joan and James and all our Lenox friends. And for the Hurleys: my mentor and soulmate Jim, his wife and my Lambada partner Gerry, and their children, my dear friends Alexis, Brendan, and Drew.

CONTENTS

FOREWORD

The Brubeck family lived in Oakland, California, but my father's touring schedule meant spending months of every year on the East Coast, especially after George Wein successfully inaugurated the Newport Jazz Festival in 1954. Dave Brubeck first played at the Music Inn in Lenox, Massachusetts, (and at Newport) in 1955. It became a regular stop and a summer base for the whole family in 1959 and 1960. Dave and Iola moved into the Ice House with five kids, me aged twelve or thirteen (my birthday is in June), Mike, ten, Chris, seven, Cathy, six, and Dan, four. Imagining what this must have been like for our mother makes me pause in wonder and gratitude. I'm now grateful that John Gennari addresses not just "gender and jazz" in relation to performers but also recognizes the role of specific women, such as Iola Brubeck, Nellie Monk, Stephanie Barber, and others who were not just helpmates but true partners, indispensable in furthering their husbands' careers.

The Music Inn experience was indeed influential. It was where crucial developments in modern jazz took place. What's more, it repositioned that music in American culture. Of course, as a preteen, I didn't understand the future impact of what I heard and saw, but looking back from the twenty-first century, the academic discourse, canon formation, and "permanent diversity" we have long taken for granted fall into place. I mean that literally.

John Gennari grew up in Lenox and is comfortable writing about its history and the Berkshire scene—relating it to broader themes, particularly race and music. His main subject is how and why a liberal artistic and intellectual culture flourished when Phil and Stephanie Barber established a school of jazz at the Music Inn. He deploys an array of disciplinary lenses through which music, archival photos, and tropes about jazz and blackness are examined. He raises the "moldy fig" question of whether studying jazz ruins it and recounts the quest for "legitimacy," recalling long-ago local history, even the abolitionist movements of the 1850s.

Lenox, including the surrounding Berkshire region, is still a cultural resort area, principally because of the 1937 bequest of the Tanglewood estate to the Boston Symphony for use as a summer home. The Boston Symphony Orchestra and the Boston Pops have presented outdoor concerts annually—except during World War II—and, over time, have created performance spaces, developed educational programs, and commissioned composers. The Music Inn itself was created from former service buildings belonging to an old estate in walking distance of Tanglewood. Bill Smith, my father's intermittent colleague from student days under Darius Milhaud, was literally camping in the woods when they collaborated on *Brubeck à la Mode*. The album's cover shot was taken in a local ice-cream parlor. I remember walking to Tanglewood with my Uncle Howard, who had earlier worked there as Leonard Bernstein's assistant. Their connection led to recording *Dialogues for Jazz Combo and Orchestra*, with a score by Howard, on *Brubeck Plays Bernstein Plays Brubeck*.

Percy Heath III ("Little Percy" to us) and Edwin Schuller were part of our small gang of children who had the run of the place. It was so safe. The Ice House was on two levels: an upper ground level that held the main entrance, a living room, and master bedroom, and a lower ground level that led into a wing of converted stables and directly onto the stage. The kids were all downstairs in bunk beds, with a hall serving as a little common area. Concerts, literally next door, were our main source of entertainment, or at least distraction.

In his unpublished autobiography, Dave recalls:

> One night the younger children had gone to bed a bit earlier than usual. It was a warm night, so only the screen door separated their quarters from backstage. They were sound asleep when Stan Kenton's band hit the stand and the brass section opened up on their first number. Six-year-old Cathy, clad in her long white nightgown, marched out the screen door and stood at the side of the stage, hands on hips, glaring at the trumpet section perched high on the risers. She yelled up to them, "How do you expect a guy to get any sleep around here?" No one in the brass section could keep a straight face.

Ornette Coleman had a room further along the stable wing. We used to giggle quietly on our side of the thin wall when he practiced. I had been playing trumpet for a couple of years, and Mike had just started saxophone lessons. For me, practice meant starting with long tones, carefully going through some warm-up exercises, then reading through short, simple pieces designed to gradually improve range and articulation. Ornette's practice routine was pop the latches on the case, take out the horn (a plastic alto sax), and play anything (*anything!*), up and down, fast and slow, out of tune; pause, squeal a little more, then put the horn away. This is how it seemed to us. Yet, in performance his music was profoundly solemn and organized.

The 1950s has been characterized as an ultraconservative decade but also, as Gennari proposes, as a Second American Renaissance. Perhaps it depends on which part you remember: The jazz, the literature, the art? Or Jim Crow segregation and restrictive social and sartorial codes? Lenox became a country retreat of choice for

Black middle-class musicians and literary figures who mixed with like-minded whites in big cities. They had much in common: a commitment to civil rights, resistance to right-wing McCarthyism, and enthusiasm for all-encompassing modernism.

Folk music was already regularly performed and studied at the Inn, and jazz came a little later. A nexus like this had never existed before, but it was consistent with the spirit of the place. I had the supremely good fortune of being there *at this time*, and this is why I personally appreciate Gennari's fascinating and uplifting study. (John was only born in 1960). I was allowed to attend Marshall Stearns's classes, where I heard Alan Lomax's Library of Congress recordings of Jelly Roll Morton for the first time and where I learned why "blue notes" don't exist on the piano keyboard.

Most of my adult career has been in jazz education. Musicians formerly associated with Lenox were of inestimable assistance when I started the first university degree program in jazz studies in South Africa. Larry Ridley came as a Fulbright professor; Jamey Aebersold gave us his whole set of play-alongs; Billy Taylor put my premiere student ensemble, The Jazzanians, on national TV in America; and David Baker welcomed the first jazz pedagogy master's degree student from South Africa to Indiana University. The School of Jazz created by the Barbers, Gunther Schuller, and John Lewis only lasted four years, but as my father also wrote:

> This fledgling school was a forerunner of what would later develop into jazz education programs and artist residencies in universities and conservatories across the country. The amazing musicians who were instructors were all consummate artists who were pushing the boundaries and shaping the future of jazz. The concepts being taught and discussed may seem obvious in retrospect, but at that time were considered innovative and contentious. It was an exciting time to be immersed in jazz.

The last time I was in Lenox was in August 2003 for an Evening at the Pops concert at Tanglewood, which featured violinists Regina Carter, Eileen Ivers, and Lara St. John as soloists in my brother Chris's "Interplay for Three Violins and Orchestra." The name Regina Carter is well known to jazz fans, Eileen Ivers is a renowned master in the Irish fiddle tradition, and Lara St. John is an internationally admired classical soloist. The Music Inn buildings had long since been converted into a condo complex, so the Brubeck party stayed at the Red Lion Inn in Stockbridge. We felt we had to visit the old site, somewhat like visiting a famous monument. Chris's syncretic piece conveyed the old Lenox spirit that I carried with me to South Africa and back again.

John Gennari's book encourages us to see the former jazz barn not as a relic of the past but as the source of so much we consider normal today. It is often said that places like Carnegie Hall or the Village Vanguard somehow hold the vibrations of the music performed there. Conversely, Gennari reminds us that "a musical performance is imbued with the history of the place where it happens." I'm delighted and enriched by his restorative and significant book.

Darius Brubeck, May 2025
Honorary Professor, School of Music and former Director, The Centre
 for Jazz and Popular Music
University of KwaZulu-Natal
Durban, South Africa

INTRODUCTION:
JAZZ ON THE HILLSIDE

"It's a long trip from dingy backroom dives in New Orleans to a sun-bathed, verdant hillside in the Berkshire Mountains of Massachusetts, but jazz has made the journey," wrote *New York Times* jazz critic John S. Wilson. "What has developed in the hills of western Massachusetts is a unique seedbed for jazz," he continued, "basically related to the seedbed function that New Orleans once performed but in other respects totally different."[1] In these opening sentences of his liner notes for the 1956 Atlantic LP *The Modern Jazz Quartet at Music Inn*, Wilson employed a trope common to jazz commentary in the 1950s, a period when critics, journalists, film and television writers, advertisers, and others were keen to emphasize the music's surging social respectability and its strengthening affiliation with the mainstream of American life. At a time when tabloids and Hollywood movies continued to link jazz with social deviance and drug use, jazz was somehow also now a de rigueur object of the middle-class living room, certified by *Good Housekeeping* as an emblem of

Left to right: John Lewis, Connie Kay, Jimmy Giuffre, Percy Heath, and Milt Jackson (squatting), at Music Inn, 1956. The album-cover photograph (which was in color) was taken by Jay Maisel for the Atlantic LP cover *Modern Jazz Quartet at Music Inn*. © Jay Maisel. Reproduction by Hilary Neroni.

midcult connoisseurship in the form of high-end audio equipment and long-playing 33 RPM albums adorned with handsome front-cover art and erudite back-cover notes. Jazz was now firmly ensconced in John Foster Dulles's State Department, where, *Variety* quipped, "the hipsters have been given striped pants and sent overseas as ambassadors of good will"—a reference to jazz concert tours deployed by the United States Information Agency as a tool of cultural diplomacy in Cold War hot spots across the globe.[2] And jazz was now on a "verdant hillside in the Berkshire Mountains," as confirmed by the front cover of this Modern Jazz Quartet album, a photograph of the MJQ's four African American bandmembers and their Italian American guest artist, Jimmy Giuffre, casually assembled in a sun-dappled meadow in Lenox.

In mapping jazz's move from roguish New Orleans to an idyllic pastoral setting in genteel New England, Wilson slid into a discursive groove common to the period, one in which jazz is magically cleansed of its affiliations with bohemian and criminal subcultures and becomes ready and eager to serve as an evangelical force of racial harmony and bourgeois normalcy. By the late 1950s, *Good Housekeeping* was pleased to give its seal of approval to a new generation of sober, well-adjusted jazz musicians, a reprieve from the social deviants of yesteryear, "murky characters with short beards and berets on their heads, or hopped up fellows who sleep all day and crawl forth at 4:00 A.M."[3] *Esquire*, meanwhile, was enthused to discover a new and bracing jazz audience—not the "ten dozen stubborn record collectors . . . mumbling matrix numbers over their drinks" of the dark past but a healthy and diverse swathe of the public represented by such figures as "a poet in San Francisco, a farm hand in Iowa, an ad man on Madison Avenue, a hipster in Detroit, a student in New Hampshire" and "the vast multitude in twenty other countries that finds most clearly in jazz evidence of the American Dream."[4] In *Variety*, *Good Housekeeping*, and *Esquire*—a small sample culled from an extensive body of commentary in music trade publications, news-papers, and general-interest magazines—jazz heralded a bright new day in which farmers in the American heartland and elite knowledge workers on the coasts could find common ground.

What united these soundings of the jazz zeitgeist was a sense that the music, its people, and its social vibrations were strongly related to *place* and *movement*; it was an art form whose progress could be measured by its spatial and cultural geographies. A tacit assumption of the period—one still very much in force more than half a century later—was that movement from Black places and spaces to white ones triggered an increase in social respectability and cultural value.[5] Never mind that the African American middle class, in working as-siduously to counteract racist presuppositions about innate Black inferiority and incivility, had made a fetish of cultural uplift, respect-ability, and dignity—or that Fletcher Henderson, Duke Ellington, Mary Lou Williams, and other African American jazz musicians had cultivated public images as paragons of civility, respectability, and dignity, while many white jazz musicians and their fans were drawn to the music as a form of rebellion against middle-class expectations of rectitude and sobriety. The issue here was the structure of the social order, the deeply embedded hierarchies of class and race that naturalize our thinking about where people belong.

For John Wilson jazz had completed a "long trip" from the sweaty dance floors and hot rhythms of early jazz to the cool, serene cham-ber music of the Modern Jazz Quartet, a "journey" from the urban vice district to the wholesome countryside, from the late night writh-ing of the urban lower class to the physically rejuvenating, intellec-tually stimulating vibe of cultivated middle-class leisure in the sunny Berkshires, dubbed by marketers as "America's premier cultural re-sort."[6] Jazz had found a new place, and this required a reworking of the cultural algorithm. To use language that gained currency in the 1950s and has retained its cultural salience ever since, jazz had moved into the *mainstream*, a term connoting the virtual space controlled by the dominant social group, the space to which minoritized groups must cross over if they are to be recognized as truly representative of the national culture.

"Jazz," observes musicologist Andrew Berish, has given us "new ways to make sense of the changing spaces and places of American life."[7] This seemingly simple formulation cracks open important avenues of inquiry. Locations where jazz is played and listened to—the physical spaces in which sound resonates from instruments and voices and enters the bodies of listeners—indelibly shape the contours of the music, what the music communicates, and what feelings and memories become associated with it. At the micro level, this registers in matters of size, spatial design, material texture, acoustics, and ambience in the differences between a recording studio, a small bandstand next to a bar, a city block–sized dance hall, a coffee house, a concert hall. At the macro level, it concerns the meanings attached to certain places owing to their histories, social arrangements, and symbolic resonances—the difference between jazz performances in a Harlem or a South Side of Chicago nightclub, say, or at an Ivy League college, a roller rink, a loft space in a deindustrialized city, the veranda of a well-manicured private mansion. The birth and development of jazz coincided with the advent of recording technologies and modes of electronic transmission that seemingly unmoored the music from its sites of production and its commodification and distribution across boundaries of neighborhood, region, and nation. Nevertheless, tracking how jazz has circulated through localized spaces and larger cultural geographies as live performance in real time tells us a great deal not just about how music functions socially but also how society functions musically.

What did it mean for ragtime and early jazz pianist Eubie Blake to conduct a lecture-demonstration in an estate carriage house in the Berkshires? For vocalists Mahalia Jackson, Anita O'Day, and Billie Holiday to sing from the stage of an indoor-outdoor concert venue fashioned from a former hay barn? For fellow musicians to listen to those singers in that setting? For Dizzy Gillespie to conduct jazz harmony classes on the lawn outside of that barn? For Jimmy Giuffre, a swing-band veteran then crafting a new style of improvisational chamber jazz, to jam with his student Ornette Coleman, herald of the free jazz avant-garde, in a makeshift nightclub remodeled from what had been a greenhouse? For Berkshire locals and out-of-town vacationers to see and hear Louis Armstrong, Duke Ellington, and Thelonious Monk after driving backcountry roads, leaving their cars in a makeshift grass parking lot, and walking a tree-lined path up to the concert site?

Only rarely can historical sources help us satisfyingly capture the full multisensorial dimensions of such richly textured experiences. But simply to ask these questions is to intensify our thinking about music as an affective, physiological, social, and interpersonal experience. "If hearing is a major component of our sense of emplacement in the world," Berish reasons, "then music, a particular, culturally determined manifestation of sound, must also contribute to a sense of place, a feeling in the listener of being meaningfully located."[8] In this sense, music "sensuously produces place." And place—physical location combined with the psychologically potent meanings imaginatively attached to it—produces music.

Second American Renaissance

This is a book about what happened in the 1950s in a barn, icehouse, and greenhouse and in the rolling meadows, winding wooded paths, and rocky brook edges of an estate property overlooking a lake in the verdant Berkshire Hills of western Massachusetts. What happened in this place unsettled conventional assumptions about the relationship between culture and landscape, art and geography, town and city, race and place. What happened there, against all odds, was a set of developments crucial to the history of jazz.

Dizzy Gillespie and student on Music Inn lawn, 1957. Photograph by Warren Fowler.

In 1950 a recently married couple, he from a theater background, she a former fashion journalist, now colleagues in a Manhattan public relations firm, opened Music Inn, a lodging establishment and cultural salon in Lenox, on the border with Stockbridge, just down the road from Tanglewood, home of the nation's premier summer classical music festival. With the encouragement of their friends Alan Lomax, Pete Seeger, Langston Hughes, and Marshall Stearns, the couple, Philip and Stephanie Barber, fashioned their inn as a center for the study and performance of various kinds of folk music, blues, and jazz. Each of these friends had been victimized by the era's anti-communist hysteria, and Philip Barber himself saw his theater career thwarted in the 1930s by the House Un-American Activities Committee. Stearns, an English professor whose antiracist activism cost him a teaching job at a midwestern state university, was fast emerging as jazz's leading public intellectual. Over the next several years, a series of summer seminars he organized at Music Inn—Jazz Roundtables, he called them—with musicians, scholars, artists, and writers became pivotal to public understanding of the music's African roots, its folk properties, and its place in American life and culture. Later in the decade, the Barbers, Stearns, Modern Jazz Quartet pianist and composer John Lewis, and others collaborated in the founding of the Lenox School of Jazz, a first-of-its-kind effort, in which the idiom's leading figures (Dizzy Gillespie, Max Roach, Oscar Peterson, Kenny Dorham, Bill Evans, George Russell, among others) served as faculty-in-residence.

In 1955 the Barbers converted the carriage house and hay barn into a concert space with seating for hundreds extending to an outdoor courtyard. Over the next five years, the Music Barn, widely recognized for its rustic facade and distinctive roof-top weathervane, became a major site for live jazz and folk music. This was a period when jazz musicians hungered for opportunities to perform in situations other than exhausting and distraction-laden four-set-a-night nightclub gigs, while major folk musicians were happy for the chance to perform publicly *at all* after being blacklisted and losing their contracts with major media companies and booking agencies. Barn concerts by Louis Armstrong, Duke Ellington, Odetta, Billie Holiday, Count Basie, Gillespie, Roach and Clifford Brown, Sonny Terry and Brownie McGhee, Stan Getz, Sarah Vaughan, the Weavers, the Kingston Trio, Ahmad Jamal, and others attracted enthusiastic notice in the national press. Lenox, a town with several thousand residents, a handful of stop signs, and one fire truck, was now not only the summer home of the Boston Symphony Orchestra but also a wellspring of American vernacular music.

What happened at Music Inn in the 1950s was a remarkable confluence of place, people, and politics that reflected and augured seismic shifts and conflicts in American culture. Over the course of two generations, a Gilded Age estate born of excessive wealth and Euro-aristocratic pretense, set in a small-town pastoral landscape strongly linked to transformative developments in American literature, had morphed into a space for jazz and folk music performance, debate, and education informed by a movement for racial equality that had been branded as un-American by powerful actors in the federal government. Under the stewardship of its savvy, charismatic, and industrious owners, a space of summer leisure tied to a growing postwar middle-class tourist economy blossomed from roots planted in the radical politics and cultural expression of the Depression and war years.

Music Inn became one of the places to be for artists and others keen to cross artistic, cultural, and social boundaries. Leonard Bernstein came, plucked love songs on guitar for his newlywed, actor Felicia Montealegre; sat in on the jazz roundtables; and chatted up the panelists during cocktail hour. Gospel queen Mahalia Jackson came from the South Side of Chicago, sang magnificently, and argued with some of the country's leading musicologists about her technique. Jacob Lawrence came and painted a watercolor sketch of the Music Barn for the Barbers' art collection. Pugilist Archie Moore came from nearby North Adams, where he was training for an upcoming fight with Rocky Marciano; sat in on double bass; and held his own on a medium-tempo blues. Nigerian drummer Babatunde Olatunji came and jammed with Italian American jazz reedman Tony Scott. Pianist Mary Lou Williams came and played an impromptu set of stunning duets in the inn's front lounge with singer Anita O'Day, who later jammed with a student trombonist and one of the inn's restaurant

Philip and Stephanie Barber attending a Marshall Stearns jazz roundtable, 1951.
Photograph by Clemens Kalischer.

Singer Anita O'Day with Potting Shed chef "Cookie" on trumpet and School of Jazz student Paul Duynhower on trombone, 1958. Photograph by Clemens Kalischer.

cooks, who was wearing a chef's toque while blowing muted trumpet. Trinidadian dancer Geoffrey Holder came, thrilled his audience, and liked the place so much he arranged for his wedding to Carmen de Lavallade to take place in the Berkshires. The Modern Jazz Quartet came six summers in a row to fine-tune their sound, record LPs, and head up the jazz school's faculty. Ornette Coleman and Don Cherry came as students and blew people's minds.

In a postwar America that projected unprecedented military, diplomatic, and ideological power on the world stage, there was a sense that the quality of the country's arts and literature—and support for them on the part of regular citizens, cultural elites, universities, philanthropies, and even corporations—were matters of national concern as never before. Jazz critics and sympathetic commentators sought to leverage the cultural nationalist politics of the moment. They complained that jazz was underappreciated but then usually complained even more about the attention it received outside of their own efforts. What most of them really wanted, both for the music and for themselves, was *legitimacy*. This was a keyword of the era, signifying a kind of sanctification or canonization bestowed only by the custodians—the secular priests, as it were—of high culture and confirmed by the attention of people with unimpeachable social prestige. The people who ran, performed at, and patronized Tanglewood could not have fit this bill any more perfectly. When these people took interest in Music Inn, not as a passing curiosity or fascination but as a deep and sincere desire to be part of the enterprise—as when composer Henry Cowell wrote a symphony influenced by Afro-Caribbean music he'd heard as an invited roundtable panelist or when the Boston Symphony Orchestra's percussion section featured jazz drummer Max Roach as a soloist—the payoff to jazz's cultural capital was enormous. The very fact that Lenox and the surrounding Berkshire environs had no organic connection to the multiracial, urban, vernacular cultures that spawned and nourished jazz—that instead it was associated with *Moby-Dick*, Beethoven, modern dance and theater, and art museums—gave the place more power as a symbol of jazz's quest for prestige and normalcy and its transformation into a symbol of tasteful living.[9]

The careful reader will have noticed in the foregoing paragraphs a furtive slide away from folk music, a sleight-of-hand in which an enterprise that started with Alan Lomax and Pete Seeger as frontline figures shifted focus to become a story about jazz and, seemingly, only jazz. A similar trajectory characterized Music Inn itself, at least as indexed by the roster of performances the Barbers staged through the years. Folk musicians would continue to perform at Music Inn, and the inn occupied a high-profile place on the map of the folk movement, a surging phenomenon in 1950s and early 1960s American culture. More important, the *idea* of a folk ethic and community saturated Music Inn's framing of jazz, starting when Stearns's round-tables privileged folklore as a field and a method for studying the music. Later in the decade, as modern jazz became more dominant in the inn's performance schedule as well as its educational mission, there would be a drift toward high-culture ideology—not just in the Tanglewood connection but in the emergence of an autonomous jazz avant-garde represented by Jimmy Giuffre, George Russell, Gunther Schuller, Ornette Coleman, Don Cherry, and several others. But even this emergent formation was imbued with the values and sensibilities of folk culture. This owed to the location, the physical and semiotic characteristics, and the community ethic and social interactivity of Music Inn itself—Music Inn as an authentic *place*.

Folklore had thrived as an amateur activity since the nation's founding, became an organized professional academic field in the late nineteenth century, and got a big boost in the 1930s when the Depression sparked a left-wing response that coupled sympathy for the working class with an investment in the notion of "the people" and a corresponding valorization of the simple, unadorned, uncommercialized aspects of American life. Professionals and amateurs alike combed the country in search of vernacular music, dance, storytelling, and material culture (tools, musical instruments, books, houses, furniture, clothing, toys, decorative arts) that enlarged public understanding of everyday, ground-level culture. Handcrafted, homespun, rustic, natural—these were powerful synonyms for *authenticity*, a concept that became sanctified in the postwar period, when suburbanization, prefabricated houses, automobile culture, processed food, plastics, and the like seemed to foretell an increasingly synthetic future. Everything about Music Inn—its pastoral surroundings and rustic wood and stone buildings, its intimate social relations and do-it-yourself artisanal vibe, its concerts held in a barn—aligned it with a folk ethic of simplicity, honesty, and face-to-face human encounter.

Louis Armstrong performing in the Music Barn, 1956. Photograph by Warren Fowler.

This ethic is racially neutral, but, as in our own time, a tendency to fetishize the natural and to express urgent concern about the despoiling of nature by the forces of industrial (or postindustrial) modernization tends to be primarily associated with the white middle and upper classes. People from other classes and races are more likely to be dependent on jobs created by the very technologies and business practices that offend the aesthetic sensibilities of comfortably situated whites. And, especially for African Americans, nostalgia for the arcadian and the premodern can feel very much like nostalgia for the racial order of the past. Music Inn in the 1950s was fascinating in the ways it sorted through these complexities.

There, as elsewhere, the concept of "the folk" came with an assumption that the people who occupied that category were themselves more natural and more in touch with their bodies and primal urges. The folk were people who remained healthily attuned to what was elemental, uncorrupted by civilization, and untouched by the anxieties and neuroses engendered by modernity. Pete Seeger was a famous folk singer and had an attractively folksy persona, but he was not one of "the folk." Odetta, Brownie McGhee, John Lee Hooker, Josh White, Mahalia Jackson, and Geoffrey Holder were not necessarily folk artists, but they were presumed to be performing authentic Black folk culture as well as to *be* real, flesh-and-blood Black folk, with all that that implied. When Black modern jazz musicians came to Music Inn, they embraced its pastoral and rustic qualities as a

Trinidadian dancer Geoffrey Holder on Music Inn stage, 1959. Photograph by Clemens Kalischer.

healthy respite from the city. And they enjoyed convening with Black musicians working in folk, blues, and other vernacular genres. But theirs was an art of urban modernism—the Western world's most significant such art. Through their music, their self-presentation, and in some cases their politics, they were trying to transform American culture and society and leave the old order—its sensibilities and especially its racial arrangements—far behind. They helped ensure that Music Inn's folk ethic was forward-looking and innovative, not stuck in the past or wallowing in nostalgia. But they were not alone in this. The folk musicians who performed at the inn were working to popularize their music and were doing so in collaboration with jazz, implicitly rejecting notions of folk purity and authenticity and angling to reshape American musical culture.

"With jazz we are not yet in the age of history but linger in that of folklore," Ralph Ellison wrote in a famous essay published in *Esquire* in 1959. Titled "The Golden Age, Time Past," the essay memorializes the Harlem jazz club Minton's Playhouse, where Charlie Parker, Dizzy Gillespie, Charlie Christian, Thelonious Monk, Max Roach, and a few others midwifed the birth of bebop in the early 1940s. Ellison describes Minton's as a "continuing symposium of jazz," its heralded jam sessions "the jazzman's true academy." In this essay and others, Ellison beautifully evokes jazz as a communal culture that had fashioned its own vernacular forms of education, appreciation, and criticism. He stresses how important it was for these young artists to have a place where they could court challenge, hone their craft, and educate themselves in a musical tradition they were both absorbing and revolutionizing.[10]

As the essay's elegiac title suggests, however, Ellison was talking about a jazz world that had passed. We can think of Music Inn as part of what succeeded it, a change in the cultural dynamics of learning, playing, listening to, and reflecting on the experiential and historical meaning of jazz. Music Inn witnessed ad hoc jam sessions, but the coin of its realm was the tutorial, the rehearsal, the lecture. Jazz musicians earlier had picked up the art willy-nilly from records, informal master-apprentice relationships, and the freewheeling discourse of the stage, the club bar, and the dressing room; now Music Inn offered lecture-demonstrations and seminars offering social and aesthetic analysis of the form. Where the national jazz conversation had been a patchwork of insider shop talk, fan magazines, specialized journals, and stray Sunday supplement features, Music Inn offered organized roundtables of face-to-face dialogue among musicians, writers, artists, and scholars. Where jazz clubs forced musicians to contend with clinking glasses, distracted listeners, and irascible owners, Music Inn offered raptly attentive audiences and the magnetic Barbers.

The story of Music Inn is the story of the mainstreaming of jazz within the frames of post–World War II American modernism, middle-class cultural tourism, the civil rights and Black freedom movements, the folk cultures of the African and Afro-Caribbean diaspora, and a body of folkloric and anthropological thought influencing the perception of those cultures. It's a story about race, culture, and place—of the cosmopolitan multiracial city meeting the traditional New England WASP small town; of racial integration carried off with an ease found almost nowhere else in American society at the time; of the high and popular arts in robust dialogue; of the formal and the casual sidling up to each other. It's a story about learning to see jazz, the Berkshires, race, culture, and America itself in new ways.

As such, Music Inn exemplifies what social theorist Raymond Williams called a "cultural formation," a concurrence of artistic form and social location that portends changes in the broader society.[11] And it fits nicely as a coda to the story Michael Denning tells in *The Cultural Front* (1996), his encyclopedic account of the transformation of American culture effected by a loose alliance of plebeian artists (Tillie Olson, Woody Guthrie, Billie Holiday, Count Basie, Josh White, Sonny Terry, and Brownie McGhee); modernists politically radicalized by the Depression (Marc Blitzstein, Archibald McLeish, John Dos Passos, Langston Hughes, Duke Ellington); and antifascist emigres (Bertolt Brecht, Kurt Weill).[12] Together these artists created a powerful democratic movement in music, literature, theater, and film that endured right-wing allegations of anti-Americanism to become, in work that continued into the 1950s and beyond, what now serves as the core of the twentieth-century American artistic canon.

In a larger historical context, we can think of Music Inn as part of a movement that portended a reshaping of American culture so consequential as to constitute a proto–Second American Renaissance, a movement in which *place* served a crucial symbolic role. The Berkshires was one of the epicenters of the original nineteenth-century renaissance associated with Herman Melville, Nathaniel Hawthorne, Ralph Waldo Emerson, radical abolitionism, and women's rights; Wheatleigh was a property whose architecture and atmosphere embodied colossal Gilded Age class divisions (a mansion for the super-rich owners and a carriage house and hay barn for the workers) that undermined the earlier moment's democratic promise. Against this backdrop, Music Inn expressed the aspiration for a purer American democracy in the art of Langston Hughes, Duke Ellington, Count Basie, Mahalia Jackson, the Modern Jazz Quartet, Max Roach, and others and in everyday practices of cross-racial intimacy and mutual respect sharply at odds with the era's dominant practices of segregation and white supremacy.

Calling a cultural formation a second American Renaissance is no small claim. This is why I'm labeling it a *proto-renaissance* rather than a fully realized one. As much as Music Inn stands out as an exception to the national pattern of 1950s race relations, it was not a frictionless environment, and the much-ballyhooed liberal integrationist spirit of the space likely concealed or even suppressed expressions of desire among Black musicians for a more thorough reconfiguration of the racial equation governing the jazz industry. The 1960s and 1970s would bring a national Black arts movement that included systematic efforts, such as those enacted by the Association for the Advancement of Creative Musicians in Chicago and the Black Arts Group in Saint Louis, to create local collectives in which jazz education and performance were linked to broader community-organizing campaigns focused on racial justice. Black musicians Max Roach, at the University of Massachusetts, and David Baker, at Indiana University, were among the many Music Inn participants who went on to helm university jazz studies programs, while Randy Weston, inspired by the Afro-diasporic culture he imbibed at Music Inn, moved to Africa to recover and replenish the connections between African American jazz and African music and dance.

In retrospect, we can see Music Inn as a middle space between the modern jazz mainstream of the integrationist 1950s and the Black arts explosion of the race-conscious 1960s and 1970s. Music Inn provided a refuge from the matrix of commercial institutions that had governed jazz for decades, with an atmosphere of cultivated leisure largely free of the necessarily convulsive politics of the years of urban unrest and Black assertion following the assassinations of Medgar Evers, Malcolm X, and Martin Luther King Jr. But we should also see Music Inn as a transitional space linking these cultural formations, still tied to sensibilities and structures of the earlier period but also anticipating and enabling the developments of the later period. Before Randy Weston wrote "Little Niles," "Bantu Suite," and "Uhuru Afrika," several of his songs of praise for Africa and African culture, he wrote "Berkshire Blues," a tribute to his experience of Music Inn and its surrounding physical and cultural landscape. More than a decade before Mahalia Jackson sat behind Reverend King at the March on Washington shouting, "Tell 'em about the dream Martin," she enraptured a Music Inn audience in song and set a group of prominent scholars straight on crucial differences between jazz, blues, and gospel.

Music Inn was far ahead of its time in centering Afro-diasporic and African American culture in the study of jazz and in seeking to understand the music in the context of larger social and political currents, in its relationship to other arts, and as a culture unto itself. It would take decades for academia to fully engage with the implications of the breakthroughs that occurred in Lenox in the 1950s. This began to happen in a serious and sustained way only in the 1990s, with the simultaneous emergence of an interdisciplinary "new jazz studies" and with the absorption into literature, history, music, and other traditional fields of the innovative methods and theories for studying jazz produced by cutting-edge scholarship in American studies, African American studies, ethnomusicology, race studies, and gender studies.[13]

Home

This story means a lot to me. I grew up in Lenox. Like most other locals, I took pride in the town's surpassing natural beauty, its rich history, and its reputation as a beacon of American arts and culture. Partly this had to do with the feeling of otherness that was gently, sometimes inadvertently but nevertheless unmistakably, visited on my family by townspeople who considered themselves the true stewards of the town, its land, and its history. My father grew up on a farm in the north of Italy and worked during my childhood as a welder at the large General Electric plant in nearby Pittsfield. My mother was a second-generation Italian American raised in northern New Jersey, just over the George Washington Bridge from Manhattan. My uncles on both sides of the family were homebuilders, and my mother and my aunts sewed and cooked with far more skill than any of our "American" friends and neighbors. Neither of my parents finished high school, and, when we moved from a rented duplex in Pittsfield to a home in Lenox built by my father and his brothers, our new neighbors, who must have heard the Gennari brothers conversing in their regional Italian dialect while pouring concrete and pounding nails, were surprised to discover that my parents spoke English.

These ethnic and class attributes anchor my personal identity—but so too, and with equal weight, does the fact that I grew up just a few miles from Music Inn, Tanglewood, Jacob's Pillow (the nation's premier dance festival and school), the Berkshire Theater Festival, the Williamstown Theater Festival, Shakespeare and Company, the Clark Art Museum, Chesterwood, and other distinguished cultural sites. That I was educated in the local public schools while some of my youth sports teammates from wealthier backgrounds attended one of Lenox's seven—yes, seven—private schools located on sumptuous estate properties once owned by the Vanderbilts, the Frelinghuysens, and other of the nation's richest families also figured strongly in my emerging worldview and class-inflected angle of vision, as did the times I cruised Stockbridge Bowl's beaches hoping to meet summer-camp city girls and winsome Tanglewood violin and woodwind students. That my superb high school English teacher assigned *Moby-Dick* and told our class when Herman Melville worked on the novel less than five miles from our school, the view from his back window of Mount Greylock, the largest and most magnificent of the Berkshire Mountains, served as a visual surrogate for the great white sperm whale—well, that too helped me understand that I was blessed to come from a very special place and was the beneficiary of an invaluable cultural inheritance. Growing up where I did and embracing the privileges it afforded me largely explains why I became a writer and cultural historian.

Born in 1960, I was too young to have witnessed the Music Inn examined in this book. By the time I made it there, it had changed hands twice, and its programming had transitioned first, in the 1960s, to folk music (Joan Baez, Bob Dylan, a young Carly Simon in a group with her sisters) and then, in the 1970s, to rock (the Byrds, the Kinks, Van Morrison, Bruce Springsteen), with a sprinkling of folk and

Aerial shot of Music Inn buildings and grounds and Stockbridge Bowl, 1970s.
Photograph by Clemens Kalischer.

blues (Richie Havens, John Prine, Mary Travers, Taj Mahal); reggae (Bob Marley, Peter Tosh); and jazz (Dave Brubeck, the Modern Jazz Quartet, Charles Mingus). If I'd been a jazz fan as a young teenager, artists of such renown coming to play in my hometown would've thrilled me. But at that age my taste ran more to the Kinks, Van Morrison, Bob Marley, funk, and disco. Music Inn, circa 1977, was a place where I caught a dose of the fading Woodstock-cum-hippie vibe I'd been too young to experience firsthand in its heyday.

In the 1970s I saw Stephanie Barber perform as a cabaret singer in several local establishments, including Wheatleigh, the mansion she then owned that anchored the estate property where Music Inn had been located. And I was mesmerized on several occasions hearing Randy Weston play at Avaloch, an inn across the street from Tanglewood, where I later washed dishes and bussed tables, and the Potting Shed, one of Music Inn's former buildings, which had been converted into an upscale northern Italian restaurant and nightclub. Twenty years later, in August 1998, following a mundane tangle of events, I found myself serving as master-of-ceremonies at a tribute for Stephanie attended by Weston and his bandmates Sam Gill and Cecil Payne, Dave and Iola Brubeck, Percy Heath, Candido Camero, and other veterans of Music Inn in the 1950s. Among my duties was the reading of testimonials from people who couldn't attend, including John Lewis, Pete Seeger, Nat Hentoff, Jimmy and Juanita Giuffre, George and Alice Russell, Bob Brookmeyer, Ahmet Ertegun, Arif Mardin, and Marian McPartland.

This event happened not long after local music writer Seth Rogovoy published a piece on Music Inn in *Berkshire Magazine* that stirred local memories.[14] Stephanie Barber was making plans to write a book about the inn during her period of ownership; unfortunately, she passed before being able to bring it to fruition. Meanwhile, a team of filmmakers and researchers (including George Schuller, son of Gunther Schuller and an excellent jazz drummer and historian) began the work that culminated in the documentary film *Music Inn*, released in 2007.[15] Each of these efforts, along with musicologist Jeremy Yudkin's study, *The Lenox School of Jazz*, have been invaluable sources of information and inspiration as I've worked on *The Jazz Barn*.[16]

Now's the Time; Here's the Place

I haven't attempted to produce a compendious chronicle of Music Inn in the 1950s and early 1960s or to focus only on the music performed there. Those already familiar with Music Inn's history will notice that I haven't given special emphasis to the Lenox School of Jazz, instead treating the Barbers' tenure at Music Inn as an integrated whole from the Marshall Stearns–led jazz roundtables, through the period of the Music Barn, and finally to the workings of the school, attentive throughout to how what was happening in Lenox and the Berkshires related to the jazz ecosystem and American culture writ large. I believe that the importance of what happened at Music Inn in the 1950s, including but not limited to the Lenox School of Jazz, is so substantial that we must reckon with the experiences not only of people who were in attendance but also of those who weren't there and yet were important to its story.

For many people in the Berkshires, there may be no musician more strongly associated with Music Inn than Randy Weston. Yet Weston didn't serve on the faculty of the Lenox School of Jazz, and he didn't perform in the Music Barn during the time the school was in operation. Still, his association with Music Inn, first as a breakfast cook, then as an auditor of the historic jazz roundtables, and finally as a major musician and culture worker who triangulated Black Brooklyn, white Lenox, and northern Africa, stands as one of the most important legacies of the institution. Equally significant is the fact that nonjazz people like Congress representative Martin Dies, the first chair of the House Un-American Activities Committee; George Lyman Kittredge, one of the fathers of American folklore; and Melville J. Herskovits, one of the country's greatest anthropologists and its preeminent scholar of African culture, played indirect but highly consequential roles in what happened at Music Inn.

At this book's core we find a scholar using his training in American studies and jazz history and drawing on his personal experience of Lenox and the Berkshires to perform an extended analysis of Music Inn and its surroundings as a physical and cultural space and as the embodiment of multiple layers of American thought and experience. I'm really interested in how Billie Holiday, Sarah Vaughan, Dinah Washington, Anita O'Day, June Christy, and Chris Conner sang on the stage of the Music Barn. But I'm also interested in how people traveled to the concerts, whether anything important happened offstage before and after the concerts, what was written about the concerts for the next day's *Berkshire Eagle*, and how the performances related to what was said by the previous week's guest lecturer. My interest is not just the chords, modes, melodies, harmonies, rhythms, and sonic textures of Music Inn in the 1950s but also its social dynamics, its circulation of ideas, its making of culture, and its forging of *place*.

Christopher Small, a pathbreaking ethnomusicologist best known for his book, *Musicking: The Meanings of Performing and Listening* (1998), has urged us to think of music not as a noun but as a verb, a set of actions and social interactions rather than an artifact like a score or a recording. He further urges us to think of musicking as a process involving not just the people we refer to as musicians but everyone who participates in musical events, makes them possible, and shapes their memory and influence. "To music is to take part, in any capacity, in a musical performance, whether by performing, by listening, by rehearsing or practicing, by providing material for performance (what is called composing), or by dancing."[17] The person taking tickets, the stagehands, the carpenters who built the stage—these folks too are part of it. Musicking is also the expressive stylizations generated in this holistic tableau: how people dress, talk, stand, move, and inhabit space while they are musicking. Musicking also involves pre- and post-event discussions, reflections, criticism, historical and cultural analyses—altogether, the creation of meaning, a process that unfolds over time and with an especially powerful attachment to place.

Musicologist Kimberly Hannon Teal observes that physical spaces and geographic locations "play an essential role in framing and defining the music heard within them; when linked with human ideas and values, both individual and shared, the venues become jazz places."[18] Music Inn became just such a "jazz place" through its cultivation of a distinctive ethos defined in part by its physical characteristics (the Berkshire Music Barn and its surrounding idyll of woods, lakes, mountains, and meadows); in part by its location (adjacent to Tanglewood and other performing arts institutions and summer camps in an area rich with literary and cultural history); and in part by its symbolic and ideological trappings (a meshing of deep-in-the-American-grain pastoralism, Cold War–inflected "What's American about America?" discourse, and a-step-ahead-of-its-time racial liberalism).[19] All these factors contributed to making the experience of playing and listening to jazz at Music Inn different than playing and listening to jazz anywhere else. For, as Teal suggests, placing jazz musicians and audiences in a distinctive setting—a setting distinguished by particular material, historical, and sensible characteristics—"encourage(s) them to engage aurally not only with the music they hear but also with the ideas evoked by the physical space from which the music is played."[20]

Engaging with jazz places means engaging the visual. Jazz in the purest sense is invisible; like all music, jazz is a sound that enters the body and vibrates its chambers. Yet jazz is also intensely optical, its history not just one of dazzling sound but also of imagery replete with beauty, cultural meaning, and social importance. The huge pictorial archive of jazz—images used for album covers, publicity, magazine and newspaper reportage, decoration and memorialization—presents a historical record of African American high achievement as well as of intimate, complex encounters across the race line in defiance of the laws and norms of a racist society.[21]

In researching and writing about the musicking that took place at Music Inn in the 1950s, my work has been informed and galvanized by a remarkable trove of photographs, a subset of which I am pleased to present in this book. Most of the photographs I've selected were taken by Clemens Kalischer; a handful were shot by Jay Maisel, Warren Fowler, Leonard Rosenberg, and Carole Reiff; and in three cases the photographer is unknown.[22] These images are intended not merely to serve an illustrative function but to stand as works of expressive art unto themselves. And I hope they elicit more interpretations and trigger more stories than I've been able to do within the book's space constraints and my own limited powers of analysis and imagination.

My decision to write this book came when I first saw and was mesmerized by a particular photograph, the one of bluesman John Lee Hooker, discussed in the final section of chapter 2, where I also furnish some background information about its creator. For the moment suffice it for me to disclose that Clemens Kalischer was a Holocaust survivor, a German Jewish war refugee, an experience that, coupled with his discovery of Jim Crow racial segregation and white supremacy in the United States, brings a special poignancy to the photographs he took at Music Inn. Important too, I think, is the fact that what little Kalischer knew of jazz, its history, and its social dynamics and implications, he was catching on the fly as he listened to the music, the lecture-demonstrations, and the roundtable conversations suffusing the Music Inn soundscape while he was doing his camera work there. Were his intention to make quick money from magazines and newspapers or to create a visual record of jazz's ca-

George Russell and students poring over class assignments, 1959. Photograph by Clemens Kalischer.

nonical great men and women, he'd have shot more photos of Dave Brubeck, Duke Ellington, Dizzy Gillespie, Louis Armstrong, Billie Holiday, and Sonny Rollins. Kalischer's Music Inn archive instead is full of photographs of lesser-known musicians, audiences, and the grounds, buildings, and rooms of Music Inn itself. Through these photographs we come to better understand the significance of the name the Barbers gave their inn: the spaces and structures and at-mosphere of the inn itself, as a place, was integral to the musicking that originated there. Kalischer and the other photographers whose work I've selected for the book were shooting a scene, which is something more than a collection of individuals. They were mapping the visual contours of a space in which men and women of different backgrounds and stations came together to create, experience, and discuss art, culture, and history. They tell stories of labor, practice, rehearsal, performance, pedagogy, conversation, and social interaction.

It is often said that a photograph freezes time. This is not true. A photograph activates time—stretches it, manipulates it, collapses it, reconfigures it. In recording a moment in time, a photograph allows its subjects and its viewers to coexist in defiance of time, to negotiate a new relationship to time. A photograph is a collaboration between photographer, subjects, and viewers both within and against time. Time itself is a cultural construct, something humans invented to organize their experience of the world. It can be reorganized, measured and experienced differently, and it always is. Every time we look at photographs, we establish a new relationship to what we are seeing, depending on when and why we are looking and what will come. What we see is behind us, with us, and ahead of us all at once; what we see is the past, present, and future of what is photographed. What we feel from looking at photographs is time itself, the subjects of the photograph and ourselves joined together in and against the flow of time. Join me as I take us back in time to Music Inn in the 1950s, and together let's make that fascinating place come alive in our own time.

1 THE TOWN AND THE CITY

The sight would have been unforgettable, if anyone had seen it. Two frail middle-aged Jewish women and a young, strapping, six-foot, seven-inch Black man traipsing through the Lenox woods under darkness of night. The women had heard there was jazz being performed a few miles from the kitchen where the three worked together. The kitchen was in a school serving as a summer camp for central European Jewish refugees, many just a few years removed from the horrific experience of the Nazi concentration camps. They'd asked for a ride over to the jazz place, but none of the car-owning locals working at the school could come back that night to take them. This place was next to Tanglewood, they'd been told, a short distance from the back of the music shed. They'd been to a concert there and were pretty sure the fastest way on foot was through the woods lying between West Street and Hawthorne Street.

All three were musicians. They'd recently performed an informal concert at the school. The women played short classical chamber-music pieces. The young man played some of the bebop tunes he'd worked on with Max and Cecil and Ray in Brooklyn and fine-tuned in his studies with Thelonious over in San Juan Hill. This was before he came up to Lenox for the summer to escape the scourge that had descended on his neighborhood when heroin came in and turned good folks into people to be feared.

They arrived at a collection of quaint buildings off to the side of a big fancy mansion that looked like a five-star luxury hotel. There they found an audience listening raptly to a lecture being given by a man who looked like Hollywood central casting's version of an Ivy League professor. The women were confused. Maybe this wasn't a place where musicians played jazz but rather some sort of salon where people talked about the music. The professor was using a phonograph player to demonstrate the contrast between two different versions of a tune called "King Porter Stomp." He seemed to know what he was talking about. Their friend, the tall Black man, intensely absorbed, nodded his head in affirmation.

"Sophisticate Abandons New York to Be a Cowgirl"

Randy Weston and his coworkers had found Music Inn, a lodging establishment and cultural salon run by Philip and Stephanie Barber. In 1950 the Barbers had purchased the outbuildings of a Gilded Age estate—carriage house and superintendent's cottage, dairy, icehouse, greenhouse, stables, and hay barn—along with a hundred acres of land surrounding the buildings. Few if any of the jazz lecture auditors knew anything about the history of the property, but many knew it was situated in an area of deep cultural richness.

In 1892 Henry H. Cook, a New York–based railroad and banking magnate, purchased a plot of land on a knoll overlooking Stockbridge Bowl (also known as Lake Mahkeenac) on the border between Lenox and Stockbridge in the Berkshire Hills of western Massachusetts. The property was nestled in an area of notable consequence to the development of American literature and the arts. A short walk from Cook's property sat the small red cottage where Nathaniel Hawthorne lived in the early 1850s and wrote his gothic novel, *The House of the Seven Gables* (1851), and a collection of children's stories,

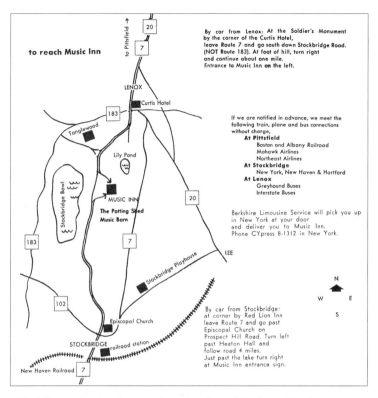

By car from Lenox: At the Soldier's Monument by the corner of the Curtis Hotel, leave Route 7 and go south down Stockbridge Road. (NOT Route 183). At foot of hill, turn right and continue about one mile. Entrance to Music Inn on the left.

to reach Music Inn

If we are notified in advance, we meet the following train, plane and bus connections without charge,
At Pittsfield
Boston and Albany Railroad
Mohawk Airlines
Northeast Airlines
At Stockbridge
New York, New Haven & Hartford
At Lenox
Greyhound Buses
Interstate Buses

Berkshire Limousine Service will pick you up in New York at your door and deliver you to Music Inn. Phone CYpress 8-1312 in New York.

By car from Stockbridge: at corner by Red Lion Inn leave Route 7 and go past Episcopal Church on Prospect Hill Road. Turn left past Heaton Hall and follow road 4 miles. Just past the lake turn right at Music Inn entrance sign.

Makeshift map showing the approximate locations of Music Inn, Tanglewood, and the Curtis Hotel in the late 1950s. Windsor Mountain School (not shown) was where Randy Weston and his coworkers set off walking through the woods to find Music Inn near the area running south past Lily Pond.

The Tanglewood Tales (1853), whose title took the name of the neighboring estate that years later would become the site of the nation's premier summer classical musical festival. One day Hawthorne and his friend Herman Melville were taking a hike up nearby Monument Mountain when a thunderstorm forced them to take refuge in a cave. A vigorous discussion of literary matters ensued. Melville had just finished writing a long, ambitious novel at his home in Pittsfield, the county seat just north of Lenox. Melville found the discussion so enriching that he dedicated the book, *Moby-Dick* (1851), to Hawthorne.

Cook was a pioneer among Gilded Age plutocrats in using extravagant architecture as a symbol of elevated social status. In the early 1880s, the building of his colossal stone mansion on the corner of Fifth Avenue and Seventy-Eighth Street—Cook owned the entire block over to Madison Avenue and up to Seventy-Ninth Street—had triggered a real estate rush among elite families that turned Manhattan's Upper East Side into the nation's most gentrified urban neighborhood. In Lenox, for the construction of Wheatleigh mansion, named after his family's ancestral English village, Cook hired the prestigious Boston architectural firm of Peabody and Stearns to design what came to be considered one of the finest American examples of a classic Italian-style palazzo, replete with yards of carved marble, numerous fireplaces, ornate stained-glass windows, and a spectacular winding staircase. The estate's gardens, terraces, and balustrades were designed by Frederick Law Olmstead, landscape architect of New York's Central Park and many other of America's most handsomely curated outdoor spaces.[1]

In 1897 Cook gave Wheatleigh to his youngest daughter, Georgie, as a wedding gift when she married Count Carlos de Heredia, a Spaniard who'd been raised in aristocratic splendor in Paris. Over the next several years, under the supervision of another architect brought over from France, the estate property was outfitted with service buildings arrayed in the manner of a European provincial farm village. After her husband died in 1917, Countess de Heredia presided over the property and a staff of close to fifty. On Sunday evenings from late spring to early fall, she hosted outdoor sunset services administered by Lenox's Trinity Episcopal Church. After the countess died, in 1946, the estate was sold to the Boston Symphony Orchestra, which recently had established its summer residency at Tanglewood.

For the next decade, Wheatleigh housed students from the Berkshire Music Center, the orchestra's prestigious school for training aspiring classical musicians. In 1950 the orchestra divided the estate, selling the service buildings and a big chunk of land to Philip and Stephanie Barber for $27,000.

Philip Barber was connected to the Berkshires through paternal ancestors who farmed in the area before migrating to the Midwest. Growing up in Mason City, Iowa, Philip, according to his son Benjamin, "yearned for the emancipation of the east coast—hoping that the secret to happiness might be found at Harvard and [in] New Haven and New York."[2] His youthful longing was shared by a first cousin with whom Philip put on amateur plays—this was Meredith Willson, later a composer, conductor, and playwright most famous for *The Music Man* (and its hit song "Seventy-Six Trombones"), a Broadway show paying homage to his Iowa upbringing.[3] Barber took a different path than his cousin into the upper reaches of the New York theater

Wheatleigh mansion, 1950s. Photograph by Frank McCarthy.

world. At Harvard he studied playwriting in George Pierce Baker's legendary "47 Workshop," then followed Baker to New Haven to assist in the founding of the Yale Drama School, where he taught playwrighting for six years and wrote *The Scene Technician's Handbook*.[4] In 1936, while working with the Group Theater in New York as an actor, dramatist, and stage manager, he succeeded Elmer Rice as director of the city's Federal Theatre Project (FTP), one of the Works Progress Administration's arts programs created by Franklin Delano Roosevelt's New Deal.

Hallie Flanagan, the FTP's national director, painted an indelible portrait of Barber while extolling his singular contribution to the project:

> There was something sculptural about Philip Barber, as if the philosophic quality of his mind, unusually just and temperate, had been rendered in blonde wood. He looked like a figurehead on a Viking ship and, in his stubborn moods, like an immovable and impervious Buddha. His judicious analysis of scripts and people was more lucid and penetrating than that of any of the directors. No one on the New York project cared more than Philip Barber did about the underlying social philosophy of Federal Theatre.[5]

The FTP pursued several goals: providing employment for actors, writers, directors, and other theater professionals put out of work by the Depression; encouraging experimentation and innovation in dramatic form and technique; and enlarging the audience for American homegrown theater, especially among citizens who'd never attended live theater.[6] Elia Kazan, Arthur Miller, Orson Welles, and John Houseman are just a handful of theater and film luminaries whose early career experiences in the New York FTP helped launch them into the big time. The program was equally significant for providing opportunities for underrepresented groups, notably women and nonwhites, and for making the theater a pillar of local community life.

Under Barber's aegis the New York FTP had an especially important impact in Harlem, where the Lafayette Theater staged some thirty plays, employing hundreds of African American playwrights, actors, directors, dancers, musicians, and stagehands—including a bold adaptation of *Macbeth* by first-time director Orson Welles, who created an Afro-Caribbean context by substituting Haitian voodoo for the Scottish medieval witchcraft of Shakespeare's original—while also sponsoring a youth program for developing neighborhood talent.[7] This racial inclusion ethic, coupled with the prolabor tilt of some of the most highly publicized FTP-sponsored plays—notably, *The Cradle Will Rock*, composer-lyricist Marc Blitzstein's allegory of working-class heroism and corporate greed, also directed by Welles—prompted an investigation in 1938 by the newly formed House Un-American Activities Committee, chaired by Representative Martin Dies.[8] Alleging communist infiltration of the program and asserting that "racial equality forms a vital part of the Communist dictatorship," the Dies Committee convinced Congress to cut off its federal funding by the end of June 1939—a foreshadowing of darker days to come, when Senator Joseph McCarthy gained control of the House Un-American Activities Committee and intensified its targeting of the arts, entertainment, and academic sectors.[9]

After World War II, Barber cofounded a public relations firm, Barber and Baar Associates, whose client list included large corporate entities such as insurance company Metropolitan Life and food manufacturer Swift and Company as well as educational institutions like Parson's School of Design and Bryn Mawr College.[10] In 1947 Philip married his firm's publicity director, Stephanie Frey—her first marriage, his fourth, with two kids. Stephanie Frey Barber was a city girl, born and raised in Jamaica, Queens, a Hunter College graduate who

Philip Barber, at Music Inn, 1951. Photograph by Clemens Kalischer.

became a fashion journalist and Manhattan woman-about-town. At Barber and Baar, she spearheaded the firm's stateside marketing campaign for Parisian designer Christian Dior's "New Look" women's collection.[11] She was a natural diva, given to eccentric clothing and extravagant custom-made hats. After she wore a black crepe sheath with no adornment, the simple sheath style suddenly became chic. The Associated Press announced her move to the Berkshires with the headline "Sophisticate Abandons New York to Be a Cowgirl." Prodded by the publicity-savvy couple, the press continued to foreground the city-country theme in subsequent coverage of the Barbers. "When you meet a city girl who looks like she belongs strictly in a Stork Club atmosphere, look out," Stephanie's husband quipped to a reporter. "She may have you milking cows before you know what's happening."[12]

The Barbers, in short, were comfortably situated in a rising urban social elite—the Madison Avenue not of the Gilded Age tycoons but of the managers and cultural mediators of consumer capitalism, corporate branding, and affluent-society fashion. Sixteen years separated the couple, but both had lived—less precariously than most Americans—through the Depression and war years. Together they were well positioned to take advantage of a booming postwar economy that enabled an emerging middle class to focus on higher education, arts appreciation, and luxury style, previously the privileged domains of what Thorstein Veblen famously called the "leisure class."[13] In

Stephanie Barber kissing her husband, Philip, at Music Inn, 1951. Photograph by Clemens Kalischer.

their heady social circle of actors, writers, musicians, designers, and business-world movers and shakers, the couple were renowned for their charm and charisma. It was a situation much to be envied.

But they wanted something different. Later they would describe themselves as having yearned "for things that couldn't be found in New York," like "fresh air and freedom, rugged individualism, beauty, trees and time and place for friends." Since marrying they'd traveled to the Berkshires for Tanglewood concerts, theater, and recreation—even tent camping, a grave challenge to Stephanie's sartorial habits but one she met with good humor. The Barbers came to think of the Berkshires as—remember these were PR professionals—"the most pleasant place to live a civilized life in the United States."[14] With a perch there, they could maintain their New York home and business interests and keep up social ties with friends who summered in the area or came in for specific weekend cultural events. Best of all, they could embark on an exciting adventure.

The Barbers decided to become the proprietors of a country inn and to take full advantage of the Wheatleigh estate's bounties: rolling meadows set against groves of pines, birches, elms, maples, and hemlocks; gracefully contoured walking paths; a now rushing, now placid brook shod with dozens of wading pools; proximity to Stockbridge Bowl as well as a smaller pond for swimming and fishing; and ample space and equipment for tennis, badminton, archery, table tennis, and croquet. Such attractive natural features and amenities were not unusual at Berkshire resort properties. The Barbers, however, had a unique calling card, a distinctive concept perfectly captured by the name they gave to their business: Music Inn.

Philip Barber was keen to create something new and vital in the American arts, something that paralleled his earlier work at the Federal Theatre Project. He loved music as much as theater—he saw the two as inseparable—and cherished his voluminous collection of classical, jazz, and folk recordings. Stephanie Barber was a performer

season rates 1955			room*	dorm*
	Memorial Day weekend	special 3 day weekend May 27 to May 30	$42	$34
	May 30 to June 6	graduation week: dinner, overnight, breakfast: $10		
	June 6 to June 30	designed for honeymooners and travellers overnight and breakfast (in bed if you prefer): $7		
	July 4th weekend	special 3 day weekend July 1 to July 4	$45	$37
Berkshire Music Festival at Tanglewood	July 4 to July 10, 6 day week	single rooms	$81	
		rooms for 2	$73, $76, $79, $81, $83, $88	$63
		rooms for 3	$71, $76, $79, $81	
	July 10 to August 14, weekly	single rooms	$91	
		rooms for 2	$83, $86, $89, $91, $93, $98	$73
		rooms for 3	$81, $86, $89, $91	
	August 14 to August 28, weekly	single rooms	$81	
		rooms for 2	$73, $76, $79, $81, $83, $88	$63
		rooms for 3	$71, $76, $79, $81	
Folk Song and Jazz Festivals at Music Inn	Labor Day week 8 days, August 28 to September 5	single rooms	$91	
		rooms for 2	$83, $86, $89, $91, $93, $98	$73
		rooms for 3	$81, $86, $89, $91	
	Labor Day weekend	special 3 day weekend Sept. 2 to Sept. 5	$45	$37
	September 5 to September 26	weekly	$60, $61, $62, $67, $68, $69	$57
		daily	$11	$9

*rate per person

Extra days beyond one week (to Thursday) prorated at weekly rate.

Although preference is given to week-long reservations during July and August, weekend space sometimes does become available.
If so, there is a 2-day minimum on reserved weekend space —
$32 per person in the rooms and $26 in the dorms.
For weekend reservations, phone us at Lenox 695 the preceding Tuesday.

American plan
3 meals a day

about the variations in rate:
We believe all accommodations will please you, but naturally the rooms vary somewhat in desirability. We have found that room preferences are largely a matter of personal taste, with guests sometimes definitely preferring a less expensive room. In general, location, size, and number of occupants, as well as bath, determine the rate.

Music Inn lodging rates in 1955.

at heart: years later she sang cabaret songs at several Berkshire night-life spots, including a cozy basement club she opened at Wheatleigh. Encouraged by Langston Hughes, Alan Lomax, Marshall Stearns, and other friends from the worlds of literature and the arts, the Barbers decided to make their inn a center for the study and perfor-mance of American vernacular music. In short order the warren of oddly shaped rooms in the carriage house became spaces for lectures, workshops, and impromptu performances. The icehouse became the Barber's living space and a site of convivial socializing among musicians and cognoscenti. Later the hay barn morphed into the Berkshire Music Barn (the Barn), site of a summer-long jazz concert series—the first ever to be held at one site—sprinkled with folk music performances, while the greenhouse was rechristened the Potting Shed and fitted out as a restaurant and nightclub. These buildings, along with their surrounding lawns, meadows, and paths and eventually Wheatleigh mansion itself, later became the physical space of the Lenox School of Jazz.[15]

American Pastoral

Jazz in Lenox? The storied history of the Berkshires seems as distant and removed from the music of Louis Armstrong, Duke Ellington, Billie Holiday, and John Coltrane as one could imagine. Like other locations in colonial New England, the Berkshires, a range of hills between the highlands of northwest Connecticut and the Green Mountains of Vermont, took their name from an area in the English settlers' homeland, a county fifty miles southeast of London. The region was one of America's first western frontiers. Stockbridge was settled in the 1730s by English missionaries as a praying town for the Mohicans who lived along the Housatonic River. When the revivalist preacher and renowned theologian Jonathan Edwards moved there in 1749, the town became a center of Puritan New England's mission to save Indian souls while expropriating their land. In nearby Sheffield, in the 1780s, in what historians have called the completion of the American Revolution, farmers aggrieved by escalating taxes mounted Shay's Rebellion, an armed uprising against the government of the Massachusetts Commonwealth. More than a century later, Springfield native Edward Bellamy, who'd become famous recently for his utopian novel, *Looking Backward* (1888), secured the event's place in American letters when he wrote *The Duke of Stockbridge: A Romance of Shay's Rebellion* (1890).[16]

The Berkshires played a significant role in the abolitionist movement that preceded the Civil War of the 1860s. Kemble Street in
Lenox takes its name from Frances Anne "Fanny" Kemble, a famous
English stage actor who settled in Lenox in the 1850s following a serious bout of "domestic infelicity," the *Pittsfield Sun*'s term for the
events that led to Kemble's divorce from Pierce Butler, one of the
country's largest slaveholders. In *Journal of a Residence on a Georgian
Plantation, 1838–1839* (1863), a book culled from letters she wrote to
her Lenox friend Elizabeth Sedgwick, Kemble explained her conversion to abolitionism, vividly detailing the appalling conditions under
which enslaved people lived and labored on her husband's plantation.
Following the divorce and her move to Lenox, Kemble evangelized
the abolitionist creed throughout New England and upstate New
York. When time permitted, she wandered over to Mrs. Sedgwick's
School for Young Ladies to read Shakespeare to the students, including the daughter of Ralph Waldo Emerson, the granddaughter of
President Martin Van Buren, and other offspring of the Eastern Seaboard's "best families."[17]

During the nineteenth and early twentieth centuries, paper and
textile mills and electricity plants located along the Housatonic River
made the region—and Pittsfield, the county's largest manufacturing
center, the site beginning in 1907 of a major General Electric facility—an important engine of the nation's industrial development.[18]
Meanwhile, the area became a center of American literature and culture from the transcendentalist movement of the 1840s and 1850s to
the turn-of-the-century Gilded Age, its landscape serving as a muse
for Nathaniel Hawthorne, Herman Melville, William Cullen Bry-
ant, Catherine Maria Sedgwick, Edith Wharton, W. E. B. Du Bois,
and others. In 1922 a majestic statue of Abraham Lincoln sculpted
by Stockbridge resident Daniel Chester French took its place as the
centerpiece of the Lincoln Memorial on the National Mall; soon it
became—and remains—one of Washington's iconic sights.[19]

Lenox was dubbed the "inland Newport" (and its public high school sports teams "The Millionaires") after Henry H. Cook, Edith Wharton, Andrew Carnegie, Emily Thorn Vanderbilt, George Westinghouse, and other members of the moneyed class built or purchased vast mansions set on expansive, rolling estates in or near the town. Families arrived by train for the summer "with retinues of servants and mountains of luggage" and "liveried footmen and top-hatted coachmen" and "Gibson girls by the dozen, all dressed up in the latest creations of the international famous fashion salons."[20] In 1902 Edith Wharton bought the plot of land in Lenox where she personally designed the mansion and grounds of the Mount, her lavish estate, the focus of much of her influential writing about gardening, interior design, and the domestic lives of the well-to-do. In her novel *Ethan Frome* (1911), the titular character and the ingenue he loves lose control of their snow sled and crash into an elm tree. In conceiving the pivotal scene, Wharton held in her mind's eye the steep tree-lined hill stretching from Lenox's Church on the Hill, a Congregationalist chapel dating to the colonial era, down into the town's village center. Wharton and the business tycoons held on to the estates until global travel, the income tax, ever-rising maintenance costs, and the Great Depression undermined aristocratic lifestyles and forced them to sell. Most of the properties subsequently became private schools for children of prosperous out-of-towners and the local upper class.[21]

Lenox, 150 miles north of New York City and 130 miles west of Boston, was distant enough from these metropoles for their inhabitants to describe traveling there as "going to the country." Yet the southern Berkshire towns were close enough to those cities and even closer to smaller regional cities like Albany, Springfield, Hartford, New Haven, and Providence, for a day trip or an overnighter to attend a single event. Lenox was geographically near enough to major cities to determine sports team loyalties—an intense rivalry between the New York Yankees and Boston Red Sox split many families—yet culturally distant enough for it not to be unusual for a town native never to have set foot in New York City or Boston, whether out of disinterest, anxiety about mixing with crowds, or an out-and-out fear of encountering people different than themselves. Many prosperous families from eastern cities and their suburbs sent their children to summer camps in the Berkshires or just over the border in upstate New York, a short drive away.[22] Lenox's proximity to New York made it possible for Philip Barber to continue running his Manhattan public relations firm while also comanaging Music Inn.

Lenox, then, had a unique connection with New York and Boston: geographically proximate, artistically linked, and yet culturally distinct. The best example was Tanglewood, owing to its cornerstone relationship with the Boston Symphony Orchestra and its role as a key conduit to the New York classical music establishment. By far the largest of the Berkshire arts institutions, with audiences sometimes exceeding ten thousand, Tanglewood received scrupulous coverage in the Boston and New York newspapers, where readers could find Berkshire property listings in the real estate section. For Boston Symphony Orchestra musicians, just as for New York–based dancers, choreographers, actors, directors, arts administrators, and stagehands who taught, performed, and worked in the Berkshires in July and August, this city-country dynamic was a continuum around which to build a career and a life. Many of these artists and administrators and an even greater number of dedicated audience members owned property in both locations and often relocated to the Berkshires full-time when their careers ended or slowed down.

So even if most Bostonians and New Yorkers never set foot in the Berkshires, and many locals resented the "summer people" and second-home owners coming from those places and elsewhere, within the arts community and among the culture-minded, the Berkshires-city nexus was one of vital importance. This geodemographic dynamic produced mild social tensions that gave rise to a colorful

Guests arriving at Music Inn, 1951. Photograph by Clemens Kalischer.

folklore among those born and raised in the Berkshires—stories about pushy, fast-talking city people complaining about their dinner orders or the pace of service at the gas station, copping attitude with innkeepers, being overly enthralled by their heartwarming interaction with a salt-of-the-earth hardware salesperson or mesmerized at the sight of cows grazing in a meadow.[23]

Place-based cultural distinctions manifested equally in the very experience of travel to and from the Berkshires. Rail lines connected the area to New York and Boston and smaller regional cities, and many out-of-towners traveled there by car or bus. Before the Massachusetts Turnpike and the New York State Thruway opened later in the 1950s, most trips were made on state roads like Route 22 and Route 23 in New York; Route 20 in Massachusetts and eastern upstate New York; Route 7 in Vermont, Massachusetts, and Connecticut; and Route 8 in Connecticut and Massachusetts. These were two-lane roads that carved through farmland and passed small town centers and hamlets every ten miles or so. Another option for the trip from New York was the Taconic Parkway, a beautifully scenic four-lane road that routed traffic around town centers while traversing lush Hudson Valley farmland and a set of handsome state parks established during Franklin D. Roosevelt's tenure as New York governor.

Travel to and from the Berkshires, then, meant passing through a landscape that harkened back to an older America, the America of an agriculture-and-artisan–centered economy and human-scale interpersonal relations. This was a nostalgia-laden vista of farmers selling vegetables and dairy products at roadside stands; quaint villages composed of a meeting hall, post office, library, school, a couple of churches, maybe a locally owned food market, gas station, and drugstore; and townspeople who all knew one another. With their wealthy tax bases, Lenox, Stockbridge, Williamstown, Great Barrington, and other Berkshire towns created especially comely New England village settings where local farmers, millworkers, and tradespeople cultivated pride in their town's verdant landscapes and genial Main Streets. During the World War II and Cold War years, the area furnished an amiable portrait of apple-cheeked American civic culture and democratic everyday life. Stockbridge was the home of Norman Rockwell, whose illustrations for the *Saturday Evening Post* and other popular magazines, many featuring Stockbridge townspeople, created a national iconography of small-town American Fourth of July parades, Boy Scout ceremonies, church social functions, Thanksgiving dinners, and drugstore lunch-counter coffee klatches.[24]

In the American popular imagination, such space was strongly coded as *white* space—not the kind of suburban white space enabled by postwar, big-government, social-engineering policies, but traditional white space organically linked to the nation's hallowed Jeffersonian vision of yeoman farmers, small-town democracy, localism, and civic virtue. In 1959 the *New York Times* described the Berkshires as having "some of the most arresting scenery and gracious towns to be found outside of the feudal south in the plantation era of the last century."[25] In the period of industrialization and urbanization in the late nineteenth and early twentieth centuries, mountains, lakes, pastoral landscapes, and fresh air became associated with whiteness, which itself was associated with bodily purity. It became customary for white Anglo urbanites to travel to such places for physical and spiritual rejuvenation—not just to counteract the effects of fast-paced, high-pressure office work but as a cleansing antidote to the clamor, grime, smell, and unsightly environs associated with undesirable ethnic populations of the city.[26]

That the population of the Berkshires was, in fact, overwhelmingly white was less important than the power of the attractive image of the Berkshires projected by tourist magazines and other media through photographs, articles, and radio advertisements for skiing, hiking, canoeing, golf, tennis, bird-watching, apple picking, and other activities implicitly assumed to be hallmarks of a middle-class white lifestyle. *The Berkshires* was a phrase that conveyed nothing about the day-to-day lives of African Americans laboring as service staff in the area's hotels, inns, and restaurants or the Irish, Italians, Poles, and French Canadians toiling in the paper mills along the Housatonic River or at the massive General Electric plant in Pittsfield, which employed more than thirteen thousand in the postwar years.[27]

The Berkshires, as an image and a concept, would come to be strongly associated with Jewish culture—not, however, owing to a belated recognition of the Jewish peddlers, merchants, and farmers who'd lived in the area for more than two hundred years as fully assimilated community members but because Jewish names like Koussevitzky, Bernstein, Copland, Fleisher, and others became synonymous with Tanglewood and because Jews were disproportionally represented in the audience base for Berkshire cultural institutions. Since the 1920s the Borscht Belt in the Catskill Mountains, 130 miles southwest of Lenox, with its string of resort hotels featuring Yiddish tummlers and a brisk summer single's scene for young vacationers from New York metro-area Jewish neighborhoods, was the center of popular entertainment with a distinctive ethnic flavor. The Berkshires, by contrast, became the favored locale for Jewish performers and audiences with a taste for elevated cultural fare such as classical music, modern dance and theater, and art museums.[28]

Race and Place

In discourse about race and geography, it is often the case that binary terms like *city* and *country* conceal a more complicated nonbinary continuum, camouflaging what is in fact a structure of mutual intimacy and interdependence. This is especially so when it comes to *white* and *Black*, terms that in America—this is the essence of how race works in this culture—have been constructed as exclusionary opposites, when in fact they have no meaning except in relation to each other. When we imagine the Berkshires as a pastoral space distinct from the city and as a white space free of Blackness, we erase a more complex and interesting reality. The Berkshires were not only *not* free of a Black presence; the Black presence in the Berkshires was crucial to the development of national and international Black intellectual and cultural life, including what was known in its own time as the New Negro movement and later as the Harlem Renaissance.

W. E. B. Du Bois, the great African American intellectual and writer, was born and grew up in Great Barrington, just south of

Stockbridge and Lenox. After graduating from Searles High School, he went to Fisk University in Nashville, supported by money raised by his childhood church, the First Congregational Church of Great Barrington. He went on to earn doctorates at Harvard and the University of Berlin, publish the classic *The Souls of Black Folk* (1903) and many other books, make seminal contributions to the new academic field of sociology, and become a leading advocate of civil rights and anticolonialism.[29] While editing the *Crisis*, the magazine of the National Association for the Advancement of Colored People (NAACP), of which he was a cofounder, Du Bois's work intersected with that of other prominent Harlem figures with ties to the Berkshires. James Weldon Johnson, a civil rights advocate, poet, author of the novel *The Autobiography of an Ex-colored Man* (1912), and lyricist (he wrote "Lift Every Voice and Sing," now known as the Black National Anthem), spent his summers living in the small cabin in Great Barrington he used as a writer's retreat. It was there, between 1926 and 1937, a year before his premature death, where Johnson wrote his most famous work, a book of sermons in verse called *God's Trombone* (1927), as well as his autobiography, *Along This Way* (1933).[30]

The premier photographer of the Harlem Renaissance, James Van Der Zee, was born in Lenox and grew up there on his family's sprawling farm. One of the first photographers to extensively document community life in Lenox and other Berkshire towns, Van Der Zee was also a skilled pianist and violinist, and in 1906 he moved with his father to Harlem to pursue a career in music. The success he enjoyed in that field—he helped found a classical chamber group—proved not as historically significant as his photography. In 1916 Van Der Zee and Gaynella Greenlee, who soon became his wife, launched a studio on 125th Street, from which he produced the most extensive visual documentation of life in Harlem from the 1920s through the 1960s. Van Der Zee shot thousands of pictures of Harlemites engaged in everyday activities, as well as formal portraits of local notables like

Black nationalist leader Marcus Garvey, poet Countee Cullen, entertainers Florence Mills and Bill "Bojangles" Robinson, preacher and politician Adam Clayton Powell Jr., and prizefighters Jack Johnson and Joe Louis.[31]

The pattern was clear: the Berkshires was a decidedly white space that nevertheless was home to (or second home to) exceptional African American writers and artists who exercised an outsize influence on American culture. This was further confirmed in the 1960s, when the venerable novelist and critic Ralph Ellison purchased a country retreat in Plainfield, a town of fewer than three hundred residents on the eastern edge of the Berkshire Hills, thirty miles northeast of Lenox. Ellison, originally from Oklahoma City, migrated to Harlem from Alabama after an unsatisfying stint at Tuskegee Institute, where he played trumpet well enough to secure an audition for Duke Ellington's band. *Invisible Man* (1952), his jazz-themed masterwork, is considered by many the greatest American novel of the mid-twentieth century, while his magazine essays on Mahalia Jackson, Charlie Parker, Charlie Christian, and Jimmy Rushing set a new standard for that genre of jazz letters. Ellison and his wife, Fanny, were drawn to Plainfield—the deep boonies to residents of Pittsfield and North Adams, the industrial centers of the Berkshires, as well as to residents of Williamstown, Stockbridge, and Lenox, the county's cultural centers—in part because it was just down the road from the Cummington home of close friends, the poet Richard Wilbur and his wife, Charlee. The Wilburs introduced the Ellisons to their social circle of Berkshire literati and scholars from the nearby college towns of Williamstown, Bennington, Northampton, and Amherst. Ralph, according to biographer Arnold Rampersad, took special pleasure in owning a home "in what once had been the center of American artistic and moral glory," affording him a place-based connection to "Emerson and Melville and abolitionism."[32]

Another group of African Americans affiliated with the Berkshires

in the mid-twentieth century were teenagers who attended two private educational institutions founded in the late 1940s just a few miles
from Music Inn. The Windsor Mountain School in Lenox was established by Max and Gertrude Bondy, German Jewish educational
reformers who'd fled Germany when the Nazis forced the closure
of their progressive international school. After emigrating in 1937,
they first reestablished their school in Switzerland; then in Windsor, Vermont; and finally in Lenox, where in 1944 they purchased
a mansion owned by the recently deceased New York lawyer and
art collector Grenville Lindall Winthrop, a direct descendant of John
Winthrop, the first governor of the Massachusetts Bay Colony. Max
Bondy implemented a pedagogical model emphasizing individual
learning, while Gertrude, who'd studied with Sigmund Freud, served
as school counselor. Windsor Mountain operated under an explicitly
antiracist progressive philosophy incorporating what would now be
called a social justice ethos. In its first years, the school's student body
and faculty were dominated by refugees from Nazi Germany, suffusing it with a distinctly left-leaning European atmosphere. Among its
enrollees in the late 1960s, when African Americans typically composed 15 percent of the student body, were children of jazz musicians
Thelonious Monk and Randy Weston, celebrity entertainers Sidney
Poitier and Harry Belafonte, and retired Brooklyn Dodgers catcher
Roy Campanella.[33]

A few miles down Route 183 in Interlaken stood the Stockbridge
School, founded by Hans Karl Maeder, a German socialist in rebellion against his father, a vicious anti-Semite who'd welcomed the
rise of Hitler and the passage of the Nazi racial purity laws. This
school also became well-known for its racial integration as well as
an ethic of internationalism symbolized by the United Nations flag
that flew next to the American one atop the school's main building.
For Maeder the Stockbridge School represented the culmination of a
deep personal commitment to antiracist education that began when

he worked on a coffee plantation in Kenya and started a school for the children of Black farmworkers.[34]

In thinking about the experience of Black students, musicians, writers, artists, and service-class workers who came to the Berkshires, it is crucial to recognize the heightened significance of place—and travel from place to place—in African American history and culture. This is deeply embedded in the shared life of a people whose defining condition under enslavement was that of not being allowed to travel and then, after emancipation, of living under Jim Crow laws that posed strict limitations on how and where they could travel. It is not coincidental that some of the most consequential moments in civil rights history centered on travel. Think of the Rosa Parks episode in mid-1950s Montgomery, Alabama; the early 1960s Freedom Riders, who challenged segregated seating on buses; and *Plessy v. Ferguson*, the court case triggered by a man light enough to pass for white but legally considered Black under Louisiana's "one drop rule." When the US Supreme Court ruled in 1896 that Plessy was not allowed to ride in the white section of an interstate train, it enshrined the Jim Crow system in federal constitutional law for the next six decades.[35]

Segregation is a system of control over place and movement, a regime that regulates where people can live and where and how they can travel—a system, that is, designed to keep people *in their place*. It was not until 1967, following the monumental civil rights laws enacted during the Johnson administration, that Victor H. Green ceased publication of *The Negro Motorist Green-Book*, a guide to lodgings and businesses that welcomed Black patrons. The folklore of jazz, blues, and rhythm and blues teems with stories of traveling African American musicians relegated to boarding houses in Black neighborhoods (while their white bandmates stayed in superior lodgings), compelled to eat their meals in cars and on buses when the only restaurants in town prohibited them from entering. Many of these musicians proudly claimed to be the original Freedom Riders.[36] Their stories exemplify how race has functioned in the United States as "a primary way of ordering American geography."[37]

Travel for African Americans was fraught and often dangerous. But it could also be liberating, a sign of freedom and escape from the racial constraints embedded in US law and custom. Not coincidentally, travel is deeply encoded in the sonic properties of jazz and other genres of Black music. The sound of the swing orchestra can be likened to the repetitive rhythm of a train rolling along on its tracks coupled with the syncopated counterpoint of its engine—what jazz scholar Joel Dinerstein calls "the music of techno-progress itself" carrying "the rhythmic drive of technological change and the promise of social mobility."[38] The Alabama-born African American writer Albert Murray names this hallmark of Black sonic life "locomotive onomatopoeia" and asserts that all Black music "played the train."[39] Murray's insight recalls not just swing but also work songs and blues sung by railroad track–maintenance workers to synchronize their movements for both pleasure and heightened efficiency as well as rock and roll pioneer Little Richard sculpting the grooves of "Lucille" and other breakout songs from his memory of trains rolling over the tracks just outside his childhood home in Macon, Georgia.[40] My generation was raised on *Soul Train*, the popular TV show that opened with the sound and image of a locomotive and featured a regular segment in which young Black men and women danced two by two—sometimes to "Love Train," by the O'Jays; "'C'mon 'n' Ride It (The Train)," by the Quad City DJs; or "Steam Train," by Lee Fields—down a line framed by ersatz train tracks.

From the underground railroad of slavery times to the rail journeys out of the segregated South during the Great Migration, from the high prestige accorded African American Pullman porters to the implications of living "on the other side of the tracks," the train held deep and complex meaning for African Americans. Duke Ellington loved riding trains and wrote songs like "Choo-Choo," "Daybreak

Express," "Happy-Go-Lucky-Local," and "Track 360," sonic pastiches that evoked chugging rhythms, whistles, and hissing steam. "Take the A-Train," the band's theme song from the 1940s, was written by Ellington's collaborator Billy Strayhorn based on the subway directions he received from Ellington when he first came to New York to meet the bandleader.

Jazz narratives and mythologies use geographic locations to signpost an odyssey, a journey carrying Black people and Black sound through the United States and on to the rest of the world. Among musical genres jazz may be singular in the strength of its attachment to place and to the movement from one place to another. Histories and taxonomies of jazz typically organize the music according to the places associated with distinctive styles forged within specific cultural contexts: New Orleans jazz (a festive music of streets, the vice and pleasure district, Mississippi riverboats); Chicago jazz and Kansas City jazz (hot music channeling the spirit of the heartland and the frontier in mob-controlled speakeasies and clubs); and West Coast jazz (a music of cool serenity redolent of sun-and-sand leisure).[41] The perpetual energy and movement associated with the music is inextricably linked to the fact that the livelihood of many jazz musicians requires travel on an almost constant basis. In a fundamental way, jazz is the story of musicians on the road, riding in cars, on buses, trains, and airplanes, moving between nodal points in the music's vast, distended, often unstable ecosystem. For this reason biographies and autobiographies of major jazz musicians often read essentially as travelogues, chronicles of incessant movement from place to place and the experience of navigating the social codes and structures of those places.[42]

"Take the A-Train" is about arriving in Harlem, a metonym for the epochal movement of vast numbers of African Americans from the agricultural South to industrial cities in the North and the Midwest and to New York from smaller inland cities such as Pittsburgh,

Detroit, Cleveland, Cincinnati, and Indianapolis. These migrations were a common defining life experience for pioneers of swing music in the 1920s and 1930s, including Duke Ellington (from Washington, DC); Louis Armstrong (New Orleans, Chicago); Fletcher Henderson (Cuthbert and Atlanta, Georgia); Jimmie Lunceford (Fulton, Mississippi, Denver, Memphis); Cab Calloway (Rochester, New York); Chick Webb and Billie Holiday (Baltimore); and Lester Young (Woodville, Mississippi; Kansas City). In the early 1940s, Harlem was the place where a restless, ambitious generation of younger musicians catalyzed by wartime demands for racial equality, a group led by Charlie Parker (Kansas City), Dizzy Gillespie (Cheraw, South Carolina), Thelonious Monk (Rocky Mount, North Carolina), and Kenny Clarke (Pittsburgh), hatched a new style called bebop, an audacious music marked by fleet tempos, mercurial chord changes, and sharp-cornered rhythms. The next wave of New York–centered innovation in the 1950s was hard bop, an extension of bebop incorporating elements of the blues, rhythm and blues, and gospel; and cool and modal jazz, styles that favored melody, lyricism, and space over hard bop's harmonic and rhythmic density. This wave featured, among others, Miles Davis (East Saint Louis); Art Blakey (Pittsburgh); Clifford Brown (Wilmington, Delaware); Tommy Flanagan, Barry Harris, and Hank Jones (Detroit); George Russell (Cincinnati); John Coltrane (Hamlet, North Carolina); and George Coleman (Memphis).[43]

The new styles mandated performance spaces that facilitated a more intimate relationship between the musicians and their listeners than had been the case for the swing music played in large dance halls like the Savoy Ballroom and Black neighborhood theaters like the Apollo in Harlem and the Howard in Washington, DC. This brought the heyday of small, urban jazz clubs with a stage just large enough to accommodate four or five musicians, a lively bar, and bosom-to-bosom seating for patrons. This style of club—Small's Paradise, Bird-

Saxophonist George Coleman at Music Inn during his band's residency there in 1958. His career took him from his hometown of Memphis to Chicago and then to New York, where he joined Max Roach's quintet. Photograph by Clemens Kalischer.

land, the Royal Roost, Café Society, and the Famous Door in New York; the Hi-Hat in Boston; the Chatterbox in Cleveland; the Flame Show Bar in Detroit; Club DeLisa and Rhumboogie Café in Chicago; Club Riviera in Saint Louis; the Down Beat and Billy Berg's in Los Angeles; and Bop City in San Francisco—became an iconic cultural space where listeners witnessed at close range the magic of a band's alchemy and the charisma and individuality of each performer.[44]

The upshot is that jazz in the 1950s redoubled its association with urban culture, even as the advent of the long-playing record, hi-fi equipment that functioned as 1950s modern-style living room furniture, and jazz's central role in the masculine style and ethos found in *Playboy* and other men's magazines together crystallized a new consumer culture that circulated well beyond urban environs both nationally and internationally.[45] Jazz was still coded as a music of the city at a time when American cities were entering a period of radical transformation driven by fundamental geographic, demographic, economic, and political changes. Government policies regarding transportation (notably the federal highway system) and housing (discriminatory mortgage-lending practices coupled with de facto segregated public housing systems) facilitated the phenomenon of "white flight" from cities to racially homogenous suburbs. Soon industrial manufacturers would begin relocating to nonurban (and eventually non-US) locations for cheaper labor, leaving cities with diminished tax bases, poorly funded schools, and a host of consequent social problems.[46]

For some, jazz's association with the city—the sound of urban bustle and sophistication combined with styles of language, dress, and presence connoting hipness and cool—still held a great deal of allure. But for many others, including no small number of jazz musicians, cities had become places of acute danger and struggle. A major factor was the scourge of narcotics that permeated the urban jazz scenes of the late 1940s and early-to-mid 1950s. The roster of musicians of the time who battled addiction, served prison time for possession, or lost their lives to drug overdoses is a virtual who's who of the jazz canon. The smoke-filled jazz clubs that attracted photographers and brought pleasure to listeners were veritable health hazards for musicians, with a promiscuous flow of drugs and alcohol, crazy work schedules playing havoc with circadian rhythms, and—with a few notable exceptions—thorny relationships with club owners. Charlie Parker, Billie Holiday, Thelonious Monk, Sonny Rollins, and Max Roach are just a few of the musicians whose drug-related brushes with the law resulted in the loss of their New York cabaret cards, preventing them from working in city nightclubs that served alcohol.[47] Police patrolled the streets outside city jazz clubs, purportedly to contain the spread of vice in the entertainment district, in truth to counteract interracial mixing and put successful Black men in their place. In a heavily publicized incident, Miles Davis was left bloody from a vicious beating by a police officer's nightstick on the sidewalk outside of the midtown Manhattan club where he was headlining.[48]

Randy Weston and the Berkshire Blues

This was the context in which Music Inn emerged for jazz musicians as a space of peace, tranquility, dignity, and the possibility of self-realization. For African American bebop pianist and composer Billy Taylor (Greenville, North Carolina; Washington, DC), living in Brooklyn in the late 1940s and 1950s and hustling for work in the hurly-burly Manhattan club scene, the trip to Lenox was a welcome opportunity "to get out of the city, enjoy the beauty, relax."[49] For fellow jazz pianist and Brooklynite Randy Weston, Lenox figured as nothing less than a life-defining experience.

Weston hailed from a family steeped in Afro-Caribbean music, racial pride, and the kind of immigrant entrepreneurial energy the US prizes when it is not swept up in xenophobia. His Panamanian father introduced him to West Indian calypso, which melded in young Randy's ear with other Caribbean styles; blues and Black church music from the streets; the Duke Ellington, Count Basie, Benny Goodman, and Billie Holiday he heard on the radio; and his parents' collection of records by "everybody from Marian Anderson to the Ink Spots." Weston's mother, Vivian Moore Weston, a gentle church-going woman from Virginia, was a domestic with a ferocious work ethic. His father, Frank Edward Weston, was an ardent follower of Marcus Garvey and a member of the local Universal Negro Improvement Association. In the family restaurant, Trios, he hung "maps and portraits of African kings on the walls," his son remembered, "and was forever talking to me about Africa." Weston worked long hours in Trios, a hub for artists and intellectuals in Bedford-Stuyvesant, then a multiethnic neighborhood of Blacks, Jews, Italians, Germans, and Irish. When time allowed, he continued honing his piano skills, building on but also veering from what he'd learned in the classical repertoire emphasized by the teacher he'd studied under since he was fourteen.[50]

Weston's interest in jazz crystallized at Brooklyn's Boys' High School, where drummer Max Roach, saxophonist Cecil Payne, pianist Duke Jordan, and trumpeter Ray Copeland, all destined to become leading hard bop players, also spent their teenage years. By the time Weston graduated, he was "only hanging out with other musicians or aspiring musicians like me." One key space for this informal but vital social mixing was Brooklyn's network of Black musicians' clubs, "cultural centers, places of black culture, where black youth [hung] out with experienced musicians." Other important spaces were the homes of musicians ("also places of culture, places to learn") like Max Roach's house, where, a few years later, after returning to Brooklyn from a year in Okinawa as a staff sergeant in the segregated army, Weston met Charlie Parker, Dizzy Gillespie, Miles Davis, and George Russell, who was living at Roach's house when he wrote "Cubana Be, Cubana Bop" for Gillespie's Afro-Cuban orchestra. An equally important grooming space was Thelonious Monk's apartment in Manhattan's San Juan Hill neighborhood, where Weston—later considered the foremost disciple of jazz's high priest—was one of many musicians who visited regularly to soak up Monk's wisdom.[51]

It was a remarkably rich and nourishing cultural milieu, a seedbed for some of the most exciting and innovative music of the period. But a dark specter hovered over it. "Most of us weren't hip to this heroin, had never heard of it, [but] this thing wound up spreading like cancer," Weston recalled. "It spread among almost all of us involved in that scene, the young people of that particular time, including myself." For Weston, who'd been bred to take immense pride in Black culture and community, the narcotics epidemic exacted a bigger cost than the damage it did to his and his friends' bodies: "This drug panic was coupled with a turn for the worse in how our people were abusing each other, due in part to systemic segregation and racism. Many of us had fought for our country in the war, only to return home to the same old Jim Crow." Weston later heard that "this heroin epidemic was being spread by organized crime." The sad result was that "a lot of my guys died, a lot of guys got sick, and this wonderful group of young musicians and friends of the music that we grew up with, who had such dignity and pride . . . all of a sudden heroin turned people into thieves and idiots and it was really the devil that entered our community. . . . I wanted to get out of there so bad."[52]

I've been quoting from *African Rhythms: The Autobiography of Randy Weston* (2010), a splendid collaboration between Weston and the distinguished jazz writer Willard Jenkins. At this point in the book, the gripping narrative takes a sharp turn, pivoting on a moment of serendipity, which Weston attributes to the presence of "grace." It reminds me of the famous scene in *Narrative of the Life of Frederick Douglass* when Douglass, in conveying how his move to Baltimore—he was still the property of his master but no longer restricted to the plantation—"opened the gateway to all my subsequent prosperity," a development he put down to "a special interposition of divine Providence in my favor."[53] Weston's providential moment came when he ran into Lefty Morris, a Brooklyn friend who was playing basketball for a semi-pro team in the Berkshires called the Lenox Merchants. Six-feet, seven-inches tall and possessed of deft court skills battle-tested in Brooklyn schoolyards, Weston saw this as his ticket out of a Bed-Stuy scene that had ravaged his body and soul. At Morris's urging ("Randy, why don't you go up to the Berkshires, it's really beautiful up there. . . . You'll get plenty of fresh air, drink fresh milk, eat fresh vegetables, and get yourself healthy again"), Weston hopped the bus for his fateful journey—in his case, reversing the poles of Douglass's passage, a journey from city to country, urban despair to pastoral hope.[54]

To say that the story is narratively constructed to convey a dramatic transformation marked by travel from a corrupted place to a redemptive one—a time-tested literary device—is not to say it is not true, only that it is not the whole story. Heroin was available in the Berkshires for anyone who wanted or needed it. Respectability and dignity were in no short supply in Bedford-Stuyvesant's Black churches, families, and businesses. In what philosopher Charles Mills calls the "moral geography" of race, white spaces like the Berkshires live in the popular imagination in opposition to Black spaces like Bed-Stuy, owing to a culturally ingrained logic by which we impute sharply contrasting traits and value to the people who inhabit places known as "America's premier cultural resort" and the "ghetto." "You are what you are because you originate from a certain kind of space," Mills explains the tacit logic, "and that space has those properties in part because it is inhabited by creatures like yourself."[55] Randy Weston became an inhabitant of *both* these spaces, and they proved to be mutually supportive in turning him into a professional musician. Contingencies of history shaped how Lenox and Bed-Stuy came to offer different material and symbolic resources. For Weston the significant value of each place—the cultural and artistic wealth of Black Brooklyn and white Lenox—meshed with each other to launch his career.

In the event Weston passed on the Lenox Merchants and started his time in the Berkshires working service jobs in resorts. Not yet

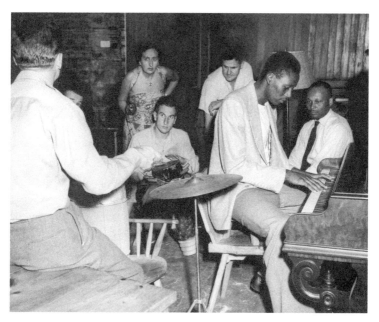

Randy Weston, with calypsonian Macbeth the Great (to Weston's left, wearing a necktie) looking on, at Music Inn, 1950. Photographer unknown.

sure he wanted to pursue a career in music, he nevertheless was pleased to discover opportunities to keep playing. As a handy man at a resort on Lake Buell outside of Great Barrington, first, and then as a breakfast cook at Seven Hills in Lenox, he practiced after his shifts on the pianos in each property's drawing rooms. "Right away I saw that all these resorts in the Berkshires area had beautiful pianos," he recalled. His next job was in the kitchen at Windsor Mountain School during the summer, when it served as a camp for elderly Jewish refugees from central Europe. Many of the refugees were musicians: pianists, violinists, singers. Some had concentration camp tattoos on their arms. When a group of them heard Weston practicing and asked him to perform in a concert they were staging, he initially declined, thinking they expected him to play Bach, Beethoven, Mozart, and other classical music he hadn't practiced in years. They assured him they wanted him to play exactly what he'd been practicing on a Windsor Mountain piano—bebop standards—and so he did.

This led to the fateful occasion when two of his kitchen female coworkers, one from Hungary and the other from Czechoslovakia, told Weston they'd heard there was jazz nearby at a place called Music Inn. "Imagine a 6'7" black man striding through the woods with these two European women. What a sight that must have been," Weston said. The group arrived a bit late for a lecture being given by Marshall Stearns, just as Stearns was drawing a contrast between Fletcher Henderson's and Benny Goodman's versions of Jelly Roll Morton's "King Porter Stomp." "Who's this cat?" Weston thought, and who, he wondered, were the hundred or so people in the audience "who had come to this particular resort for music."[56]

Weston frequented Music Inn in the coming weeks and years for more roundtables and performances, enthralled by Stearns's capacious pan-African approach to jazz and the Afro-diasporic performers he invited to Lenox, especially master drummers Babatunde Olatunji from Nigeria and Candido Camero from Cuba, Trinidadian dancer Geoffrey Holder, Guinean choreographer Asadata Defora, and the Savoy Ballroom hoofers Al Minns and Leon James. "I had never before heard or read any other jazz critic or educator making the clear connections of jazz origins to Africa," Weston said. "Everybody else told that same old 'up the river from New Orleans' story, leaving Africa completely out of the picture. I said 'Who is this guy?' I *had* to know him." After hearing Weston play, Stephanie Barber hired him as the Music Inn's breakfast chef and encouraged him to practice on the piano in the front lounge. Soon Marshall Stearns asked him to accompany his lectures with demonstrations of modern jazz styles. Weston seized the opportunity to form a trio with two friends from Brooklyn, bassist Sam Gill and drummer Willie

Jones, and bring them up to Lenox. Later in the decade, Stearns and the trio together conducted jazz-history presentations in colleges and universities across the country.[57]

Given his race pride and wide-ranging intellectual and cultural interests, Weston cherished his time at Music Inn not just for its crucial impact on his musicianship but also for introducing him to notable African Americans like poet Langston Hughes, actor Butterfly McQueen, journalist and pianist Dan Burley, and Spelman College folklorist Dr. Willis Laurence James. His summers in Lenox spanning the 1950s were also a boon to Weston's family life. He brought his children up to the Berkshires for July and August so they could "get out of the city, get some fresh air, and enjoy the beauty of the land," knowing that the "sisters who worked in the big hotels" would help him out when he needed someone to look after them. "Just to get the kids out of New York for the summers was great," Weston recalled.

> And in my case I was so grateful because that Berkshires experience enabled me to rid myself of drugs and be far from the other madness. Not to mention how the place was like a music paradise, with the opera, the Boston Symphony, people like Leonard Bernstein and Lukas Foss in residence, jazz at the Music Inn, plus all the people coming in to do the lecture series. Those ten summers in the Berkshires were a real cleansing experience for me, and I was able to further develop myself as a player and finally gain the confidence to where I was able to reconcile myself to making music my profession.[58]

A heartwarming story like Randy Weston's makes it very easy to romanticize the Berkshires. But the area was part of the United States, and this was the early 1950s. If Black musicians had not been invited by the Barbers to stay at Music Inn, they and their families may not have been able to rent a room from another lodging estab-

Randy Weston listening to Professor Willis Laurence James on the grounds at Music Inn, 1957. Photograph by Warren Fowler.

lishment in Lenox or Stockbridge. It was customary at this time for rural and small-town hotels and inns across the country—not just in the South—to not accept Black or Jewish guests. The Berkshires were no exception. When Weston first arrived in Lenox, he lodged with a woman named Gerty, one of the Black women who would "rent rooms to black men or black women who were working domestically in the area because we couldn't stay in the segregated white hotels."[59] Stephanie Barber remembered it this way: "Black people were not popular in New England. In the early days, when we over-flowed . . . we had problems finding beds at local inns for artists who happened to be black. People in the village did not approve of what we were doing. But in good New England fashion, they believed we had the right to do it."[60] Benjamin Barber, who worked for his father and stepmother at Music Inn as a young teenager, characterized the situation as one of bilateral tension: "The presence of so many black musicians, many with urban habits, had to be startling to the com-munity—but no more startling than the open skies, woodlands and rural landscapes were to the artists."[61]

There are additional reasons to wonder whether the Berkshires happening to be the place where certain exceptional African Amer-icans were born or spent significant time had produced a facade of racial progressivism concealing indifferent, ambivalent, or even hos-tile local feelings toward Black people and Black culture. When Ralph and Fanny Ellison's Plainfield home burned to the ground—it was there where Ralph worked on his follow-up novel to *Invisible Man*, much later published as *Juneteenth* (1999)—the fire marshal ruled the cause as faulty wiring. According to Ellison's biographer Arnold Rampersad, however, Ralph and Fanny believed that "some local per-sons or person had deliberately burned them out." When neighbors took up a collection and presented them with a check for a couple hundred dollars "to get something for your new home," Fanny re-sponded "graciously if perhaps ambiguously, too," saying, "We had no idea how much we were welcome until the fire."[62]

The long and remarkable career of Lenox native son James Van Der Zee—he died in 1983 at age ninety-seven—lasted well into the 1970s. In 1969 several of his portraits of Harlem luminaries and casual shots of anonymous neighborhood residents were featured in *Harlem on My Mind: Cultural Capital of Black America, 1900–1968*, a highly con-troversial exhibition mounted by the Metropolitan Museum of Art as part of its centennial celebration. These photographs, and others shot by famous *Life* magazine photographer Gordon Parks, were displayed not as works of fine art but as design elements in a narrative social history of Harlem otherwise composed of newspaper clippings and timelines. The exhibition did not include a single painting, drawing, sculpture, or other work of fine art produced by an African American, leading to a spirited protest by Black artists and intense scrutiny of the Met along with the entire art world establishment for its virtually total absence of racial diversity.[63] What was true of the art world of the time also characterized the way Lenox framed its own history. If Van Der Zee received mention in town historical materials—and often he did not—it was not done in a way that placed him in the genealogy of venerated Lenox cultural figures like Nathaniel Hawthorne and Edith Wharton. Lenox boasts a superb local history society, which in recent decades has been exemplary in its commitment to racial inclusion. Unfortunately, however, to this day Van Der Zee—whose life and work have been honored and analyzed in excellent recent scholarship—has not been officially memorialized by the town.[64]

And then there's the case of W. E. B. Du Bois. Despite his global renown as a writer, scholar, and activist, it was not until the 1980s, two decades after his death in 1963 and a Sisyphean struggle to memorialize him in his hometown, that Du Bois's birthplace in Great Barrington became a commemorative site the town finally was proud to highlight in its tourism marketing. The property had been purchased in the late 1960s by a foundation financed by high-profile donors such as Norman Rockwell, Sidney Poitier, Ossie Davis, and Ruby Dee. When the foundation announced its intention to develop a public park honoring Du Bois, it was met with fierce local opposition that forestalled any significant development of the property for many years, even after it was designated as a National Historic Landmark in 1976. Today, happily, the site, on Route 23 a few miles outside of Great Barrington's thriving downtown, features interpretive plaques and informational tours professionally curated by the University of Massachusetts. Few of the site's visitors know how difficult and protracted an effort it took to honor the man whose name adorns major research institutes at the University of Massachusetts and Harvard and whose work is taught in hundreds of college courses across the country.

In that late 1960s moment, as the Vietnam War convulsed American society and the civil rights movement gave way to Black Power, the local chapter of the Veterans of Foreign Wars slandered Du Bois as an anti-American traitor for the left-wing sympathies he'd developed after World War II, when he became a tribune of world peace and freedom and then expatriated himself to Ghana in the last years of his life. Great Barrington's town council blocked a dedication ceremony planned by the memorial foundation, while the *Berkshire Courier*, the town's community newspaper, called for the site to be vandalized. As carefully documented by historian Amy Bass, Du Bois's local detractors over the decades not only excoriated his politics but also accused him, patronizingly, of breaking faith with the community that had raised money for him to go to college. These purveyors of bite-the-hand-that-feeds-you denunciation showed scant interest in reading anything from Du Bois's remarkable body of work. Doing so may have helped them understand the circumstances that led the man who helped found the NAACP to later join the Communist Party and adopt a pan-African approach to the struggle for Black freedom and equality.[65]

Bed-Stuy, the Berkshire Pastoral, and the Sound of the African Village

In 1965 Randy Weston entered a New York studio to record a solo performance of "Berkshire Blues," a tune he'd written in 1962 and recorded with a sextet in 1964. He was especially keen to record a solo version when invited to do so by Duke Ellington, who'd pinpointed

Weston as one of the first artists he intended to feature on a new record label he was launching with his sister Ruth.[66] Weston's piano style was primarily influenced by Thelonious Monk; like Monk, Weston's sound was situated in the harmonic innovations of bebop but still firmly grounded in the swing and stride traditions, wary of the blistering tempos and flashy technical displays that had become bop hallmarks in favor of medium tempo swing grooves and ballads tethered to the song's melody. But he also idolized Ellington, worked hard to develop a keyboard touch just as distinctive as his (in Weston's case, a supple touch both muscular and delicate), and, like the master, approached the piano as an orchestra unto itself.[67]

Weston wrote "Berkshire Blues" as an homage to the Berkshires landscape, a sonic memory of the time he spent there "usually at night," when he "used to take a walk, and breathe the air, take in the trees, and just sort of get with the place itself."[68] The tune is a waltz, a form Weston was drawn to for its swinging lilt and an insinuative feel he associated with the gentle syncopated pulse the calypsonian Macbeth the Great used when Weston heard him at Music Inn. Weston's pianism on "Berkshire Blues" strongly echoes both Ellington and Monk, validating as much as any tune in his oeuvre the view widely held by jazz experts that Weston is the premier successor to those two venerable figures in the canon of jazz pianist-composers.[69]

Given the strong sense of place evoked by "Berkshire Blues," it is instructive to consider where the recording falls in a career strongly marked by an acute consciousness of place and culture. Like W. E. B. Du Bois, Weston married his ardor for African American freedom and equality to his identification with the African struggle for self-determination.[70] Seeing the civil rights, African decolonization, and Black Power movements as part of the same revolution, Weston began in the late 1950s to make music in collaboration with arranger and trombonist Melba Liston that spoke directly to contemporary African issues, most notably the 1960 album *Uhuru Afrika* (Swahili for "Freedom Africa"). Weston turned to Langston Hughes for lyrics and liner notes and used a twenty-four-piece big band featuring an all-star percussion section that included Candido Camero, Babatunde Olatunji, and Max Roach (on marimba)—all, like Hughes, Music Inn veterans.[71] In 1964 Weston's *Uhuru Afrika* joined *We Insist! Max Roach's Freedom Now Suite* and Lena Horne's civil rights–themed LP *Now* on a list of recordings banned by South Africa's apartheid government.[72]

Weston made two trips to Africa in the early 1960s, sponsored by the State Department and the American Society of African Culture, including one in 1961 to Lagos, Nigeria, with Langston Hughes. After touring the continent with his sextet in 1967, Weston, drummer Ed Blackwell, and bassist Vishnu Wood stayed on in North Africa. Weston settled down in Morocco, studied and collaborated with Gnawa and Jilala musicians, and ran a music, food, and culture establishment called the African Rhythms Club. His experience of living, performing, and studying in Africa, the basis of the Afrocentric aesthetic and ethos that suffused the rest of his career, was memorialized in compositions like "Lagos," "Tangier Bay," "Roots of the Nile," and "Marrakech Blues." While Weston's interest in Africa and the African diaspora came first from his family upbringing in Black Brooklyn—he titled another of his tunes "African Village Bedford-Stuyvesant"—his passion for African music also came from "being at Music Inn, meeting people like Geoffrey Holder, Babatunde Olatunji, Langston Hughes, and Dr. Willis James. They were all explaining the African-American experience in a global perspective, which was unusual at the time."[73]

This was a time when the dominant US jazz narrative cast the music as uniquely and indigenously American, "a kind of equal-opportunity soundtrack to [US] racial integration."[74] Weston's own experience fit snugly into that Cold War–era formulation, and he profited from it with his State Department sponsorship.[75] But Weston was writing a larger narrative, one in which Africa figures not just as the place of the music's origin but also as a vital location of its present and future. He was writing a narrative in which jazz is fiercely attached to place and yet also transcends place through its incessant and far-reaching mobility.[76]

Weston said of Ellington that he "used the sounds of the city, but [in] whatever he does, you can always hear the blues. And I think that so-called blues feeling, its rhythm and sound, is the sound of the African village."[77] In Randy Weston's blues, and in all his music, we hear a remapping of the history of jazz—a history rooted in the spaces where it was played and heard, from an urban club to a country barn, a history steeped in place and travel, from the streets of Bedford-Stuyvesant to a patch of woods in the Berkshires to the Moroccan seaside and back again.

2 MARSHALL STEARNS, McCARTHYISM, AND THE JAZZ ROUNDTABLES

"Who's this cat?" Randy Weston posed an excellent question when he happened on Marshall Stearns at Music Inn. At the time not many people would have known the answer. Stearns had been writing about jazz since the 1930s, but only as a side hustle. His day job as a college professor teaching medieval English literature somehow had failed to bring him to the attention of the broad American public. Over the next several years, however, he'd garner significant notice in the national press, where he was variously described as a "horned-rimmed, clipped mustached, apotheosis of The College Professor," "the Toynbee of jazz," and a "man whose mind is closely attuned to the disparate beats of Chaucer and Ellington."[1] His jazz writing appeared in *Harper's*, *Esquire*, and the *Saturday Review*, and he had a popular New York City radio program called *Jazz Goes to College*. In 1956 he found himself in the Middle East with Dizzy Gillespie's band, representing the US government on a mission to thwart the spread of communism.

Crucial to this trajectory was the time Stearns spent at Music Inn every summer through the 1950s, first as the originator and organizer of yearly programs he called jazz roundtables, then as a founder and faculty member of the Lenox School of Jazz. The roundtables brought together a multiracial group of jazz, classical, blues, and African and Afro-Caribbean musicians and dancers, poets, critics, and scholars from a range of disciplines including folklore, ethnomusicology, anthropology, sociology, and psychology—a remarkably inclusive gathering of thinkers engaged in rigorous holistic study of jazz in its fullest historical, cultural, and aesthetic dimensions.

Stearns was just then starting a new job at Hunter College in New York after earlier appointments at the University of Hawaii, Indiana University, and Cornell. Decidedly more committed to his jazz work

Marshall Stearns lecturing on the roots of blues and jazz at Music Inn, 1951. Jazz historian Rudi Blesh is seated on the front couch to the far right. Dancers Leon James and Al Minns are seated beside the stuffed chair. Photograph by Clemens Kalischer.

than to teaching *The Canterbury Tales*, he was the recipient that year of a Guggenheim fellowship, the first awarded to a jazz researcher, and would go on to publish two foundational books in the field, *The Story of Jazz* (1956) and, with his wife, Jean, *Jazz Dance* (1964).[2] Musicologist Mark Burford is right on the mark when he says, "It would not be a stretch to call Stearns the father of academic jazz studies."[3]

Stearns was both scholarly and good-humored and took immense pleasure in socializing. At his Greenwich Village apartments—his first, the top floor of a brownstone walkup at 32 West Tenth Street previously occupied by Leonard Bernstein, and then a flat at 108 Waverly Place spacious enough to house his collection of more than twelve thousand records and equally exhaustive volumes of jazz periodicals, photographs, and memorabilia—he hosted legendary parties whose guests included culture-minded couples like Philip and Stephanie Barber and writers, artists, and jazz musicians of such renown as Dizzy Gillespie, Charlie Parker, Billy Taylor, and John Lewis. These jazz luminaries and others made guest appearances in a jazz history course Stearns taught with John Hammond and George Avakian at New York University.[4] Stearns's collection of jazz materials became the original archive of the Institute of Jazz Studies, formally chartered in 1952 and run out of Stearns's apartment until his passing in 1966.[5]

This was vitally important cultural work at a time when jazz was still an object of widespread derision, devaluation, and misunderstanding. Still tainted by sensationalist associations with brothels, narcotics, and the criminal underworld, its real history was largely unknown, and its ballyhooed qualities of vanguard style, hipness, and erotic allure rubbed against the puritanical and Victorian sensibilities of white and Black elites alike. Many of its white supporters favored white musicians who were seen through a frankly racist lens as more learned and sophisticated than Black ones. Even among whites who credited Black folk culture as the matrix of the music's origin, many believed only white musicians possessed the intelligence and cultural equipment to elevate jazz into a legitimate art form.

Typical of the era's popular mindset was the 1947 film *New Orleans*, a Hollywood feature that purports to tell the story of jazz, tracing the music's rise out of vice-infested Storyville to commercial and artistic glory in Chicago, New York, and then the rest of the world. Louis Armstrong and Billie Holiday play supporting roles as muses to a high-society white female opera singer whose vexed romance with a casino and jazz club owner drives the plot. In a painfully hackneyed happy ending, the movie culminates in a triumphant scene set in Carnegie Hall, where the opera singer lamely croons a blues song she stole from Holiday, backed by the combined orchestras of Carnegie Hall and white jazz bandleader Woody Herman. Lady Day and Satchmo are nowhere to be seen.[6]

Stearns's commitment to elevating the cultural status and understanding of jazz, and of Black culture more generally, was matched by an equally strong passion for Black civil rights and equality. During his posting at Indiana University in the mid-1940s, Stearns headed the local chapter of the NAACP and spearheaded efforts to desegregate the campus as well as the surrounding Bloomington community. This was a tall order at a university where administration, alumni, trustees, and many students tilted strongly toward status quo conservatism on racial issues and much else and in a region where the Ku Klux Klan was still strong. Stearns earned a reputation as a troublemaker after intervening on behalf of a small contingent of Black students—among other actions he was an advocate for a newly constituted Black sorority and pressured the university news bureau to include images of Black students in yearbooks and other campus publications—and for leading the effort to force local off-campus restaurants and other businesses to end Jim Crow practices tacitly supported by the university. NAACP posters publicizing the desegregation campaign were torn down by the KKK, and the white supremacist terrorist organization draped trees and poles in the downtown area with ropes and images of white-hooded figures.[7]

When Stearns's contract came up for renewal in 1946, the university chose not to reappoint him. Historian Mario Dunkel has closely examined the available evidence and concluded that Stearns was let go because of his civil rights activism. In the emerging Cold War climate, not even a relatively centrist organization like the NAACP could escape suspicion of communist infiltration. Like many US universities, Indiana capitulated to the Red Scare by instituting mandatory loyalty oaths and purging faculty members suspected of being communists or even sympathetic to causes supported by the Communist Party USA. Stearns had never affiliated with the party and like several other left-leaning jazz writers—notably John Hammond—regarded the CPUSA's approach to race issues and its specific effort to appropriate jazz as opportunistic and ham-handed. In coming years his jazz writing—such as a 1951 *DownBeat* piece titled "Reds Can't Comprehend Jazz, So Put It Down"—would so strongly align the music with US policy that in 1956, when the State Department sent Dizzy Gillespie and his band on a tour of the Middle East as a soft-power initiative to promote American culture as a bulwark against the Soviet Union's insurgency in the region, Stearns wrote the promotional materials and accompanied the band on the trip as an adviser.[8] Dunkel argues convincingly that Stearns's anxiety about maintaining employment during the McCarthy era led him to pull away from overt, ground-level campaigns for civil rights and instead embed his antiracism in cultural work. He believed that teaching Americans about jazz could be "a subtle way of ingraining the values of racial equality and democracy."[9]

Folklore, Anthropology, and "Africanisms"

For Stearns part of what it meant to be a righteous jazz scholar was to be aligned with folklorists, anthropologists, and cultural brokers determined to recover the history of Black folk music and proselytize it as a crucial foundation of American culture itself. Zora Neale Hurston, Willis Laurence James, Lawrence Gellert, John Hammond, and Alan Lomax were among the most important figures engaged in this project. Hurston, the splendid African American novelist and essayist, studied folklore and anthropology at Columbia University—she was one of Franz Boas's students—and joined Langston Hughes in favoring the vernacular culture and everyday folkways of lower-class Blacks against W. E. B. Du Bois, Alain Locke, and others who preferred a strategy of racial uplift in which exceptionally gifted artists (part of Du Bois's "talented tenth") drew on the cultural inheritance of the race but emulated Euro-American high-culture aesthetic norms. James, like Hurston, was born in Alabama and then raised in Florida. He was an African American singer, composer, conductor, folklorist, and Spelman College professor who'd been collecting Black southern folk songs since the 1920s. Gellert and Hammond worked in the context of the Popular Front movement of the 1930s, linking the folk music of Black southern farmers and laborers to the fight against racial oppression and economic injustice. Hammond, a Vanderbilt scion who grew up in a Park Avenue mansion, also took it upon himself to monitor Black jazz musicians to ensure they were staying true to their folk culture and not turning jazz into a bourgeois, Europeanized travesty.[10]

The leading folklorists of the time were John A. Lomax, who had started his career collecting cowboy songs and frontier ballads in Texas, and his son Alan, who first collaborated with his father while traveling the backroads of the South recording Black folk music, then later serving an informal apprenticeship with Hurston. Much has been written about the Lomaxes as scholar-adventurers of the American open road, tireless collectors of work songs, prison songs, sea shanties, field hollers, ring-shouts, hymns, spirituals, sermons, square dance tunes, and children's game songs.[11] Father and son hustled speaking engagements at libraries, historical societies, social club banquets, and scholarly conference smokers. As white southerners of sharply divergent political orientations, John's paternalistic conservatism clashed with Alan's bohemian radical antiracism and critique of structural oppression. Above all, they were known for their "discovery" of Lead Belly (Huddie Ledbetter), a Black man they found in a Louisiana prison serving time for murder, a veteran of pool halls, saloons, lumber camps, and cotton fields, whom they shepherded to fame singing "Rock Island Line," "Goodnight Irene," "The Midnight Special," and other folk songs for predominantly white middle-class audiences—an immensely impactful but controversial episode of cultural brokerage in which, by John Lomax's own reckoning, Lead Belly became "the most famous [Black man] in the world" and he "the most infamous white man."[12]

Neither the discomfiting dynamic of John Lomax's relationship with Lead Belly, with the singer serving as his benefactor's chauffeur and following southern protocols of racial deference, nor suspicion of the Lomaxes among folk purists of their flair for self-promotion could gainsay their most important achievement. They had broadened the racial inclusiveness of the American folk song canon. More to the point, they had found in the songs of Black washerwomen, sharecroppers, railroad workers, churchgoers, and convicts an unmistakable bardic genius, a distinctive American sound telling singularly American stories. The poet Archibald MacLeish, librarian of Congress from 1939 to 1944, later heralded the Lomax collection of African American field recordings held at the Library of Congress as "a body of words and music which tells more about the American people than all the miles of their quadruple-lane expressways and all the acres of their billboard-plastered cities."[13]

The eruption of Lead Belly and the Lomaxes into broad public consciousness in the mid-1930s happened at the same time Marshall Stearns was launching his jazz-writing career with a series in *Down-*

Beat, "The History of 'Swing Music,'" the first jazz history produced by an American critic that was unequivocal about the pioneering role of Black musicians at every stage of the music's evolution.[14] This convergence was not a coincidence. Later, in *The Story of Jazz*, Stearns drew heavily on the Lomaxes for his discussion of work songs, minstrelsy, spirituals, and blues as crucial to the origin, evolution, and continuing development of jazz. Stearns had absorbed the view held by Alan Lomax and common among other folklorists that blues and jazz's urbanization and commercialization threatened the purity of Black folk music. While he chafed against the purist creed, he wanted to show that the best jazz remained organically immersed in Black everyday life. And the Lomaxes inspired Stearns and other people in the jazz world with their conviction that music was the most powerful form of culture; its performance and reception the most deeply affecting of experiences; its evocation of feeling and emotion linked to time, place, and social context the most illuminating evidence of how people live and have lived.

Stearns was born into the kind of Boston family that considered matriculation at Harvard a Brahmin class prerogative and regarded his interest in jazz—he played C-melody saxophone in high school and college and collected all the records he could get his hands on—as a youthful passion he'd surely leave behind when he came to his senses as a respectable adult. After graduating from Harvard College in 1931 and attending Harvard Law School, Stearns duplicated the journey taken by Philip Barber (Harvard '25) by relocating to New Haven.[15] In 1935, while a graduate student in Yale's English department, Stearns cofounded the United Hot Clubs of America, a jazz appreciation organization patterned after the group formed by pioneering French jazz critic Hugues Panassié earlier in the decade.[16]

Dedicated to the simple but for some outrageous proposition that jazz is a "worthy object of study," Stearns and his collaborators (the ubiquitous John Hammond, Boston-based critic George Frazier, and New York record retailer Milt Gabler) hosted meetings of jazz aficionados in New York, Boston, and New Haven, using their own record collections for sessions of intense listening and exacting analysis. Hammond had started his legendary career as a jazz producer and evangelist by overseeing recording sessions for the UK wing of Columbia Records and writing for *Melody Maker, Gramophone*, and other British music publications. While linking music and social justice in columns for the left, radical *Nation* magazine and the *New Masses*, the CPUSA's quasi-official journal, he organized labor protests in the factory where the records he produced were being manufactured. Hammond and Stearns were authoritative voices in the pages of *DownBeat*, the new jazz trade magazine, where they showed special interest in asserting the music's African American provenance.[17]

The idea that Black aesthetic and cultural properties were the defining features of authentic jazz was taken for granted within the Negritude movement in France. But it was controversial in the United States, where the title "King of Jazz" was held by Paul Whiteman, the appropriately surnamed symphonic jazz maestro, and where fan polls consistently rated white bandleaders like Benny Goodman and Artie Show higher than Black ones like Duke Ellington and Count Basie. Hammond and Stearns worried that jazz's African American progenitors risked erasure from public memory as their recordings from the late 1910s and 1920s were quickly going out of print. Under the banner of the United Hot Clubs of America, they lobbied the major companies (Columbia, Victor, Decca) to reissue the most important of those recordings, guaranteeing sales of at least a thousand copies of each through Gabler's Commodore Record Shop. Their success, resulting in reissues of recordings by King Oliver, Jelly Roll Morton, Freddie Keppard, Sydney Bechet, Louis Armstrong, Fletcher Henderson, the New Orleans Rhythm Kings, and others, ensured the availability of a textual record of early jazz that foregrounded

Black musicians and the few white ones who played convincingly in a Black-influenced style.[18]

Stearns's approach to understanding these musicians, their music, and their milieu reflected the strong influence of his studies in academic fields that seemed remote from jazz until his own work forged connections between them. One of his professors at Harvard was George Lyman Kittredge, a man of vast erudition who taught popular classes on Chaucer, Shakespeare, the epic, and the ballad.[19] Following the death of his mentor Francis James Child, who had done definitive work on the history of English and Scottish balladry—Child was Harvard's first professor of English, Kittredge the second, and a seminal figure in the professionalization of both English studies and folklore in the United States—Kittredge became recognized as America's preeminent scholar of the ballad. It was Kittredge who sparked in Stearns the specific literary interests he pursued more deeply at Yale and later taught in the English classroom: Chaucer, chivalric romance, Arthurian legends of the mystical quest for the Holy Grail, and the Knights of the (wait for it) *Round Table*. More broadly, Stearns fully absorbed Kittredge's interest in folklore, oral culture, and the search for American bardic genius in vernacular forms of expression—the search for a distinctive American voice and sound.[20]

This was a moment in America's history, Alan Lomax's biographer John Szwed has written, "when its citizens had begun to think seriously about the culture they had developed, and about where they stood among the nations of the world."[21] Stearns had witnessed the beginnings of a systematic effort to delineate the features of American culture in a course he took with literary historian F. O. Mathiesson, who began his career in Harvard's English department just as Kittredge was bringing his to a close. A decade after he taught Stearns, Mathiesson's book *American Renaissance: Art and Expression in the Age of Emerson and Whitman* (1941) gave shape to the American literary canon and played a pivotal role in the advent of the new

John Hammond enjoying a performance in Music Inn's carriage house, 1951.
Photograph by Clemens Kalischer.

scholarly field of American studies. Tellingly, however, there's no evidence that Stearns, who later energetically recruited American studies scholars into his jazz network, regarded Mathiesson as an important influence on him beyond showing that American cultural history had earned some measure of esteem in the academy.[22]

Mathiesson's concept of an American Renaissance—his book coined and popularized the term—held that Ralph Waldo Emerson, Henry David Thoreau, Nathaniel Hawthorne, Edgar Allan Poe, and Walt Whitman had collectively fulfilled the role of the American Homer or Virgil. But these writers of New England and the Eastern Seaboard had remained geographically and temperamentally linked to America's colonial landscape and cultural idioms at a time when the national story—and the sound of its telling—had moved south and west. It was in the sonic vernacular creativity of those regions where the American bardic impulse flourished. Stearns's passion for jazz and his absorption of the work of the Lomaxes and other folklorists had pointed his compass toward the US South and even farther south than that.

By the time of the Music Inn jazz roundtables, Stearns's sense of what tools were needed to understand jazz had prompted an even deeper interest in folklore and a new engagement with anthropology and ethnomusicology. His reading in these fields convinced him that reckoning with the aesthetics, social role, and cultural distinctiveness of African American music required an understanding of musical practices in West Africa and the Black Caribbean. He was especially drawn to anthropologist Melville J. Herskovits and folklorist Harold Courlander, whose fieldwork in Africa and throughout the African diaspora revealed transatlantic cultural survivals (Africanisms) in religious belief and practice, language, music, foodways, family structures, and social organization. Stearns traveled throughout the US South and to Cuba, Haiti, and the Bahamas in the late 1940s and early 1950s to witness firsthand the Afro-diasporic music practices he knew were not just part of jazz's prehistory but were continuing to shape its development.

In 1942, as Allied troops invaded North Africa, Dizzy Gillespie composed "A Night in Tunisia," which starts with a nimble ostinato bass line, setting a different groove than jazz's standard straight quarter-note walking bass, and features an oscillating pattern of half-step chord changes. These elements, which gave the tune a seductively mysterious feeling, were common in Afro-Cuban music, a style that had been percolating in East Harlem, the Bronx, and other parts of New York City where large numbers of migrants from the Caribbean had settled over the previous decade. After the recording session, Gillespie launched his big band, using "A Night in Tunisia" as its signature theme song. In September 1947, at a well-publicized Carnegie Hall concert, Cuban master conga player Chano Pozo joined Gillespie's band for the premier of "Cubano Be, Cubano Bop" and "Manteca," tunes that originated the subgenre of Afro-Cuban jazz or, as it was later known, Latin jazz. "Manteca" quickly became a popular hit, its mambo cymbal bell pattern and clave pulse proving at once irresistible to dancers and alluring to bebop connoisseurs.

After Pozo was murdered in Harlem in December 1948, Stearns traveled to Cuba to research his life. He interviewed Pozo's father and grandmother and searched for the roots of Pozo's musicianship. He observed drummers playing rhythms dedicated to the Yoruban thunder god, Chango, and witnessed performances of African-influenced mambo, rhumba, and conga dances. He participated in religious rituals that he likened to those carried out in evangelical ceremonies led by Daddy Grace and Father Divine in African American communities.[23] These experiences inspired Stearns to take up African and Afro-Caribbean drumming. Once, in a lecture-performance with the Randy Weston Trio, illustrating affinities between traditional African rhythm and modern jazz, Stearns related his own experience taking lessons from master drummer Asadata Dafora at Music Inn:

"It took me a whole month to do four with one hand and nine with the other. An African drummer does that 4-over-9 combination in his right hand alone."[24]

In 1953 Stearns traveled to Haiti with Courlander, who was conducting the field research that would lead to his book *The Drum and the Hoe: Life and Lore of the Haitian People* (1960). There Stearns participated in a vodun ceremony led by a priest who, he said, looked "so much like Charlie Parker that it made me uneasy." What he observed in the ceremony struck him as very similar to the rituals, ecstatic behavior, spirit possession, and general ambience he'd observed on his visits to Baptist revival meetings in South Carolina and Georgia.[25]

Herskovits, founder of the first academic program in African studies in the United States, at Northwestern University, had studied with the great German American anthropologist Franz Boas and carried forward his mentor's paradigm-shifting arguments about race and culture. Before Boas anthropologists purported to document disparities in the intellectual capacity of different populations through skull measurements and other putatively scientific procedures. This buttressed an evolutionary model in which races and cultures were sorted vertically into a hierarchy from "primitive" non-Europeans to "civilized" Europeans. Boas held that race was a social invention and not rooted in biological differences and, further, that every culture's values, behaviors, and forms of expression and social organization had internal logic and integrity and could not be ranked objectively as higher or lower than those of any other culture.

This was the basis on which Herskovits studied African and African-descended cultures. His book *The Myth of the Negro Past* (1941) argued that African Americans had inherited a rich culture from their African forbears—a heavily debated issue at the time, with other scholars arguing that slavery had destroyed any appreciable remnant of African culture in Black American life—and that they were in no way inferior to white Americans. Despite its having virtually nothing to say about jazz, this book was the first reading Stearns assigned in his history of jazz courses at New York University and the New School. Before his students listened to King Oliver or Jelly Roll Morton, he wanted them to appreciate the critical importance of studying Black culture.

The Red Scare and the Roundtables

In June 1950 a right-wing subscriber-based newsletter called *Counterattack* released *Red Channels: The Report of Communist Influence in Radio and Television*, with a list of 151 people alleged to be engaged in the subversion of American freedom. This became the blueprint for the House Un-American Activities Committee's infamous blacklisting of actors, writers, musicians, journalists, and others, effectively barring them from national broadcast media, publishing and recording companies, and other outlets crucial to their livelihoods. Included on the *Red Channels* list were two of the headliners at Music Inn's very first event, held the next month: Alan Lomax and folk singer Pete Seeger.[26] Another of the Music Inn inaugural headliners, folk singer Woody Guthrie, was not on the *Red Channels* list, but only because he'd already been condemned by the House Un-American Activities Committee for his prounion, pro–civil rights, antifascist, and antiwar views. Lomax had been instrumental in bringing Guthrie to the attention of the broad American public in the late 1930s, featuring him on his CBS network radio program *Back Where I Came From*. In a typical segment, Guthrie would blow "Lost Train Blues" on his harmonica while Lomax rhapsodized about him (the son of a wealthy land speculator) as a man who'd "gone into the world and looked at the faces of hungry men and women. He's been in hobo jungles. He's performed on picket lines. He's sung his way through every bar and saloon between Oklahoma and California."[27]

Guthrie and Seeger were the most visible figures in a so-called folk revival that raised awareness among urban and suburban middle-

Pete Seeger (left) and Woody Guthrie (right) performing at Music Inn's first concert, July 2, 1950. Dan Burley sits to Seeger's right, Reverend Gary Davis to Guthrie's left. Photograph by Leonard Rosenberg.

class whites of the song traditions of rural Americans, Appalachians, African Americans, and other ethnic groups. The Almanac Singers, the group Guthrie and Seeger cofounded in 1941 with their friends Lee Hays and Millard Lampell, paired this repertoire with protest songs aimed at various forms of social injustice, especially labor exploitation, songs Robert Cantwell has described as "dividing the world into stiff-jawed workers and porcine bourgeois bosses." The writer Theodore Dreiser said, "If we had six more like these boys, we could save America." The FBI disagreed. After it branded the musicians anti-American seditionists, a flurry of negative press and harassment forced the group to disband in 1942.[28] Over the next two decades, some of the most powerful people in the US government continued to libel these deeply patriotic artists as anti-American subversives. Despite—or because of—this persecution, the folk song movement blossomed into one of the singular American cultural developments of the 1950s and early 1960s, fostering a sense of moral righteousness among young people on college campuses and in summer camps across the country, culminating in the emergence of Bob Dylan and Joan Baez as culture heroes and champions of the civil rights movement.[29]

The *Red Channels* list included others who frequented Music Inn in the 1950s: classical and music theater notables Leonard Bernstein, Aaron Copland, and Marc Blitzstein; English-born folk balladeer Richard Dyer-Bennet; and two prominent African American cultural figures, the Harlem-based poet and writer Langston Hughes and the blues, gospel, and protest song performer Josh White, a matinee idol and darling of white café society. Sonny Terry and Brownie McGhee, a folk blues duo who were favorites of the Barbers and Music Inn audiences, were not named in *Red Channels*. But as veterans, like White, of labor and civil rights activism in the Piedmont region of the Carolinas and Virginia, they too were branded as dangerous radicals and effectively blacklisted by the major networks and booking agencies.[30] When a *New York Times* photographer balked at including Pete Seeger in his pictures of the Music Inn concert because of his suspected communist affiliation, Stephanie Barber was emphatic: "He stays in the shot, or there is no picture."[31] Seeger wrote to Barber many years later, thanking her for helping keep his career afloat during the "frightened Fifties": "I will never forget singing at Music Inn back in the days of the Blacklist."[32]

In Music Inn's opening event, Lomax, Seeger, and Guthrie were joined by Reverend Gary Davis, an African American street singer and veteran of the Piedmont blues and gospel scene, in a program of folk songs played for the inn's weekend guests. Lomax had been as important a supporter of Seeger as he'd been of Guthrie. Seeger's father, Charles Seeger, a distinguished musicologist and folklorist, moved his family from Connecticut to Washington, DC, in 1935, around the time Lomax started his work as an assistant to his father at the Library of Congress. After Alan became the top man on the library's folk song project (at age twenty-three), he hired Pete (nineteen at the time) as his assistant, tasked with cataloging and transcribing songs. When the young Seeger started his singing career, Lomax helped him develop important contacts, facilitated his performances, and eventually recorded him, as well as the Almanacs, for Commodore. Bess Lomax, Alan's sister, sang with the Almanacs. It is fair to say that Pete Seeger and Woody Guthrie would not have become household names but for Alan Lomax's tireless advocacy.[33]

Lomax himself had become a performer, strumming his guitar and singing folk tunes and ballads at labor union events, in local bars, and at parties held in the homes of Washington bureaucrats and politicians. When Charles Seeger was put in charge of programming the entertainment for a White House state dinner for King George VI and Queen Elizabeth of England, he called on Alan to sing cowboy songs from his father's collection. Lomax was honored, and the evening proved to be a watershed in his life—but decidedly not in the way he'd anticipated. A midwestern woman had contacted the FBI with information about Lomax's political views and loyalties. When Lomax arrived at the White House, he was frisked and bullied by Secret Service men who'd been alerted by the FBI. Badly shaken, he stumbled through his performance, even though Eleanor Roosevelt caught on to what had happened and offered warm solicitude. The FBI would continue to track and harass Lomax for the next thirty years.[34]

Lomax took the occasion at Music Inn to play tapes of songs and interviews he'd recorded with New Orleans pianist and composer Jelly Roll Morton in 1939 for the Library of Congress. This material formed the basis of Lomax's newly published book, *Mister Jelly Roll: The Fortunes of Jelly Roll Morton, New Orleans Creole and 'Inventor of Jazz'* (1950), a story of Morton's career editorially curated by Lomax but vividly told in Morton's own self-aggrandizing "sporting-life

Alan Lomax performing at Music Inn's first concert, July 2, 1950. Photograph by Leonard Rosenberg.

lingo."[35] Lomax had held on to his folk-centered view that blues and jazz had been corrupted by commercial forces—recordings of the music were played on the radio!—until he was able to gain access to the masters in New York record company archives (Columbia, RCA, and Decca; he ended up producing records for the latter two) and see how much important noncommercial music the companies had recorded. His antijazz argument also lost some of its potency when he heard Morton's stories about jazz's early development as a neighborhood music played by and for a small community of Blacks and Creoles, where it had all the hallmarks of a racially authentic folk music. Lomax's book would become one of the bibles of the "moldy fig" movement, embraced for bolstering Rudi Blesh's argument in his manifesto *Shining Trumpets* (1946) that real jazz died when it left New Orleans.

Just three months after his appearance at Music Inn, Lomax, fearing the implications of the recently passed McCarren Act, which empowered the government to arrest and detain persons suspected of subversive activity, set sail for Britain, commencing a long period of political exile. Based in London, he hosted BBC radio programs; worked on a massive multi-LP anthology of world folk music; took extended fieldwork trips to record regional vernacular music in Ireland, Scotland, Spain, and Italy; and tussled with cultural bureaucrats across Europe who threw up roadblocks to his work. These projects internationalized the scope of Lomax's seminal ethnographic research, expanding and bolstering his already pivotal work in the folk music movement.[36]

Shortly before Alan Lomax left the country in September 1950, Music Inn held the first of its jazz roundtables. Marshall Stearns intended these seminars to pursue several interlocking goals. The primary one was to systematize and codify the study of jazz, asking big questions about the music and its place in American life that were not being addressed in the jazz writing and commentary then dominated by highly fractious polemical debates between modernists and traditionalists about what constitutes real jazz. Importantly, this goal entailed exploring the roots of jazz back to Africa and through vernacular styles like blues, gospel, and calypso, an approach that emphasized jazz's cultural capaciousness and mitigated against strict policing of its stylistic borders. Even as the roundtables stressed jazz's folk roots, they also aimed to elevate jazz's cultural standing through the legitimizing force of academic authority coupled with Music Inn's location in the Berkshires next to Tanglewood, as well as combat caricatures of jazz by generating positive media attention that would disabuse Americans of their misconceptions about the music and the musicians. Finally, and of no less importance than these other goals, the roundtables undertook to contribute to the civil rights and Black freedom movements by furnishing a model of productive interracial collaboration, showcasing Black excellence and providing a platform for Black artists, writers, and intellectuals (not just African Americans but also Africans and Afro-Caribbeans) to shape public discourse about themselves and their art.

The inaugural jazz roundtable was a five-day affair that began on August 29, a Tuesday, two days after Tanglewood completed its summer season. Attendees spent the afternoon listening to recorded jazz, calypso, and Afro-Cuban music, then heard an evening lecture by Stearns on characteristics of African music such as communalism, improvisation, and polyrhythm. Stearns posited that Afro-Cuban music retains more African qualities than American jazz owing to the slave trade's longer presence in the island's economy, the Moorish influence on the music of the Iberian Peninsula, and the religious syncretism of African deities and Catholic saints, a vital cultural link

Marshall Stearns (back partially turned, with glasses) leading jazz roundtable discussion in 1952. Dr. Willis Laurence James is seated to Stearns's left. Photographer unknown.

not found in the parts of the Americas colonized by the Protestant countries of northwest Europe.

As the week wore on, attention focused increasingly on African rhythm. Ethnomusicologist Arthur Alberts presented drum and string music he'd recently recorded in Africa. Macbeth the Great performed calypso and spoke about the steel drum bands of Trinidad. Asadata Dafora, from Sierra Leonne, thrilled everyone with his drumming and dancing. A few days later, after the legendary Savoy Ballroom duo of Leon James and Al Minns performed everything from the cakewalk to the Eagle Rock, both Dafora and dance scholar Mura Dehn identified continuities between African and African American vernacular dance. In sum a Herskovitsian theme pushed by Stearns echoed strongly throughout the five days: jazz was an Afro-diasporic music with deep multinational roots that continued to be replenished.

There was more. Chicago-based African American journalist and pianist Dan Burley claimed that the blues had originated in Texas and played some tunes he'd heard there along with several of his own compositions. Stearns claimed that blues and jazz used the *perfect scale* instead of the *tempered scale* favored in classical music since the time of Bach, further asserting that part of what made these styles so compelling was that they drew from a more expansive tonal range than most European music.[37] Discussions sprinkled across the five days addressed factors working against Black performers, such as Jim Crow union halls, lower pay rates, and difficulty securing plum engagements in major hotels and national media outlets. Sociological analysis of "Negro stereotypes" surfaced, including the trenchant observation that "the negro is considered to have mystical powers which make him at once a friendly and a dangerous person."[38]

Announcements of the inaugural roundtable appeared in local and regional newspapers and the jazz press, while more publicity came via word of mouth in the Barbers' social network. A turnout of more than 250 people across the five days brought huge relief, as the July folk program had attracted only the guests who were staying at the inn. If public attendance at this first jazz roundtable had not been so robust, the Barbers might well have reconsidered the viability of their whole concept. *Record Changer* hailed the event as a major success, albeit in terms that inadvertently diminished the role of the Black performers. Under the headline "Jazz at Tangle-

Leon James and Al Minns, legendary members of Whitey's Lindy Hoppers from Harlem's Savoy Ballroom, on stage in the Music Barn, 1958. Photograph by Clemens Kalischer.

wood"—an early example of the conflation of Music Inn and the neighboring classical music festival that would repeat over the decade—writer Peter Drew enthused about "the eminently respectable and erudite Professor Stearns whose dynamism stands the best chance of upsetting this false and dangerous stereotype [about jazz's lack of respectability]." "Particularly gratifying," he continued, "was the fact that the listeners, a far less 'hep,' less automatically sympathetic group than the usual jazz-lecture audience [he was talking about the Tanglewood holdovers] not only stayed on for all five days, but in some cases volunteered contributions to Stearns's Institute project."[39]

There were nine Music Inn jazz roundtables held from 1950 to 1956, with two in 1951 and 1956, and one in each of the other years. The first seven tilted heavily toward Stearns's folkloristic and anthropological orientation; these sessions foregrounded the jazz styles and jazz-adjacent roots forms about which he was most knowledgeable (ragtime, early New Orleans, blues, swing, gospel, calypso, and Afro-Cuban) and spotlighted African American and Afro-Caribbean dance, later the subject of his book *Jazz Dance*, the seminal work on the topic and still an important dance studies text more than half a century later. Over their first five years, the roundtables included the calypsonians Macbeth the Great and Lord Burgess (Irving Burgie, writer of many of the songs that made Harry Belafonte famous); the Nigerian drummer Babatunde Olatunji; the Piedmont folk duo Brownie McGhee and Sonny Terry; bluesman John Lee Hooker and the blues duo of Jimmy "Baby Face" Lewis and Estelle "Mama" Yancey; gospel singers Mahalia Jackson and Ernestine Washington; blues and jazz singer Myra Johnson; ragtime and early jazz pianist and composer Eubie Blake and his theatrical collaborator Noble Sissle; boogie woogie and jump blues pianist Sammy Price; and swing band stalwarts trumpeter Rex Stewart and singer Jimmy Rushing. Despite Stearns's friendships with leading bebop musicians and working relationship with Randy

Weston, the only straight-up modern jazz players featured in the roundtables before 1956 were reedman Tony Scott in 1951 (when he jammed with Olatunji, thrillingly by all accounts); pianist Billy Taylor in 1952 and 1954; and composer and French horn player Gunther Schuller in 1955.[40]

The final roundtable, in 1956, took a new direction with an effort to smooth over the friction between older musicians playing in traditional styles and younger musicians playing modern ones. It was a remarkable session that involved Pee Wee Russell, Willie "The Lion" Smith, and Wilbur de Paris from the traditionalist camp, along with a who's who of modernists including the Modern Jazz Quartet, Jimmy Giuffre, Sonny Rollins, Dizzy Gillespie, Max Roach, Oscar Pettiford, Ray Brown, Charles Mingus, Teo Macero, and Quincy Jones. This valedictory weeklong roundtable—which we'll examine in the next chapter—culminated in a historic concert recorded by Atlantic Records and helped set the agenda for the Lenox School of Jazz, which opened the following summer.

The "Main Stream" and Its Discontents

The connective thread of the Stearns-led roundtables was the idea of jazz as a cultural web in which the music was inseparable from the various forms of vernacular expression that fed into it. This had been a core tenet of the UHCA's ideology in the 1930s. John Hammond proselytized the idea in two *Spirituals to Swing* concerts at Carnegie Hall, placing the Count Basie Band (in the 1938 concert) and the Benny Goodman Sextet (in 1939) in programs otherwise featuring Black "roots" musicians Sister Rosetta Tharpe, Big Bill Broonzy, Big Joe Turner, Ida Cox, Sonny Terry, the Golden Gate Quartet, and others. Hammond famously favored Count Basie over Duke Ellington, seeing Basie's rough-hewn, hard-swinging Kansas City style as more racially authentic than Ellington's allegedly Europeanized symphonic concoctions. This ran directly counter to the modernist idea of jazz as a high art informed by its vernacular sources but elevated to a superior status above them. Duke Ellington, for instance, was regarded by Alain Locke and other Harlem Renaissance modernists as an artist who drew on the blues, work songs, spirituals, and other folk forms but turned them into formal art works of disciplined mastery in his scored-through compositions. Modernist jazz critics Barry Ulanov and Leonard Feather embraced Ellington on the same grounds and championed Charlie Parker as a next generation vanguardist who rose above his source material (popular songs and blues) with unprecedented technical virtuosity and creative fecundity: he was a small bop combo *artist*, not a dance band *entertainer*.

The modernist angle on jazz implicitly cast the music in hierarchical and evolutionary terms: jazz represented artistic progress beyond the vernacular forms it drew on, and jazz's modern styles represented progress beyond earlier ones. There was even a new postwar genre called *progressive jazz*, mainly associated with Stan Kenton's big-band compositions, held by its supporters to be more ambitious, complex, and high-mindedly experimental than everything that came before. This was the basis for the sectarian culture war in the jazz world of the mid-twentieth century, in which adherents of the traditional small-group, polyphonic, blues-based style associated with New Orleans and Chicago resisted developments like New York big-band swing, bebop, and progressive jazz, while champions of these modern styles often denigrated the older music as archaic and unsophisticated. Stearns pushed against this cleavage. If we think of each jazz style as a culture, Stearns took the Boas-Herskovits position that each jazz culture was of equal value, each had its own norms and standards, and it was intellectually invalid to rank them into a hierarchy or construe them as following a linear path of progression. Importantly, however, whereas post-Boasian anthropology tended to think of cultures as isolated and autonomous, Stearns saw each jazz style (or culture) as intertwined in an organic and unified continuum held together by a common foundation in blues tonality and swing rhythm.

We see a partial representation of this in a blackboard chart that Stearns used throughout the two roundtables held in 1951. Titled "The Blues," the chart visualizes a genealogy of American music from antebellum marches, hymns, ring shouts, and reel jigs down through early New Orleans jazz and on to what is labeled as a post-1920 "Main Stream." Quite possibly this was the first use of a term that became widespread in the 1950s: *mainstream jazz* or the *jazz mainstream* signified a consensus forged around the proposition that for all the differences between, say, Louis Armstrong, Benny Goodman, Charlie Parker, and Thelonious Monk, their music shared a great deal and cohered into a recognizable tradition. Stearns's chart seems to imply that the entire development of jazz after 1920 constitutes an unbroken line held taut by its secure anchoring in the blues. The overarching importance of the blues, not just as a music, but as a language, an aesthetic, and a Black cultural ethos, gained more traction when Sterling Brown, the African American poet, folklorist, and Howard University professor, introduced his powerful voice to the roundtables in 1952 and 1953.

The second of the 1951 roundtables, titled "Definitions in Jazz," stands out for several reasons. One was the importance of Stearns's blackboard charting of "The Blues" and a particular photograph in which it appears. A second was the meeting's effort to come up with a concise, bulletproof definition of jazz, led by Stearns and ethnomusicologists Richard Waterman and Willis Laurence James. Waterman had studied under Herskovits and become a seminal figure in Afro-diasporic musical studies with his 1948 paper "Hot Rhythm in Negro Music," published in the prestigious *Journal of the American Musicological Society*. James, the Black folk song collector and Spelman College professor, had conceptualized an aesthetic practice he named the "Negro folk cry," which Mark Burford has described as "a

Ethnomusicologist Richard Waterman leading a jazz roundtable discussion, with John Lee Hooker to his left, 1951. Photograph by Clemens Kalischer.

spontaneous, prelingual cry, an *ur*-expressive device that was apparent in many folk musics but was uniquely fundamental to African American musical aesthetics."[41]

After extensive deliberation the group reached consensus on a streamlined definition consisting of a single sentence: "Jazz is an improvisational American music, utilizing European instruments, and fusing elements of European harmony, Euro-African melody, and African rhythm." While semantically efficient, the definition was a bare-bones, least common denominator affair that left out the most interesting parts of the roundtable discussion, such as explanations of how jazz musicians achieve rich expressiveness by employing "displacements" (James) and "flexible intervals" (Waterman) in their use of the diatonic scale, and Waterman's elucidation of his subtle concept of "metronome sense," a feature of African and Afro-diasporic musicianship in which players maintain a strong feeling for the music's underlying pulse.[42] Stearns cannot have been pleased that the definition did not more strongly emphasize jazz's African ingredients and failed to include such terms as "Afro-American" or—given the time—"Negro."

Several years later, in *The Story of Jazz*, Stearns revised the roundtable definition: "We may define jazz tentatively as a semi-improvisational American music distinguished by an immediacy of communication, an expressiveness characteristic of the free use of the human voice, and a complex flowing rhythm; it is the result of a three-hundred-years blending in the United States of the European and West African musical traditions, and its predominant components are European harmony, Euro-American melody, and African rhythm."[43] Notable here was an emphasis on the epochal history of transatlantic cultural blending and a more powerful illumination of the music's dynamism and pulse through such terms as "immediacy," "expressiveness," and "flowing." Waterman's fingerprints are obvious, and Stearns's reference to "the free use of the human voice" reflected the heavy influence of James. All the same, his close relationship with the Spelman professor—James had designed Stearns's itinerary for visiting Black Baptist churches in Georgia and South Carolina—did not save Stearns from inadvertently bolstering an enduring stereotype of Blackness by counting only African rhythm, and not also African melodic inventiveness, as a core element of jazz.

The third standout feature of the 1951 roundtable was the presence of gospel matriarch Mahalia Jackson. She told the story in a *Saturday Evening Post* article later in the decade, and it is worth following her narrative closely. "In 1950," she said, "the man who had always arranged for my appearances in the colored churches in New York told me about a symposium on the origins of jazz music which was going to be held up in Massachusetts. Music professors from the Julliard School of Music, Columbia University and a lot of other big places had been invited, and they wanted me to sing some gospel songs for them." The inn was full, and the Barbers had to put Jackson up in the barn. "They gave me an old horse stall to sleep in, and I thought to myself, 'I finally made it into the white folks world and look where it landed me!'" Jackson sang a program of songs with her piano accompanist, Mildred Falls, including "Didn't It Rain, Lord," "Jesus, Savior, Pilot Me," and "Movin' on Up." Then things got interesting. "As soon as I finished, a great big fuss busted out. The professors started arguing with one another and asking me where I had learned to sing that way. Who had taught me? Where had I learned such tonal shading and rhythm?"

> They got out tape recorders and played some African bongo drums and asked me if it sounded familiar. I told them I didn't know anything about jungle drums, but the beat sounded good; it did something for me. . . . They kept me singing there half the night. When I woke up in my horse stall in the morning, I heard tape recordings of my own voice coming from the carriage house. I told my accompanist, "We're into something here with these crazy people." They kept analyzing my style and disputing with me why I did it just that way.

Jackson concluded her account on a positive note. "'Mahalia,' Philip Barber told me, 'If you'd started down to the lake while you were singing "Shall We Gather at the River," all those experts would have followed you right into the water to be baptized.'" Finally, she expressed gratitude that "all those professors spread the word," which

Mahalia Jackson, her piano accompanist Mildred Falls, and "the professors" (left to right: Dennis Strong, John Mehegan, Richard Waterman, Marshall Stearns, John Hammond, and Willis James), at Music Inn, 1951. Photograph by Clemens Kalischer.

she credited with leading directly to her appearances on Ed Sullivan's television show and at Carnegie Hall.[44]

The *Saturday Evening Post* had a long tradition of depicting African Americans as premodern fol k characters, and this piece ran under the happy-go-lucky title "I Can't Stop Singing."[45] But the story Jackson tells—doubtless with heavy editorial intervention—is not inconsistent with other evidence of what happened in Lenox during those late summer days, though it underplays the extent to which Jackson was at odds with the line being pushed by the roundtable's leaders. Waterman and James were keen to have Jackson affirm that all Black music shared the underlying aesthetic properties of blue tonality, the folk cry, and metronome sense. Jackson refused to assent to any analytical scheme that failed to emphasize the religious purpose and meaning of what she sang. She was especially disinclined to acknowledge any connection between her music, blues, and jazz. When an auditor asked her which parts of gospel come from jazz, she thundered, "Baby, don't you know the Devil stole the beat from the Lord?"[46] Jackson grew even more emphatic on this point in coming years, when her appearances at the Newport Jazz Festival drew widespread attention. "Reporters always try to link my singing with jazz and blues and find some common roots," she told an interviewer in 1963. "There is no comparison."[47]

This didn't deter Stearns from pointing to Jackson's singing in the first chapter of *The Story of Jazz* as his primary illustration of blue tonality, which he describes as a common feature of Black music, in which "two areas of the octave—the third and seventh in the scale (E-flat and B-flat in the scale of C) are attacked with an endless variety of swoops, glides, slurs, smears, and glisses." "In other words," he added, "a singer, or instrumentalist, takes certain notes and cradles and caresses them lovingly." Jackson "creates an almost solid wall of blue tonality" at her annual concerts at Carnegie Hall, Stearns observed. "She breaks every rule of concert singing, taking breaks in the middle of a word and sometimes garbling the words together, but the full-throated feeling and expression are seraphic."[48]

Stearns continued his effort to frame jazz as part of a unified Black musical matrix, especially in the longest and largest of the roundtables, a three-week affair from August 15 to September 5, 1954. Stearns's apparent goal was to make a case for Afro-diasporic and African American music as a multidimensional folk culture that was

Mahalia Jackson seated next to Marshall Stearns during a 1951 jazz roundtable.
Photograph by Clemens Kalischer.

an underrecognized pillar of American culture writ large. The folk
theme became clear in Stearns's press release announcement that the
roundtable would culminate with "a jug band playing square dance
music of the deep South." Pete Seeger, Brownie McGhee, and Sonny
Terry performed together and talked about the multiracial roots of
American folk music. Trinidadian American dancer and anthropologist Pearl Primus, trained in the modern idioms of Martha Graham
and Charles Weidman but increasingly drawn to African culture,
took up where her mentor Asadata Dafora had left off four years
earlier. Lord Burgess and Macbeth the Great once again added their
distinctive flavor to the proceedings, seemingly turning Music Inn's
great room into a Harlem or Bedford-Stuyvesant West Indian social

club. Langston Hughes read his poetry, talked about Black life, and mapped out intersections between jazz, blues, folklore, and literature. Finally, S. I. Hayakawa, a linguist and semanticist (later a conservative US senator), delivered a paper comparing popular love songs and the blues, derogating the former for their "unrealistic idealization" and praising the latter for their sincerity and tough-mindedness. He was accompanied by the Sammy Price Trio and singers Jimmy Rushing and Myra Johnson, who demonstrated the difference.[49]

A stout challenge to the jazz mainstream concept came from art and music historian Rudi Blesh. Drawing his own conclusions from the work of Herskovits, Lomax, and Waterman, Blesh advanced a view that veered from Stearns's model (and the "Definitions in Jazz" symposium's findings), arguing that the blues was an African music with no European influences, and only those jazz musicians who played an authentically African-inflected blues idiom were playing real jazz. At Lenox he took the same peremptory position he'd developed in *Shining Trumpets*: "To this day, with rare exceptions, only Negroes from New Orleans can play real jazz." Only New Orleans, that is, with its "tumultuous echoes of dancing, shouting, and chanting in Congo Square" retained a sufficiently palpable memory of Africa to ensure the music's purity in the face of assaults by poisonous European elements, modernization, and commercialization. For Blesh even the jazz musician generally considered the best to ever come out of New Orleans had lost his way. By 1928 Louis Armstrong, in his Hot Five recording of "West End Blues," flirted with apostasy, Blesh alleged, by allowing pianist Earl "Fatha" Hines to traffic in nonblues, Chopinesque sentimental harmonies. By 1930, in what Blesh considered jazz's great tragedy, Armstrong had fully severed his connection with New Orleans collective polyphony by choosing to showcase his individual virtuosity in the putatively corrupt realm of commercial big-band swing. In Lenox, Blesh and his partner, Harriet Janis, continued their advocacy of simon-pure "real" blues and jazz, hyping musicians they were recording on their Circle label, among them Edward "Kid" Ory, Thomas "Mutt" Carey, and Bertha "Chippie" Hill.[50]

MOST COVERAGE OF the roundtables dutifully channeled Stearns's press releases or gave him space to write under his own byline. In the *Berkshire Eagle*, Milton Bass said of his attendance at the July 1951 roundtable that "it is the first time I have ever been able to hear one of my favorite types of music without being blinded and choked by cigarette smoke, and without somebody's elbow being crowded onto my large and sensitive nose."[51] Trad jazz magazine the *Second Line* reported on the 1952 roundtable, singling out the presentations by psychiatrist Maurice Green on the relationship between jazz and sex and Wellesley College psychology professor Irene Pierce on social groups affected by jazz. This lengthy piece described Willis Laurence James as "probably the greatest living ethnomusicologist"; praised Olatunji Babatunde (in the primitivist language of the time) for appearing "in the full regalia of his tribe . . . [and] completely captivat[ing] the large audience by his drumming, his dancing of ritual dances, and finally [by] the role of goodwill ambassador from the Dark Continent'; and said visiting sketch artist Bruce Mitchell "was as busy as the proverbial one-armed paper-hanger." These features evidently were not diverting enough to protect the writer's brain from the assault of the roundtable's dense, high-volume discourse: "One more syllable a day, and the collective cerebellae would have rebelled. And one decibel more, and the incus and malleus of each guest would have suffered permanent derangement."[52]

A brazenly sarcastic and elitist takedown of the whole jazz roundtable concept appeared in the *Washington Times-Herald* in 1951. Glenn Dillard Gunn, a classical pianist, conductor, and critic, was outraged that jazz was being taken seriously just up the road from Tanglewood. "An imposing cast will preside over this abrupt transition from the music of art to the music of entertainment," Gunn snarled. "It seems to be drawn principally from the universities. Guggenheim fellow Dr. Marshall Stearns, we are told, will 'chair' the discussions. Coming from Lenox with its traditions of great American literature this modern distortion of English suggests that jazz has invaded our current habits of speech as well as of song." Gunn might have found the following year's roundtable more palatable, the one that included a psychiatrist and a psychologist, for he was disappointed that "an authority on mental disturbances and psychic abnormalities" was missing from the one he did attend. "Devotees of jazz are not crazy," he reckoned. "They are just unfortunate. Their contacts with great music have been insufficient to develop standards of taste."[53]

Contrary to Gunn, key figures from Tanglewood gave Music Inn their full support and found substantial enrichment in its programs. After hearing a steel drum band at the 1954 roundtable, composer Henry Cowell devoted a movement in one of his symphonies to that instrument. Marc Blitzstein and Leonard Bernstein regularly attended jazz roundtables—Aaron Copland came to at least one—and were not shy about sharing their views. Bernstein, who was on the verge of becoming one of the most famous and popular figures in all American music, had been a student at Tanglewood in the 1940s, the prize pupil of Boston Symphony Orchestra conductor Serge Koussevitzky. But he was deeply interested in all genres of music and the connections and crossovers between them. He'd grown especially interested in jazz while writing his Harvard senior thesis, "The Absorption of Race Elements into American Music," in 1939. In 1953 a *Business Week* reporter writing a story on Music Inn found Bernstein on the inn's grounds playing guitar and singing "Arabian folk songs" to a group of listeners that included his newlywed, Felicia Montealegre, and the couple's friend, Stephanie Barber. Later in the decade, Bernstein's celebrated musical score to *West Side Story* drew heavily on elements of Afro-Latin jazz, doubtless at least in

Marc Blitzstein (left) and Leonard Bernstein (right) at a Music Inn party. Behind them is jazz pianist and Julliard teacher John Mehegan, 1951. Photograph by Clemens Kalischer.

part because of that music's heavy presence at Music Inn, owing to Stearns's belief that it was important to jazz's future.

The roundtables were known to many more jazz musicians—especially New York City–based ones—than those who made it to Music Inn. Billy Taylor, whose presence at the 1952, 1954, and 1956 seminars made him a crucial bridge figure between the traditionalists and the modernists, embraced Music Inn as a space where musicians could share ideas in a more deliberative way than was possible in the flow of their demanding professional lives. "We discussed this stuff after hours" he observed, "but Music Inn brought everything into focus." Lenox "combined elements of the school and the club" and "had tremendous impact because people came back to New York and put it [the fruit of the Music Inn discussions] out on the table."[54] Taylor would go on to become widely known as "Dr. Billy Taylor"—not just for his University of Massachusetts doctorate and his multiple honorary degrees but also for his extraordinary work as the public face of the jazz education movement, for his ubiquitous presence in radio and television jazz programming, and eventually for his role as the inaugural artistic director of jazz at the Kennedy Center in Washington, DC. This trajectory started for Taylor at Music Inn, as it later would for Max Roach, Gunther Schuller, David Baker, and others.

Leading jazz critics prized the roundtables and proselytized them. Nat Hentoff was a year into his stint as *DownBeat*'s New York editor when he came to Lenox as an invited panelist for the 1954 roundtable. He returned multiple times, and his thorough field reports in *DownBeat*, *Saturday Review*, and other publications helped raise awareness of Music Inn's importance across the country. "It was really in some respects like being on shipboard," he later recalled, "because there were really no delimitations as to hours or place, in terms of when you could talk to musicians and when they could talk to each other. It was a continuous flow, extraordinarily relaxed." John Hammond, whose maternal family owned an estate in Lenox, attended the important "Definitions in Jazz" roundtable in 1951, returned several times throughout the decade, and helped spread the word about Music Inn's importance and uniqueness.

Coda: Clemens Kalischer, Music Inn, and the American Promise

One visitor to Music Inn has left us an especially illuminating record of the jazz roundtables—a photographer who had just arrived in the Berkshires when he brought his camera to the two gatherings in 1951. Clemens Kalischer was a refugee from Hitler's Germany, where the Nazis had vilified jazz as a degenerate Black and Jewish creation polluting the great German classical music tradition of Bach, Beethoven, Brahms, Strauss, and Wagner. Born in 1921 to a middle-class Jewish family, he grew up first in Nordhausen, southwest of Berlin, and later in Berlin itself, where his mother was a physiotherapist and his father, a psychotherapist, worked with disturbed and delinquent children. When Hitler came to power in 1933, Kalischer's father perceived from his therapeutic practice significant anxiety and antagonism brewing in Germany's working class and lower-middle class. Presciently sensing looming danger, he insisted the family flee Germany as soon as possible. Kalischer, his sister, and their parents first briefly relocated to Switzerland before settling in Paris.

When the Nazi-friendly Vichy government came to power in France in 1939, Kalischer was taken prisoner along with other Germans. Separated from his parents and sister, Kalischer spent three years in a succession of eight labor camps before landing in Albi, an internment facility in southwest France. There, miraculously, he found his father and learned that his sister and mother were located at a nearby farm. Just as tanks and planes of the German blitzkrieg came within sight and hearing, the Kalischers were rescued from Albi, shepherded to Marseilles, put on a freighter to Casablanca, and then transferred to a transatlantic passenger ship that took them to Bermuda and then, finally, to Baltimore.

The narrow escape hinged on the benevolence of Anna Freud and Princess Marie Bonaparte, great-grandniece of the French emperor, Sigmund Freud's most famous patient, and herself a prominent psychoanalyst. Freud and Bonaparte were colleagues of Kalischer's father and succeeded in having his name included on a list of Jewish and anti-Nazi writers, artists, and scientists who received US visas through the Emergency Rescue Committee, a private American relief organization led by journalist Varian Fry and supported by Eleanor Roosevelt. The group included such luminaries as Heinrich Mann, Hannah Arendt, Marc Chagall, Claude Levi-Strauss, Arthur Koestler, and Marcel Duchamp.[55]

After their arduous journey, Kalischer and his family arrived in New York in 1942. Struggling financially and still frail from his brutal internment experience, he nevertheless was eager to avail himself of the city's cultural riches. While toiling in a series of jobs in Manhattan department stores and as a copy boy at the French News Agency, he enrolled first at Cooper Union to study fine arts and later in evening classes with Berenice Abbot at the Photo League, then housed at the New School for Social Research, an emerging center of European émigré intellectual life. The Photo League, a collective that included such notable figures as W. Eugene Smith, Paul Strand, Lisette Model, and Robert Frank, was founded in 1936 as an explicitly leftist organization following the model of the worker-photography movement in Europe. In 1947 it was accused of being a communist organization and placed on the Department of Justice's blacklist; it ceased operations in 1951.[56]

Kalischer eschewed strong ideology of any stripe and distanced himself from the Photo League's political culture. He viewed the organization largely in instrumental terms: his association with it gave him access to a first-rate darkroom. He was already familiar with the pioneering European photographers André Kertész and Henri Cartier-Bresson and admired their aesthetic of formally rigorous pictures of everyday street life. He knew what and how he wanted to photograph; what he needed was the equipment that would enable him to realize his vision.[57]

Kalischer was fascinated by New York City's architecture, its workers, and, especially, its marginalized ethnic populations. He combed the streets for scenes that spoke with quiet contemplation to the grace and beauty of everyday life, developing a bracing, clear-eyed documentary focus and keen knack for capturing subtle details of human presence and interaction, Traversing Harlem, the Lower East Side, Little Italy, the Garment District, Pennsylvania and Grand Central Stations, Madison Avenue, city parks and schoolyards, the Hudson River docks, and more, Kalischer, a self-described "silent observer," calmly trained his camera on food vendors, garment workers, longshoremen, shoeshine boys, store windows, news-stands, train passengers, and children draped on a climbing bar in a housing-project playground. The *New York Times, Time, Newsweek, Fortune, Harper's Bazaar*, and other major periodicals, both in the United States and Europe, published his pictures. His work garnered praise from art and photography critics and curators for its human empathy and compositional clarity. Kalischer's most widely recognized and celebrated work was *Displaced Persons*, a series shot in 1947 and 1948 of Jewish refugees arriving in New York by ship from Bremerhaven. In coming years Kalischer's photographs were displayed on several occasions in the Museum of Modern Art (MoMA), most notably in *The Family of Man*, Edward Steichen's landmark exhibition of photography that expressed global solidarity in the wake of World War II.

In the summer of 1948, Kalischer traveled through the American South and Appalachia, landing at Black Mountain College in North Carolina, at the invitation of Beaumont Newhall, curator of MoMA's photography department. At Black Mountain he encountered and contributed to an extraordinary arts scene that included composer John Cage, choreographer Merce Cunningham, painters Josef Albers and Elaine and William de Kooning, and many others. As exciting and enriching as Black Mountain was for Kalischer, however, just as memorable and transformative was an incident that occurred during his travels. Kalischer had started his journey south by rail. While waiting to change trains in Washington, DC, he came face-to-face with Jim Crow. Knowing nothing about American racial norms, he innocently sat in the "Colored" section of the station waiting room, only to startle a Black woman on the bench beside him. The episode—in the nation's capital, no less—awakened him to a harsh reality of American life and redoubled his interest in the lives of American minority groups.

Unlike Gjon Mili, Francis Wolff, and other émigré Jewish photographers who were passionate about jazz and worked from inside its culture, Kalischer came to the music by happenstance and did not make it the center of his life. After moving to the Berkshires in the early 1950s, he found his way to Music Inn—if not quite as haphazardly as Randy Weston and the two Jewish woman who accompanied him through the woods. What he saw there fascinated him. Kalischer came from a Jewish intellectual family and community in which vibrant discussions of literature, art, and politics were a vital form of social and ethical engagement. Here, just a mile and a half down Hawthorne Street from the simple cabin where he was living, were scholars, writers, and musicians digging into the aesthetics and history of an important modern art form, engaging in robust debate, and squarely addressing the race issue that was critical to his understanding of his adopted country.

Kalischer shot dozens of photographs at the crucial "Definitions in Jazz" roundtable in early September 1951, including those seen in this chapter of Mahalia Jackson, Marshall Stearns, John Hammond, and others. The one that has enjoyed the widest circulation captures John Lee Hooker sitting silently at a table in a makeshift academic setting. Hand across his forehead, head slightly cocked, Hooker casts a wide-eyed, penetrating gaze across the table. On the blackboard behind him is the Marshall Stearns chart discussed earlier in the chapter. We know why Hooker was there and how he fit into Stearns's agenda. He'd grown up in a Mississippi Delta sharecropping family and moved to Detroit as part of the migration of African Americans from the rural South to the urban North. His sound was craggy and serrated, equal parts country backroad and city swagger. His tangible air of Black folk authenticity served for Stearns a purpose not dissimilar to the one Lead Belly did for the Lomaxes.

The pellucid black-and-white composition and simple backdrop of Kalischer's photograph evoke a homespun rusticity reminiscent of Black Mountain College, a fitting analogue for Music Inn's setting as well as its similar atmosphere of purposeful artistic and intellectual labor. Hooker has about him an aura of alertness and sincerity. At this point in his career, Kalischer was cultivating a style not dissimilar to that of the American Scene photographers associated with the New Deal's Farm Service Association and Works Progress Administration initiatives. Like Walker Evans and Dorothea Lange, Kalischer married a social documentarian ethos to an elegant formalism, capturing a broadly inclusive vision of American life, rural as well as urban, at all class levels but with special interest in the marginal and disfavored. He tried to represent such people as dignified and self-possessed.

But look at Hooker's facial expression: Is it one of curiosity, satisfaction, skepticism, boredom, or something else? Hooker's contact with the white world at this point in his life was limited mostly to situations of radically unequal power, if not outright racist abuse. A letter Stearns received from a white Detroit talent manager who'd been in contact with Hooker before he came to Music Inn reveals not just a casually patronizing racial attitude typical of the era but a reasonable account of Hooker's concerns about what he could ex-

THE BLUES
MARCH
HYMN
RING SHOUT-CRIES
WORK SONG
DANCE-GAMES
RAGTIME
SPIRITUALS
JUG BANDS
N.O. BRASS BANDS
EARLY BLUES
1820?
GOSPELS
N.O. JAZZ
1900
THE BLUES
1910-
HILL BILLY
DIXIELAND
MAIN STREAM (1920)

John Lee Hooker seated in front of Marshall Stearns's blues genealogy chart at a jazz roundtable discussion, 1951. Photograph by Clemens Kalischer.

pect in Lenox. Stearns had asked the manager to intercede when the invitation he'd sent directly to Hooker went unanswered. "Hooker had received your letter and wanted to answer it but was unable to understand your intent in writing him," wrote the manager.

> He was under the impression you were a "prophet" [not professor] and couldn't quite get the drift of the whole thing. He is a trusting simple soul and has been taken advantage of by nearly all those with whom he has had dealings in the music industry. . . . A Negro friend and I have convinced him that you're a "right guy" and that this could be the break he's been waiting for. . . . He seems quite congenial, tho [sic] his speech is sometimes hampered by stuttering. He stopped drinking on his doctor's orders, and so far as I am able to discover (and I believe it reliable) he has no "habits."[58]

Hooker, who had a wife and two children and was working as a janitor in a Detroit steel mill at the time, wasn't so trusting and simple a soul as to not ask for travel expenses and advance payment for the ten days he'd be at Music Inn. While there's no evidence that his Music Inn appearance significantly boosted his career—he wouldn't be financially secure until the 1960s, when he was discovered by British blues-rock bands and their audiences—there's also none to suggest he found his time there anything other than agreeable. All the same, one of the things we can perhaps read into Hooker's expression in the Kalischer photograph is evidence of the heavy burden of being a Black man in a white space, not knowing if he was among the kind of white people who'd wonder if he had a "habit." This underscores a crucial point: however racially progressive Music Inn's ethos and productive its cross-racial collaborations, it was still a white-owned space in an even whiter place, a reality that its African American, Afro-Caribbean, and African visitors could not ignore.

John Lee Hooker performing during a Music Inn jazz roundtable, 1951. Photograph by Clemens Kalischer.

CLEMENS KALISCHER'S STORY gives us a tangible sense of the deep cultural richness and social importance of Music Inn in the 1950s, its reframing of American cultural history, and its connection to kindred post–World War II efforts to bolster the American arts. After recently surviving labor camps and courageously launching his own career as a visual artist, he now found himself in the company of dancers Leon James and Al Minns taking flight to execute their Lindy Hop steps, gospel queen Mahalia Jackson pursuing catharsis through religious ecstasy, and bluesman John Lee Hooker giving sonic shape to the Black Great Migration. His journey south opened his eyes to American racism, and his time at Black Mountain College gave him a sense of the vitality of the American arts and his own place within them. Where better than at Music Inn, a space dedicated to excavating the roots of Black music and analyzing its unique place in American culture, for Kalischer to discover both the nagging complexities and the bright promise of America? When we count Kalischer as one of the participants in the musicking that took place in Lenox, what we see there are men and women from radically different backgrounds testing their shared belief in the redemptive possibilities of suffering, the expressive freedom enabled by constraint, the lyricism borne of catastrophe, the highest joy wrested from the deepest sadness.

In 1950 Music Inn was caught in the swirl of anticommunist hysteria for welcoming artists and cultural workers who'd been condemned by their own government as anti-American seditionists. By 1956 Philip and Stephanie Barber, Marshall Stearns, and all the musicians, scholars, and writers they'd brought to Lenox had made Music Inn a center for the study and performance of an art form that the same government was now using to promote democracy around the world.[59] And they had created something more: a social laboratory for addressing the challenges of interracial collaboration, developing more honest and accurate configurations of American history and culture, and contemplating more deeply and critically what the country is really all about.

THE BARN, THE *EAGLE*, AND THE "NEGRO GENTLEMAN"

In April 1955 newspapers across New England heralded the upcoming opening of the Berkshire Music Barn in Lenox and its series of summer concerts featuring Coleman Hawkins, Dizzy Gillespie, Count Basie, Thelonious Monk, Art Farmer, Teddy Charles, Richard Dyer-Bennet, and other top-drawer jazz and folk acts. Some of the headlines conflated Tanglewood and Music Inn ("Series of Jazz Concerts Planned at Tanglewood," "Tanglewood Gets Jazz Barn").[1] Others primed readers for a culture clash ("Jazz to Vie with Symphony at Lenox," "Lenox to Have Musical Extremes," "Long Hair, Boogie Woogie to Mingle in Bay State").[2] The *Boston Globe* moved in the opposite direction, characterizing the Lenox arrangement as a "family reunion," in which "professors and mechanics, students and business people respond to [jazz and folk] just as they do to the familiar beauty of Bach and Beethoven."[3] The *Worcester Telegram* hyped the Music Barn as a hip, finger-popping, jive-talking alternative for those who found Tanglewood wearying: "If Brahms, Beethoven and Bach pall on you at Tanglewood, drop down a few squares to the Music Barn and pick up on some of these swinging sounds, pops. It should be the most."[4] In a tongue-in-cheek editorial, the *Berkshire Eagle* leveraged the area's vaunted cultural history into a swipe against the

Newport Jazz Festival, which had opened the previous summer to much ballyhoo: "Performers such as Dizzy Gillespie and Thelonious Monk, Einsteins of bop, will certainly add a fourth dimension to the sylvan glades of Lenox. It is only right that this type of music should gravitate to Berkshire County where it will be treated with the dignity and care it deserves. The social upstarts at Newport were a little forward in presenting their gaudy two-day festival of jazz. They should stick to their tennis and quiet dinner parties and leave the important cultural events to us."[5]

These various ways of framing the advent of the Music Barn reveal how challenging it was for gatekeepers to make sense of jazz's location in the American cultural field. Jazz was wed to classical music in its mission to be seen as serious, legitimate art. Jazz was an alternative to classical music because its swinging, improvisational approach matches the twentieth-century American pulse better than fastidiously composed and conducted German orchestral music from past centuries. Jazz and classical were musical extremes. Jazz and classical could be brought together, but their audiences were different and uncomfortable with each other. Jazz and classical were part of the same family and jointly appeal to a wide cross-section of Americans. And so on. All these positions, and their contradictions, wove their way through the cultural discourse of the 1950s.

One thing was clear: while jazz continued to operate in the commercial realm—it was still a business beholden to the bottom line, and it was organized into managerial and laboring classes—no longer was it considered commercial music in the same way it had been before World War II, when big-band swing was America's popular music and the heartbeat of a national youth culture. That space was just now yielding to the surging phenomenon of rock and roll. Like swing, rock and roll was a dance music marketed to teenagers as carefree pleasure and freedom from parental strictures, the fulcrum for a new youth culture with its own lingo, attitude, affect,

Dizzy Gillespie, with Nelson Boyd on bass and Charlie Persip on drums, at Music Barn, 1955. Photograph by Warren Fowler.

dress styles, and other accessories. Many jazz and classical musicians, critics, and fans deemed rock and roll not merely inferior music but an industrially manufactured, least-common-denominator travesty with little or no artistic value. This attitude enhanced jazz's claim to artistic integrity and merit: jazz had ascended the cultural hierarchy to a perch above the degraded commercial realm and was moving closer to the exalted status of classical music. Music Inn symbolized this trajectory more than any other place in the country—because of its physical proximity to Tanglewood and, even more, because journalists, tastemakers, and cultural brokers, even in New England, persisted in conflating the two institutions.

The jazz-classical relationship would intensify at Music Inn after 1956, when it became an epicenter of the third-stream movement, an effort to merge the two musical approaches, and when the Lenox School of Jazz fashioned itself largely after classical music–education models in its pursuit of artistic validation. Nevertheless, jazz's more natural affinity at Music Inn was the one that had been established at the inn's very first event in 1950 and nurtured in the roundtables, the one now being enshrined in the Barn's own programming. Folk music—and, even more, the notion of folk naturalism—was part of Music Inn's DNA and integral to the way it conceptualized jazz and presented it to the public. The Barn's yearly program booklets, like its publicity campaigns, gave equal billing to jazz and folk, even though a typical season featured three or four jazz events for every folk one. After the opening of the Barn, the Potting Shed became a semi-autonomous operation within the Music Inn fold, programming folk headliners, with late-night post–Barn concert jazz jam sessions as auxiliary fare.

But the inn's pastoral folk identity went much deeper than its staging of folk music. Music scholar Steve Waksman observes that the mid-twentieth-century vogue for outdoor music was "built upon a Romantic belief that encounters with nature could heighten aesthetic experience."[6] One sees this belief clearly reflected in early press coverage of the Music Barn. While the headlines differed, April's syndicated stories parroted the Barbers' press releases in noting that the Barn and the famous Tanglewood Shed "just down the road apiece" shared the architectural distinction of being indoor-outdoor spaces. This theme grew stronger in reviews of the concerts in July and August. *New York Times* music critic Howard Taubman, in a piece titled "Country Jazz," enthused about the design of the Music Inn concert space, a "fine old barn of French provincial architecture" with a "resonating backyard," which "has the look of a Renaissance courtyard theater." Writing in the *New York Herald Tribune* under the headline "Jazz Moves Outdoors into the Country Air," John Hammond reported that the Count Basie Band's performance in Lenox "was the most satisfying jazz concert" he could remember, "outdoor or enclosed." "The weather was good," the acoustics "nearly ideal," and the audience so "appreciative and attentive" that "every member of the band played as though inspired, and even the usual reticent leader was so overcome by an excellent piano and the surroundings that he played chorus after chorus on his own."

Business Week's story on Music Inn in 1953—the one that caught Leonard Bernstein singing folk songs to his wife—was a four-page spread with photographs of college students and twenty-somethings singing and playing acoustical instruments all through the inn's buildings and over its grounds. "Every Man for Himself in Upsurge in Music-Making" announced one heading, while photo captions read, "Guest finds outlet for his musical instincts in a paper-covered comb" and "Rhythm section beats it out on tuned drums made from steel oil barrels." The magazine's focus was US commerce: there was money to be made in folk music ("Music Inn has been doing 20% more business than last year"), the story assured its readers. Still, the key theme of the story was the inn's ethic of homespun craft and democratic participation ("Music Inn is thriving because it caters to

Music Barn stage and adjoining courtyard, designed by Philip Barber, 1955.
Photograph by Clemens Kalischer.

people who want to make music, not just listen to it"), core values of the folk movement.[7]

The folk authenticity trope permeated Marshall Stearns's thinking. "In a society of increasingly mass-produced, assembly-line entertainment, when every individual is treated like an empty pitcher to be filled from above," he wrote, "jazz retains something of the spirit of the handicrafts of yesteryear. The print of the human spirit warms it."[8] A common theme of 1950s social criticism was the lament that postwar American culture, in everything from mass entertainment to packaged convenience food, had been industrialized and standardized to the point that individual sovereignty and self-realization had given way to alienation and narcotizing conformism. What better way to counteract the numbing homogeneity of mainstream culture than to spend a weekend fashioning one's own musical instrument,

Count Basie Band, with Joe Newman on trumpet and Frank Wess on flute, at Music Barn, 1955. Photograph by Warren Fowler.

participating in a backwoods drum circle, or attending concerts in a barn?

There was an important underlying—though seldom acknowledged—racial dimension to the mass-culture critique. Tellingly, Stearns went further in the same passage: "Deep down, jazz expresses the enforced and compassionate attitudes of a minority group and may well appeal to us because we all have blue moods and, in a fundamental sense none of us is wholly free."[9] The "us" here reveals Stearns's blithe assumption of a primarily white middle-class readership or, what may be the same thing, an unintended but paradigmatic conflation of Americanness and whiteness. And the notion that white America's pursuit of true freedom called for sympathetic identification with—even masking and playacting as—Black Americans recycled a conceit dating to the plantation and the minstrel show, when the nation's most unfree people were envied for their expressive vitality, emotional honesty, and physical gracefulness. The same logic was in play in post–World War II America, where bland, white middle-class conformism found its opposite in Black vitality, and one of the remedies for mass-culture inauthenticity was—to riff on Du Bois—the soulfulness of Black folk. "The print of the human spirit warms it," Stearns's lovely phrase, might just as easily have been written by Rudi Blesh in one of his reveries about King Oliver or Jelly Roll Morton. Blesh *did* write the line "none of us is wholly free" before Stearns borrowed it. For both men the point was to try to convey the profound humanity of the blues.

The roots of the mass-culture critique lay in antitotalitarian responses to the rise of Stalin, Mussolini, Hitler, and, for that matter, American big business corporatism. One strain of 1940s jazz leftism was the "moldy fig" movement, which fashioned itself as antifascist in embracing trad jazz as warm, intimate, and virtuous in contrast to the cacophony of mechanistic big bands and—I'm channeling the fig position here—the affectless detachment of the beboppers. Swing orchestras were militaristic bureaucracies led by cult-of-personality celebrity bandleaders who dominated and infantilized their audiences. Bebop was an insidious conspiracy propagated by enemy-of-the-people pseudo-intellectuals. Progressive jazz was the sinister conceit of marquee bandleader Stan Kenton, an Ayn Rand–inspired, self-styled jazz businessman-superhero who wrote cold, bombastic orchestral works seemingly glorifying America as a superpower in the atomic age. Against these fascistic travesties, trad jazz—or simply *jazz* for the figs, who regarded the modern styles as apostasy against the real article—stood for honesty, authenticity, artisanship, homespun democracy, and human-scale sociality.

Music Inn's claim on those same values, even when it presented modern jazz, was strengthened by its contrast with the Newport

Jazz Festival. The two enterprises were tightly linked and supportive of each other. The Barbers and Newport's founder George Wein
were friendly and consulted with each other about artist bookings.
The advisory boards of the two enterprises were virtually identical.
While the Barbers' innkeeping responsibilities prevented them from
visiting Newport, Wein came to Lenox several times—he attended
the 1956 musicians' roundtables and played piano at Music Inn's historic end-of-season concert—and supported the School of Jazz by
funding student scholarships. Wein turned to Marshall Stearns and
Nat Hentoff, his fellow Bostonians, for help in organizing educational
panels, which closely paralleled the Music Inn roundtables. In 1959,
when Wein staged his first Newport Folk Festival, it was Stearns who
organized and moderated a Sunday morning panel discussion on the
state of contemporary folk music. One of the panelists, recently back
from abroad, was Alan Lomax.[10]

In envisioning the Newport Jazz Festival, Wein's primary model
was Tanglewood, which he saw as the "American Salzburg," a season of outdoor concerts in a bucolic setting with the imprimatur of
the field's most accomplished figures and an international reputation
for artistic excellence. Newport in its early years showed significant
promise in this direction. Starting in 1957, however, Wein began to
program rock and roll alongside jazz in hopes that larger revenues
would help him meet the increasing fees demanded by major jazz
artists. What had started as a quaint, boutique event ballooned into
a vast and ungainly operation, capped in 1960 by a youth "riot"—a
similar but much smaller fracas had broken out at a Kingston Trio
concert at Music Inn the previous summer—and a musicians' "rebel
festival" protesting Wein's alleged duplicity. Leading jazz critics had
begun to excoriate the festival even before these developments.[11] In
1956 the *New Yorker*'s Whitney Balliett decried the "fat hand of big-
ness" that he claimed had begun to strangle the festival in 1955 when
it moved from Newport's historic tennis casino to Freebody Park, a

municipal baseball facility.[12] Richard Gehman described the festival as a "huge supermarket" set up for the benefit of a "vast and generally tasteless public."[13] Wein's old friend Nat Hentoff—Hentoff's first-hand knowledge of jazz came from hanging out in Wein's Boston jazz clubs, and he introduced the impresario to his future wife, Joyce (Alexander) Wein—threw in with the rebel musicians, lamenting that Newport had become "a money-grubbing enterprise of the same category as any giant midway, staffed with shell games, taffy candy, freak shows, and thrill rides."[14]

Music Inn, meanwhile, had a lake, a brook, starry nights, the smell of freshly cut grass, a barn, and, very soon, a school.

The Lively Arts

The *Washington Post* press critic Ben Bagdickian once declared that there are only three great newspapers in the world, each of a certain kind: the *New York Times*, *Le Monde*, and the *Berkshire Eagle*.[15] A journalism trade meme circulated for many years touting the *Eagle* as "the *New York Times* of small dailies." *Time* magazine published an article on the *Eagle* in 1973 anointing it the best newspaper in the country for its size.[16] Purchased in 1891 by former Pittsfield mayor Kelton Bedell Miller and owned by the Miller family for the next century, the *Eagle* entered a golden period in the 1950s that lasted over the next several decades. The paper was known in the trade for hiring top graduates of journalism schools, the Ivy League, and elite small colleges like Williams, Amherst, and Smith, grooming them for long careers at the paper or preparing them for jobs at the *Boston Globe*, the *Times*, the *Post*, *Time*, and other larger publications. The Berkshires' proud and often feisty local town populations, coupled with the metropolitan sophistication of much of the summer crowd, made for a diverse and demanding readership. While excelling at nuts-and-bolts coverage of routine town-by-town civic matters, the *Eagle* also featured a stable of first-rate editorial page writers, eventually boasting of a

Pulitzer Prize. Its pages were occasionally graced with the voices of local figures of national and international renown such as Williams College political science professor James McGregor Burns and Lenox resident William Shirer, the legendary CBS radio war correspondent and chronicler of the rise and fall of the German Third Reich.

Tanglewood, the Williamstown and Stockbridge theater festivals, the Jacob's Pillow dance festival, and other Berkshire arts and culture institutions attracted ever-growing audiences in the postwar period, generating significant advertising dollars for the *Eagle* from those organizations as well as lodging and restaurant businesses whose clienteles expanded correspondingly. These heightened revenues, the swelling numbers of arts and culture-minded readers, and the sense among editors and writers that this sector was both newsworthy and integral to the identity of the area led to the hiring of writers with backgrounds in the arts or at least a willingness to try their hand at the beat. Like other small regional papers, the *Eagle* relied on wire services like the Associated Press and other syndicates for national coverage of the movie, television, and recording industries. But one of the reasons the *Eagle* punched above its weight was that it also employed its own music, theater, movie, and art critics of similar caliber to those working at the big-city papers.[17]

The key player in the *Eagle*'s beefed-up arts coverage was Milton Bass, who started at the paper in 1951. A Pittsfield native with a bachelor's degree from the University of Massachusetts and master's from nearby Smith College, Bass served as the paper's arts and entertainment editor for almost four decades while also building a career as a writer of popular westerns, detective fiction, and traditional novels. His regular column, "The Lively Arts," where he reported on the local scene and commented on national cultural trends, was one of the *Eagle*'s most popular spaces. Bass came into the position with an appreciation for jazz, some experience hearing it played live in New York clubs, and an affection mostly for its more crowd-pleasing styles, but nothing approaching the level of expertise or deep immersion typical of the era's well-known jazz critics.[18]

In Music Inn's first years, the Barbers and Marshall Stearns knew that the *Eagle* would be crucial to the fate of their operation. Stearns at first was unsure about Bass, claiming the *Eagle* writer "initially knew nothing about jazz," and later expressed surprised when Bass showed some progress, quipping "his conversion to jazz was gratifyingly close to a miracle."[19] Bass quickly grew into the job and wrote capably about Music Inn's jazz events over the decade. Sharply opinionated, trusting of his own spontaneous reactions, he didn't hesitate to publish lukewarm reviews of famous or soon-to-be-famous Barn headliners and often captured concert high points with sound judgment and fresh, snappy prose. By the end of the decade, Bass was writing occasional jazz pieces for the *Atlantic*, where he examined new developments in the music, including ones he heard at Music Inn and didn't like.[20]

Thorough local newspaper coverage endows an event or series of events with local meaning, makes the events part of the local conversation, turns their participants into local characters, and makes them a part of local history and sense of place. If a paper like the *Eagle* runs an interview with a national celebrity or an artist of national reputation who appears at a local venue, readers are made to feel a personal connection to that person. Dave Brubeck appearing at Music Inn, with the performance advertised, previewed, reported, and reviewed in the *Eagle*, made readers look at this international star as a part of their own lives, an indigenous feature of their native ground. Like many School of Jazz faculty members, Brubeck brought his family to Music Inn. His children swam in Stockbridge Bowl and played on the beach with other Lenox and Stockbridge children. This effectively anointed these musicians and their family members as honorary members of the community. Locals who harbored ambivalent or even hostile feelings toward the "summer people" felt differently about a Dave Brubeck, Dizzy Gillespie, John Lewis, or Leonard Bernstein. When one of those men dined at a Manhattan restaurant, it was a routine event of no special moment. When they dined at a restaurant in the Berkshires, they became part of that restaurant's history and identity. If Earl at Loeb's Market in downtown Lenox were to exchange banter with Dizzy Gillespie while ringing up his copy of the morning *New York Times*, the encounter would become part of local community folklore.

Conversely, when Milton Bass wrote about a Music Inn concert, he became part of the performance, a mediator in the public experience of the event, and, most important of all, a custodian of its memory. He was an integral part, as it were, of Music Inn's musicking. Did those who attended the Ahmad Jamal concert share Bass's disappointment in the "tepid renditions of several well-known songs" and the pianist's "showman's knowledge of what will titillate an undiscerning audience, playing each gimmick for all it's worth"? Did they come away feeling that Jamal plays "jazz style rather than jazz"?[21] Maybe not, if the *Holyoke Transcript Telegram* was to be believed, for that paper's reviewer observed an audience that "sat in rapture for almost three hours" before "their beloved saint."[22] How did Charles Mingus and his admirers feel when Bass, in reviewing his performance with the Teddy Charles Quartet, complained that "the bass is essentially a harsh, blunt instrument and no matter how virtuoso the performer, there is a certain loss of melodic line when the instrument is too dominant in a group," as Bass deemed it to be on this occasion?[23] How did gospel fans feel when Bass praised Mahalia Jackson when she played the Music Barn but put down her genre, asserting that "gospel songs are for the most part contrived compositions with naïve lyrics, [and] adaptations of the simplest homiletic clichés"?[24]

What did drummers think about Bass's judgment that Louis Bellson's solo in the Dorsey Brothers concert "was not as imaginative as

Left to right around the table: Dave Brubeck, Angela Kalischer, Cornelia Kalischer, and Chip Barber, at Music Inn, 1959. Photograph by Clemens Kalischer.

those delivered on the same stage recently by Max Roach and Chico Hamilton" or that Roy Haynes, playing behind Sarah Vaughan, "showed his admiration for Max Roach in a couple of solos but did not demonstrate any of Mr. Roach's ability" or that Dave Brubeck's rhythm section of bassist Norman Bates and drummer Joe Morello formed "the most solid backstopping available to any jazz group anywhere"?[25] What were the reactions and counterreactions to Bass's saying of Vaughan that her "'cuteness' quite often gets the better of her musical judgement, and there are times when she completely destroys a mood just for the sake of an audience chuckle"? Or, on the occasion of Billie Holiday's death, what was the response to his recalling that "when she sang at the Music Barn in Lenox two years ago, she was trying to substitute alcohol for narcotics and it proved a sad and sorry affair."[26]

These were some of Bass's most pointed provocations. But every

Billie Holiday, with Mal Waldron on piano and Chuck Israels on bass, at Music Barn, 1957. Photograph by Warren Fowler.

review provokes someone. People who care about musicians and what they play care equally about how musicians and their music are represented in print and then talked about; such caring is integral to the feelings and meanings the music accrues as part of the musicking process. Impossible though it is to measure the volume of discussion engendered from a concert review, or in most cases to follow this or that particular discussion in detail, there develops within a community, particularly a relatively small one, the felt presence of a public conversation, a sense of the direction of that conversation, and a potentially infinite set of either publicly voiced or privately contemplated thoughts on the part of individuals who engage with the conversation, even if only in their own minds. We can dismiss this as nothing more than a parade of gossip. Or we can recognize it as the social alchemy that turns art into public culture.

The Newport Jazz Festival took place over a single weekend. Music Inn, starting with the opening of the Barn in 1955, mounted a *season* of concerts over the course of ten consecutive summer weeks, sometimes staging two in the same week. Most of the performers stayed at the inn for a whole week leading up to their performance.[27] Couple this with the buzz generated both about and within the jazz roundtables and later the School of Jazz, and the jazz conversation in Lenox became especially robust and multilayered. And then this conversation went national when outside newspaper and magazine journalists and jazz critics wrote about Lenox, amplifying its reach and intensifying its impact within the jazz ecosystem. This is the process by which Music Inn mediated between the local and the national, making jazz's connection to the culture of Lenox and the Berkshires consequential to the shaping of the music's own larger culture.

A good arts writer and editor knows that reviewing concerts is just one way a newspaper brings a season of music alive and gives it context and coherence. There are also "color" stories to be written, providing texture and dimension to the season, making it feel like something more than a succession of this concert, then the next one, and then the next one after that. Bass wrote a story about Robert Reisner, impresario of the Open Door, a modern jazz club in New York, who managed the Music Barn in the summer of 1955. Reisner, later the author of *Bird: The Legend of Charlie Parker* (1962), an oral history he compiled in the years following Parker's death, was the *Village Voice*'s first jazz writer and a tireless tout for new styles of modern jazz. "He started a one-man campaign to make Greenwich

Village conscious of cool jazz," Bass informed *Eagle* readers. "He carried signs, posted bills, delivered circulars, tangled with cops and spread the word. The response was strictly nowhere. So he took out an ad in [the *Voice*] which read 'Bob Reisner says the three greatest life experiences are sex, psychoanalysis, and cool jazz.'" Intrigued by Reisner's manner of speech, Bass observed that "his Brooklyn soprano has been blitzkrieged by [the] jazz idiom."[28] Now Reisner was more than a manager; he was a character who brought flavor to the scene.

The Barbers and Marshall Stearns counted on Reisner, who was also serving as the Institute of Jazz's librarian, to help facilitate relations with the modern jazz headliners in the 1955 Music Barn season—Dizzy Gillespie, Art Farmer, Thelonious Monk, Teddy Charles, and each bandleader's sidemen—and to shape publicity about what Music Inn was hoping to accomplish. "With poetry and painting all being done in the abstract now, the road [modern] jazz has taken is the only logical one," Reisner told Bass. (Reisner was also an art historian and taught a course at the New School on graffiti, later writing a seminal book on the history of the form.) Reisner was aware that a certain segment of the public was put off by the cool demeanor of many jazz modernists. "The musicians aren't aloof; they're just shy," he told Bass. "Most of these modern jazz musicians are classically trained, and in their week's stay at Music Inn they plan to rehearse, compose, cogitate."[29]

Bass's story on Reisner provided important context for a phenomenon the *Eagle* writer and others met with ambivalence, if not mild resistance. Throughout the mid-to-late 1950s, Bass's concert reviews revealed his preference for blues-based swing acts like Count Basie and his shout singer Jimmy Rushing, Louis Armstrong (who appeared with singer and dancer Velma Middleton), and Duke Ellington. Along with millions of other Americans, Bass seemed to expect from jazz an experience of uncomplicated happiness, joy, and excitement, one he was able to also access from a jocular, audience-pleasing bebopper like Dizzy Gillespie or a warm, straight-ahead hard bop act like the Max Roach–Clifford Brown group. With the notable exception of Brubeck, whom he credited with playing "some of the finest jazz ever heard in this area," Bass appeared to be on the fence, and often puzzled, about the strain of modern jazz that was moving in the direction of abstraction.[30] One can taste the snark dripping from these lines in one of "The Lively Arts" columns: "From now on Dixieland will be reserved for the funerals of close friends. Big bands will be relegated to weddings and bar mitzvahs. As far as music is concerned, it is going to be strictly that air-conditioned, chamber-room jazz."[31] Reviewing the Gerry Mulligan Quartet, Bass raved about Mulligan and trombonist Bob Brookmeyer's playing but bemoaned their drift into a West Coast "smooth, easy jazz which is more interesting than exciting."[32]

Bass was especially chilly toward Jimmy Giuffre, or at least the direction the reedman and composer was taking in his chamber-style music. Concerning Giuffre's trio with Brookmeyer and guitarist Jim Hall, Bass conceded that the three "cannot be denied as musicians, but one can dispute what they are doing with their talents." He added, "There is a world of difference between intellectual jazz and the introverted material that was played last night. To me, Giuffre seems to be refining himself out of musical existence, and if you look closely you can see that the emperor has no clothes." Clarifying what he meant, Bass said Giuffre's "improvisations grip neither the mind nor the emotions."[33]

Historic Jazz Concert at Music Inn

Rehearsal, composition, cogitation, cool demeanor, introversion: these were activities and affects more commonly associated with classical music than with jazz. Even a Greenwich Village bohemian like Bob Reisner knew as much and perceived the drift of things.

He, the Barbers, and Marshall Stearns recognized that jazz's struggle for legitimacy entailed not just the blessing of high-culture priests but an activation of their own agency in the building of their own practices of self-examination, education, evaluation, and historical memorialization. Jazz musicians were keen to create their own conversations—high-level, serious exchange and debate as practiced in the jazz roundtables, but now under their own leadership and attuned to their own concerns. As a result, the final set of roundtables, held in August 1956, were organized differently than the previous ones. A call went out to 150 musicians, inviting them to Music Inn for a set of musician-centered discussions. The 60 who showed up, Bass reported, were eager to "discuss their peculiar problems."[34] The results were historic.

"This is the first time musicians have sat down and discussed what bothered them musically," John Lewis said, in what was surely an overstatement. "Usually you just talk about a shortage of gigs and money."[35] Discussing "what bothered them musically"—an adroit phrase—took the shape of roundtables focused on issues like what makes for an effective rhythm section, the nature of jazz composition and its relationship to improvisation, jazz sonorities and the specific features of different instruments—in other words, artists talking about the nuts and bolts of making art. A separate but related purpose was gently pushed by Stearns and Lewis but also emerged organically, owing to the specific musicians present and the thoughts and feelings generated by the process of their talking and playing with one another. This was the matter of lingering tension between traditional and modern players, a situation less of their own doing than a consequence of fierce partisan passions among critics and fans coming to dominate jazz's public discourse. *New York Times* jazz critic John S. Wilson nevertheless put the blame on the musicians: "One of the stumbling blocks of the modern jazz musician has been his lack of knowledge or understanding of the background of the music

Roundtable with Leonard Feather, Dizzy Gillespie, George Wein, Willis Conover, Teddy Charles, and others, 1956. Photograph by Carol Reiff.

he is attempting to play. This ignorance has been encouraged by the schism between the older forms of jazz and the newer ones, a split in which it has become fashionable for musicians on one side of the fence to offer little but scorn to those on the other side."[36]

In the rhythm-section symposium, Sammy Price, a veteran boogie-woogie and jump blues pianist, and Wilbur de Paris, a Dixieland and old-time swing trombonist, regaled a group of young modernists with stories of coming up in minstrel shows, movie pit bands, marching bands, and tab shows. Eventually the discussion came around to the question of where swing originated, what it is, and whether there are different ways of playing it—an issue that jazz critics and musicologists would grapple with for decades to come, never quite satisfied with their efforts to explain something so fundamental to jazz and yet so difficult to capture in language. Max Roach asked Price and de Paris if they knew when and where the emphasis of the beat switched from the one and three of the marching band to the two and the four of the early swing bands. No clear answer was proffered, but everyone agreed that this was the right question. Roach said his earliest model was Jo Jones, the way he locked into a steady and propulsive groove with bassist Walter Page, guitarist Freddie Green, and Count Basie on piano, adding that what became known as "The All-American Rhythm Section" were masters of inflection and dynamics. Later, in another session, he hailed his bebop contemporary Kenny Clarke for showing how a drummer could still swing, and maybe swing even harder, using "broken rhythm." The point Roach most wanted to emphasize was that drummers swing only if they have a subtle feel for tension and release in the flow of the music.

Connie Kay, Clarke's successor in the Modern Jazz Quartet drum chair, suggested that the key to understanding swing is to not focus on the rhythm section but rather to try to grasp how a band like Basie's swings as a tightly integrated unit. A friendly disagreement surfaced between Jimmy Giuffre and de Paris when Giuffre—whose just-released LP *Tangents in Jazz* inaugurated his period of chamber jazz that soon led to his using drummerless trios—attempted to explain his interest in what he called "felt pulse," a quality in which a tune's rhythm need not be sounded to be present. De Paris admitted to being confused ("I don't get it"), the more so when Giuffre said a key influence on his innovation was a recent Louis Armstrong record. Modern Jazz Quartet bassist Percy Heath jumped in to support Giuffre, perceptively observing that what Giuffre was going after is a music that is "swinging itself."[37]

The "composer in jazz" event featured Jimmy Giuffre, Teddy

Charles, Teo Macero, Quincy Jones, John Lewis, Willie "The Lion" Smith, Oscar Pettiford, Charles Mingus, and Bill Russo—an absolute powerhouse of a group. Russo, a student of pianist Lennie Tristano who'd written for the Stan Kenton Orchestra and later would teach composing, arranging, and ensemble playing for the Lenox School of Jazz, set the terms by asserting, somewhat peevishly, "I don't trust improvisers anymore. I'm not going to let anyone butcher my efforts. What's more important, the writing or the playing?" Russo was asking a question that remains pressing for musicologists in our own time: Where does music's essence reside, in the text or the performance? Jazz strongly emphasizes performance but in doing so begs the question of what jazz composition really is. Russo was expressing a position commonly held in classical music, where master composers (Mozart, Beethoven, Mahler, et al.) are canonized and remembered while performers of their music rarely are. Others roundtable participants pushed back. Teddy Charles said that jazz composition must involve improvisation—composers must write with improvisers in mind—or it is not jazz. John Lewis doubled down on the primacy of improvisation: "To take and play this music, you have to improvise to really make it come alive." Oscar Pettiford concurred, delivering a keen insight that applies to more than just jazz: "There was improvisation before a man learned how to write music."[38]

To the surprise of no one who knew them, Pettiford and Mingus were especially vocal throughout the week. Pettiford, of African, Choctaw, and Cherokee descent, took every opportunity available to admonish the congregants and jazz historians for neglecting the American Indian contribution to jazz, which he argued was especially critical to the idiom's approach to rhythm. Mingus exclaimed joyously several times when the discussions and the music performed during the week confirmed that his own ideas and methods, considered idiosyncratic by many, had precedents or analogues in the work of earlier generations of jazz artists. "Hey, I've got roots!" he shouted after Willie "The Lion" Smith finished a stride piano demonstration. A reporter noted that "Mingus was overjoyed to hear Pee Wee [Russell] expressing the principal of the Dixieland front line, because it has some connection with his own rather peculiar way of combining composition and improvisation." At other times Mingus spoke thoughtfully about where jazz was headed. "I went to church [one] Sunday and listened to the preacher and the people sang. They came together. There was more jazz [in that church] than what I hear today."[39] This foreshadowed Mingus's recording of "Wednesday Night Prayer Meeting," the opening tune on his 1960 LP *Blues and Roots*, as well as the entire soul jazz movement of the late 1950s and early 1960s, in which Mingus, Horace Silver, Bobby Timmons, Jimmy Smith, and others drew heavily on gospel, blues, and rhythm and blues in an effort to reconnect jazz with the Black community.

"It's difficult to verbalize how stimulating the week was," Nat Hentoff reflected. "First of all, it was the first time that a large number of jazz musicians of varying backgrounds had had the time and place to communicate *to each other*." Hentoff noted the warmth that developed between the different generations of musicians after some initial mutual wariness. This détente culminated in a concert held on August 30, 1956, the last night of the gathering, which was recorded by Atlantic and released two years later with the title *Historic Concert at Music Inn*. Hentoff chronicled how the concert somewhat miraculously came off despite there being no designated leader or program plan. After musicians started showing up in the Barn around eight o'clock,

> this writer and others present began to try to organize the night. What first became evident was that rather than having to worry about getting enough players of homogenous styles to agree to make up a set, the main concern was to avoid too heterogenous a grouping. Contrary to legend, the younger players wanted

Atlantic LP cover, *Historic Jazz Concert at Music Inn*, 1958. Photograph by Clemens Kalischer.

badly to play with the older ones, and it worked the other way around. The result was a succession of entirely spontaneous performances and much mixing of personnel and ages.

The highlight of the evening, witnesses agreed, was a rendition of "Blues in E-Flat" with a rhythm section of George Wein, Oscar Pettiford, and Connie Kay backing Jimmy Giuffre and Pee Wee Russell, each on clarinet. Hentoff was so taken by Giuffre and Russell's easy rapport that he and Whitney Balliett restaged the duet for the CBS-TV *Sound of Jazz* program they produced the following year. By all accounts everyone left Music Inn feeling that something extraordinary had just taken place. John Lewis was exuberant, proclaiming the week of roundtables, along with the concert, collectively as "one of the most exciting events in the history of jazz."[40]

The Jazz–Classical Conundrum and the Third Stream

Music Inn, I've been arguing, was a space where jazz was positioned in a trilateral relationship with classical music, folk music, and the pastoral ideal. A particularly beautiful Kalischer photograph illustrates this well. The photo catches four young musicians—two male double-bass players, a female violinist, and a female flutist—standing just outside the carriage house. Framed by a wall-size door against a backdrop of the inn's potting shed, lush greenery, and soaring sky, the musicians are attractively arrayed in a horizontal line. Kalischer finds vertical balance across the line as the two bassists bow their strings at waist level, while the violinist and flutist hold their instruments up to their chin and lips. The deep indoor-to-outdoor vista, the blissful summer atmosphere, and the elegant symmetry of the well-groomed performers all contribute to one's sense of a rustic, pastoral idyll caught in a golden moment of perfection.

The identities of the musicians are lost to history, unfortunately; almost certainly, however, the two white women and the two men, one white, one Black, were not enrolled in the School of Jazz but rather were Tanglewood students boarding in Wheatleigh for the summer. These interlocking features of the photograph—its classical form and genteel human subjects coupled with its location in a place that had been coded as a jazz space—serve to illustrate the intersection of the cultures of jazz and classical music and the pastoral ideal in Lenox in the 1950s.

Willie "The Lion" Smith (*left*) and Miles Davis (*right*), watching the end-of-season jazz concert, at Music Inn, 1956. Photographer unknown.

Four students from the Berkshire Music Center (later called the Tanglewood Music Center), the Boston Symphony Orchestra's summer academy, standing in the doorway to the Music Inn carriage house and barn, 1959. Photograph by Clemens Kalischer.

More than any other individual, John Lewis provoked—even personified—the question of what the relationship between jazz and classical music should be. Should the goal be for jazz to garner the same level of cultural prestige as classical music, perhaps even to be recognized as America's own classical music? Would validation on these terms inadvertently reinforce rather than challenge classical music's hegemony? Would such validation concede to the classical world the power to determine which forms of music other than those produced in a small number of locations in Europe and now America under peculiar circumstances—access to certain forms of training and support within an already privileged cultural infrastructure—deserved such certification? Or should the goal be to overturn the whole system of hierarchical cultural valuation that assigns "classical" status to some forms of music and not others, substituting something like an art world analogue to the Boas-Herskovits model of cultural relativism, with each form afforded equal value and deemed deserving of study by scholars attuned to its uniqueness and its indigenous criteria of evaluation?

These were important issue regarding institutional and ideological power. The direction Lewis was taking in his work in the 1950s posed a more practical and immediate question: to what extent should jazz musicians import techniques and formal devices associated with classical music into their own music? This question, too, leads us into the realm of cultural ideology. Lewis was a middle-class college graduate—he studied anthropology and music at the University of New Mexico—and Manhattan School conservatory-trained musician with expertise in the classical idiom. He was an African American musician whose professional and personal development took place in the center of the jazz world, playing with musicians who were inventors and masters of its contemporary modernist styles. He was also a cultural cosmopolitan who loved European cities and was deeply conversant in their history and culture. What exactly was Lewis's "own" music? And if Lewis continued to be labeled a jazz musician, what exactly was jazz? For that matter, what exactly was an African American?

That John Lewis, Gunther Schuller, Henry Cowell, Leonard Bernstein, and other eminent figures would jump the border between jazz and classical music in a certain sense was natural and unremarkable. The notion that these two genres stood in opposition to each other had less to do with the music itself than with race and social caste and with a need felt on both sides of the divide to assert, for ideological and psychological reasons, difference and distinctiveness. The reality is that modern classical composers like Darius Milhaud, Maurice Ravel, Paul Hindemith, Igor Stravinsky, Erik Satie, Dmitri Shostakovich, and Aaron Copland were fascinated by jazz and wrote significant work under its influence. Claude Debussy did not live to see the Jazz Age, but his use of chromaticism and whole-tone scales influenced beboppers like Charlie Parker (who also idolized Stravinsky) and Thelonious Monk. The jazz big band is the American analogue of the European symphony orchestra. Duke Ellington called his group an orchestra and played in both dance halls and on concert stages. Ellington was not just a successful pianist and bandleader but a significant composer. His orchestra—and other jazz big bands— played written parts that the bandleader and arranger worked on together to fashion into a collective sonic blend. While Miles Davis later disavowed his experience studying European music at Julliard, the salutary effect of that education was obvious in his orchestral works from *The Birth of the Cool* to his later collaborations with Gil Evans on *Miles Ahead* (1957), *Porgy and Bess* (1959), and *Sketches of Spain* (1960).

The ideologically constructed divide between jazz and European music was a lingering effect of early jazz's association with seedy vice districts and European music's with the genteel conservatory. Other false binary associations—jazz with the urges of the body and

John Lewis playing piano, at Music Inn, 1959. Photograph by Clemens Kalischer.

European music with the cultivation of the mind; jazz with dark, primitive emotions and European music with enlightenment and rationality—fell easily into place. Many of jazz's most ardent supporters down to this day have reinforced these loaded binaries by overemphasizing the role of improvisation in the music or misunderstanding what a deeply rational, intellectual business improvisation is and underemphasizing the importance of composition, arrangement, and rehearsal.

In what they thought was a celebration of musical genius, both European and American commentators depicted Black jazz players as primitive noble savages untouched by the corrupting influence of civilization. The influential French composer and critic André Hodeir insisted not only that Thelonious Monk had no interest in "serious music" but that he "probably doesn't even know that such music exists." Similar nonsense came from an American pianist who claimed that Monk had no knowledge of the history of his instrument for the "simple reason that Monk is not [a] Western man. He is a Black man." In fact, as Robin D. G. Kelley's biography reveals, Monk was schooled not just in the stride style of the great African American pianists who preceded him but also in the European classics. As the son of a bootstrapping mother determined to instill in her children uplifting habits of work and culture, Monk, at age eleven, started formal piano lessons with an Austrian émigré who'd studied under the concertmaster of the New York Philharmonic. Monk learned to play Rachmaninoff, Liszt, and Chopin so quickly and so well that this teacher, after just a few lessons, told the parent of another student, "He will go beyond me very soon."[41]

Since the time of slavery, when plantation laborers played violin for social events in the master's big house, African Americans have been deeply immersed in European music. Music education, much of it delivered by highly trained women, was a central feature of Black schooling during the long era of Jim Crow segregation. Music later coded as "Black" (gospel, blues, jazz, rhythm and blues) was at the center of the recreational culture of the church, the jook joint, the dance hall, the club, and the street corner. Most of the music Black children were taught in school, however, was part of the European tradition. The music departments of Howard, Fisk, and other historically Black colleges and universities for many years taught a largely Eurocentric curriculum, sometimes adding blues and jazz at the margins but just as often regarding these forms as a dangerous incursion into the space of serious music. It is misleading to label as "white" the European music that Black educators taught their students; this music was part of their own heritage as Americans, and it was the music that an educated, cultured person of the time was expected to learn and appreciate. Some of those students, like Charles Mingus, turned to jazz only after trying to make it as a classical symphonic player and being rebuffed by the Jim Crow discrimination ruling that world.[42]

John Lewis on a Music Barn stage, leading a class, 1959. Photograph by Clemens Kalischer.

Max Roach, along with Kenny Clarke, revolutionized jazz drumming in the 1940s, moving away from the martial four-to-the-floor style of swing bands, instead playing flexible and flowing swing rhythms on the ride cymbal and, in one of the most thrilling features of bebop, accenting horn and piano players' fractured, serpentine phrasings with abstract, almost ironic snare drum riffs and bass drum "bombs" deftly dropped in odd corners of the meter. Roach was also interested in Afro-Caribbean music and traveled to Haiti in the late 1940s to study with a master drummer. He approached the drum kit not just as a rhythm instrument but also a melodic one, paying careful attention to the tuning of each drum and shifting his attack from one part of the kit to another to add tonal color and texture. These qualities made Roach one of the most admired drummers in the world. Still, he felt he had more to learn. At the height of his jazz career, Roach enrolled at the Manhattan School of Music from 1950 to 1953 to study composition and classical percussion. When he came to teach at the Lenox School of Jazz in the late 1950s, an opportunity arose to collaborate with the percussion section of the Boston Symphony. A Clemens Kalischer photograph taken in the late summer of 1958 finds Roach fronting that Boston Symphony Orchestra section in a concert led by percussionist, composer, and conductor Harold Farberman. The performance, which was recorded live and released as *Max Roach with the Boston Percussion Ensemble*, is anchored by Farberman's composition "The Music Inn Suite."[43]

John Lewis did not regard his childhood lessons and conservatory training in classical music at the Manhattan School as a matter of rejecting jazz or abdicating his African American identity. These

Max Roach on drum kit and Vic Firth on tympani, with Harold Farberman conducting "The Music Inn Suite," at Tanglewood, 1958. Photograph by Clemens Kalischer.

experiences, on the contrary, were integral to his jazz musicianship and his role as a model of African American excellence. We must remember that, in the 1950s, the concept of color blindness was not, as it is widely understood today, a mechanism with which to avoid addressing issues of historical and structural oppression. In the civic realm, it was the legal basis on which African Americans would be afforded their full civil rights as American citizens. In the artistic realm, it was the predicate that allowed African American artists to express themselves in ways that were not constrained by racial ideology, not delimited by strictures of racial authenticity. For John Lewis, Thelonious Monk, Charlie Parker, Max Roach, and others, color blindness entailed uninhibited access to all the cultural resources that they desired to realize their creative ambitions *as African Americans*.

The Barbers invited Lewis and the other members of the Modern Jazz Quartet to spend an extended time in residence at Music Inn in the summer of 1956. Then composed of pianist John Lewis, vibraphonist Milt Jackson, bassist Percy Heath, and drummer Connie Kay, the MJQ had fashioned a new style of chamber jazz, featuring fugues, baroque counterpoint, and other devices of classical music, sometimes collaborating with groups like the Beaux Arts Trio and the Stuttgart Symphony. Music Inn was a key laboratory for the development of third-stream music that sought to combine the improvisation, blues tonality, and emotional power of jazz with the formal architecture of European classical music.

John Lewis joined with Gunther Schuller in 1955 in founding the Jazz and Classical Music Society. Schuller already had crossed these boundaries as a performer, playing French horn in the Cincinnati Symphony at age seventeen and the Metropolitan Opera Orchestra at nineteen, at the same time as he explored the New York bebop scene, later recording with John Lewis, Dizzy Gillespie, and Miles Davis on Davis's *Birth of the Cool* sessions. As a young boy, while his father was a violinist in the New York Philharmonic, Schuller's parents sent him to a boarding school in their native Germany. At the very same time as photographer Clemens Kalischer's Jewish family was leaving the country—something the two would later discuss—Schuller's schoolmates were being conscripted into Hitler Youth. He came back to New York with his mother in 1936 and set about precociously on a career that would see him become one of the great figures in postwar American music. Schuller, who coined the term *third stream* in a lecture at Brandeis University in 1957, composed more than two hundred works in a variety of genres while serving at different times as artistic director of the Tanglewood music school and president of the New England Conservatory. At the Lenox School of Jazz, Schuller led ensembles and taught an analytical history of jazz course that formed the basis for his two later books, *Early Jazz* (1968) and *The Swing Era* (1989), both landmark works in the study of jazz based on careful scrutiny of recorded performances.[44]

Schuller and Lewis were simultaneously theorizing the third stream and writing compositions that exemplified it. The best known of Lewis's work in this vein were three fugal pieces, "Vendome" (1952), "Concorde" (1955), and "Versailles" (1957), which the MJQ recorded and performed live in concert. The group also played Schuller's "Concertino for Jazz Quartet and Orchestra" (1959) with the Stuttgart Symphony.[45] All were generally well received among classical music audiences and the part of the jazz audience that had classical leanings. But the reception in that part of the jazz audience pining for a "re-blackening" of jazz along the lines of soul jazz was one of disappointment and allegations that this group of first-rate African American musicians was abandoning jazz. This reception pattern did not follow straightforward racial lines. There were plenty of African American listeners who liked the direction Lewis and the MJQ were taking, and plenty of white and other non-Black listeners who felt that the music lacked the soulfulness and funkiness that jazz should have. The MJQ itself was divided. Milt Jackson, the group member whose stylistic tendencies positioned him closest to the soul-funk school, said of Schuller, "I don't want to run him down, because he's an excellent composer, but he's not writing jazz—he's not from the jazz environment."[46]

Just what it means to be from the "jazz environment" is no less tricky a question than the perennial head-scratcher, what is jazz? And it begs the question whether someone who is presumed to be the product of a jazz environment is obligated to play jazz. Ornette Coleman can reasonably be said to have hailed from a jazz environment, as conventionally construed, with his upbringing in a Black neighborhood in Fort Worth, Texas, and his experience cutting his musical teeth in southwestern honky-tonk bars before moving to Los Angeles, living on Skid Row, and performing in Central Avenue jazz clubs. But when Coleman moved further in his experimental modalities, encouraged to do so by John Lewis, Gunther Schuller, Percy Heath, and critic Martin Williams when all were together in late August 1959 at Music Inn, Jackson was openly critical.

In his book *John Lewis and the Challenge of "Real" Black Music* (2016), musicologist Christopher Coady brilliantly addresses many of these issues, carefully unpacking the racial dynamics of the 1950s jazz world. He argues that while Lewis adroitly navigated a path around and through authenticity traps, neither he nor the discourse about him resolved the problems that were responsible for setting those traps, which have remained thornily pertinent down to our own time. Coady frames Lewis as a cosmopolitan modernist in both personal style and musical aesthetics. Lewis, he asserts, "managed to conjure European compositional conventions through the innovative deployment of what have traditionally been perceived to be African American vernacular tropes." A key example is how Lewis transposed collective improvisation, the hallmark of traditional New Orleans jazz, into "independent improvised counterpoint," a performance technique consonant with the procedures of classical music composition. As we saw in the earlier discussion of the 1956 roundtables, Charles Mingus's writing had moved in the same direction. The same could be said of Dave Brubeck, Miles Davis, Bill Russo, Teddy Charles, and other jazz composers who were part of the Music Inn circle.[47]

Such advances in modern jazz composition during this period eventually became part of the jazz canon. But with the rising tide of Black consciousness in the late 1950s and through the 1960s, this groundswell of cross-racial creativity would become a ripe target for self-appointed arbiters of racial authenticity. In perhaps the best example, the African American poet, playwright, and jazz critic Amiri Baraka (LeRoi Jones), in his classic 1963 book *Blues People*, praised John Lewis as "one of the most moving blues players in jazz" and credited the Modern Jazz Quartet with "some of the most exciting jazz of the last few years," but he disparaged Lewis's efforts to combine classical music and jazz as one of the "frightening examples of what the *final* dilution of Afro-American tradition might be."[48] Milton Bass was nobody's idea of a Black nationalist, but he sounded a similar criticism after first hearing Lewis with the MJQ at Music Inn in 1956, writing that "pianist Lewis is almost Joycean in his approach to jazz, seeming to attempt to refine the music out of existence."[49]

"Carefully Tailored and a Gourmet"

Like other jazz critics of the time, Nat Hentoff felt obligated to combat stereotypes of jazz musicians driven by age-old racial primitivism as well as recent figurations of the hipster and the Beat bohemian. His easiest targets were a pair of essays, separated by a decade, written by major figures in New York intellectual and creative life: Anatole Broyard's "A Portrait of the Hipster" (1948) and Norman Mailer's "The White Negro" (1957).[50] Both romanticized the jazz player as a virtuoso trickster of edgy street language, lustful sex, mind-blowing drugs, and existential angst. Both essays were symptomatic of anxiety about mass-culture conformism, a sense that the lingering traumas of war and the Depression, combined with impersonal Cold War bureaucracies and technologies, had fatally corrupted the American soul. These were powerful cultural jeremiads, high-pitched pleas for a renewal of authentic experience, passionate calls for alternatives to American mainstream culture and psychology, akin in spirit if not style to the effusions of Jack Kerouac, Alan Ginsberg, and other figureheads of the Beat movement. In Kerouac's iconic novel *On the Road* (1957), white hipster Sal Paradise renounces his "white ambitions" of status and affluence, wishing he were Black because "the best the white world had offered was not enough ecstasy for me, not enough life, joy, kicks, darkness, not enough night."[51] Kerouac's jazz-inspired "bop prosody" and aesthetic of spontaneity marked a watershed in American literature. At the same time, as historian Douglas Brinkley has observed, much of Kerouac's writing about jazz itself "sounds like he's describing African jungle sexual rituals."[52]

Hentoff counted many Black (and white) jazz musicians as personal friends, and he'd been a firsthand witness to their cultural work at Music Inn, where they plumbed the depths of jazz's history and the specifics of its artistic procedures with the rigor of button-downed college professors. The year of the publication of both *On the Road* and "The White Negro" (1957) was the same year that saw the opening of the Lenox School of Jazz, where the faculty appointments of these musicians drew significant national and international attention. For him, and others whose disenchantment with postwar America included concerns about mass conformity but focused more pointedly on the race issue, Kerouac's jazz-as-"heartbreaking grope" and Mailer's jazz-as-"rage . . . joy, lust, languor, growl, cramp, pinch, scream, and . . . orgasm" sounded like so much childish, and frankly racist, nonsense. Mailer's "conception of the jazz musician, especially the Negro player, as the apotheosis of the purely existential 'hipster,' the Prometheus of orgasm," Hentoff wrote, "is not too far

Jazz writer Nat Hentoff at Music Inn, 1956. Photograph by Warren Fowler.

from the legend that 'all God's chillum got rhythm,' particularly the darker ones."[53]

This context helps us grasp the significance of Hentoff describing John Lewis as "carefully tailored and a gourmet" who "has been known to fly to London from New York for a few days of rest walking around the city."[54] Nobody who knew Lewis, or the other members of the MJQ or Max Roach or any number of other jazz musicians, could see any validity whatsoever in Mailer's and Kerouac's portrayals of the species. These were well-educated, middle-class men and women who were paragons of dignity and respectability, even if they were also mediums of badly needed vitality and soulfulness.

Social mobility was one of the signature features of postwar America, the most important of the peace dividends bequeathed by the Allied victory and the emergence of the United States as a global superpower. The rise of working-class ethnic Americans into middle-class status, as marked by increasing rates of education, single-family home ownership, cutting-edge appliances, ever-larger automobiles, resources for leisure pursuits like family vacations, book and magazine reading, interest in international cuisines, and other signifiers of tasteful living. This change in *lifestyle*—the word itself was a new coinage of the time meant to capture the new economic dispensation—was an aspiration for African Americans and other non-white Americans and for some in these populations a partially achieved reality despite racially discriminatory real estate industry practices and federal government policies and resource allocations. A key difference for African Americans, however, was that they had already built a middle-class *decades before* the emergence of the non-Anglo, ethnic, white population that descended from Ellis Island immigrants. This Black middle class was built by African Americans who'd achieved freedom before the Civil War and others who benefited economically from Reconstruction and made money as bootstrapping farmers and laborers, setting the stage for the development

of a class of Black business owners and college-educated professionals in the early twentieth century.[55]

That all of this was accomplished by people who were battling
against Jim Crow segregation, lynching, and other forms of racial
terrorism elevated the poignancy of their embattled middle-class status, as well as the symbolic power of those few African Americans
who rose to a position *above* the middle class. This happened—if it
did—primarily in the entertainment business, owing to that industry's publicity resources and power to shape popular images of success. African American writers, artists, and musicians who worked
outside the popular sphere often struggled economically, sometimes
even more so than manual laborers, but working in the fine art field
endowed them with a unique and exalted status. Jazz musicians, especially, were culture heroes revered for not just their music but also
their elegant style of dress and cool deportment—as John Szwed has
suggested, successors to the English gentleman as globally emulated
models of sartorial and verbal style.[56]

Coady, in his scholarly monograph on John Lewis, helpfully in-
vokes the persona of the "Negro Gentleman" in situating the composer and MJQ pianist in the context of 1950s African American
sociology and cultural politics. The term was coined by the *New York
Age*, one of the African American newspapers whose pages in this
period—the same was true of magazines like *Ebony* and *Jet*—were
filled with photographs, advertisements, society page reporting, and
editorial content aimed at what sociologist E. Franklin Frazier called
the "black bourgeoisie." In this journalistic discourse, Coady notes,
qualities such as gentility, refinement, poise, and cosmopolitanism
were seen as "evidence not of a rejection but [rather] a recommit-
ment to African American values."[57]

"Impeccably attired, with the bearing, manner, and appearance
of gentlemen in the employ of Schweppes beverages," wrote jazz
critic Joe Goldberg, "[the MJQ] play some of the most respectable

music ever to be called jazz."[58] As witnessed in their active participation in the Music Inn roundtables, the MJQ's concert attire and the musical forms it played did not quell their desire to dig deeply into the history and aesthetics of jazz. Far from seeing themselves as having in any way abandoned jazz, they were singularly responsible for the development of an institution dedicated to studying, honoring, preserving, and innovating the art form. This earned them the deep respect of other jazz musicians. "I still remember," trombonist Bob Brookmeyer recalled years later, "the sense of pride and honor I had being around the MJQ, whose individual members I secretly lionized, not only for their music but for the way they carried themselves, the way they talked and dressed and reacted to the world. I wished deeply that someday I would have the dignity and composure I was observing."[59]

The Negro Gentleman, the Sultry Blonde, and the Birth of the Cool

In a Clemens Kalischer photograph, John Lewis, wearing a pinstriped suit and tie, leans against a railing while listening to Stephanie Barber, who sits cross-legged on a stairstep below him, sporting braids and a white smock adorned with circles and sunbursts. The conversation could be about anything—music, perhaps, but just as likely some stray matters of administrative minutia. They look neither happy nor sad. They look purposeful and engaged. Each in their own signature fashion appears to be a professional at work, even as it is not clear exactly what that specific work is. Lewis holds a paper cup in his right hand, suggesting he might be catching a break from something. Or perhaps we are seeing a moment before or after a performance, a rehearsal, or a class.

The social significance of the image surely is not as striking to a random viewer today as it would have been in its own moment in the mid-1950s. The photograph shows a Black man and a white woman

John Lewis and Stephanie Barber at Music Inn, 1958. Photograph by Clemens Kalischer.

as social equals. If we favor Lewis's bespoke tailoring over Barber's funky getup, we might even say that the Black man is figured as the white woman's cultural superior. The Black man clearly enjoys the respect of the white woman; he might even have more power and authority than she does.

Kalischer shot this picture not long after Emmett Till, a young

Black teenager from Chicago, was brutally murdered by a posse of white men in Mississippi after being falsely accused of giving unwanted attention to a white woman in a grocery store. Throughout American history allegations of Black men's sexual desire or disrespect for white women had set lynch mobs in action. Jazz, since its inception, had been seen by many whites as a dangerous space of racial mixing, posing a dire threat to the virtue and purity of white women. The 1950s witnessed the blossoming not just of talented and fearless civil rights leaders like Martin Luther King Jr. but also of attractive and charismatic Black male entertainers like Nat King Cole, Sidney Poitier, and Harry Belafonte and athletes like baseball players Jackie Robinson and Willie Mays, boxing champions Floyd Patterson and Archie Moore, and basketball players Wilt Chamberlain and Bill Russell. By the end of the decade, Miles Davis was a celebrity whose persona combined romance, danger, and mystery and whose cool masculinity expressed the dignity, elegance, and sovereignty of an emancipated Black man. White fear of that identity—fear of Black men liberated from constraints put on them since slavery—radiated from the fantasy of white women's innocence and vulnerability linked to the specter of white male sexual inferiority.

Kalischer's image of John Lewis and Stephanie Barber can be read within the grain of this grim history but also as a powerful antidote to it. By spotlighting a moment of casual socializing, it projects something of a cool ambience redolent of affluent-society, middle-class leisure and summer performing arts culture. Lewis's and Barber's body language and the physical distance between them suggests an affable but purposeful workaday relationship. The key compositional element of the photograph is the positioning of the two bodies, with Lewis looking down at Barber, seated beneath him. Without attributing any explicit intention to this arrangement, we might read it as the case of a white woman who is *not* occupying the exalted social position known during Victorian times as the pedestal, the metaphorical space of white female purity and virtue born of that era's ideal of proper womanhood. Barber clearly is not a woman who has stepped off that imaginary pedestal. She's not a "fallen woman" who has surrendered her virtue; she's a liberated white woman who has chosen to locate herself beside—and in alliance with—a Black man.

Just as John Lewis and other jazz musicians were crafting new models of African American masculinity, Stephanie Barber was reshaping postwar female-gender norms. These transformations were closely related in their challenge to the status and authority of white men. Lewis was no revolutionary, but his career had revolutionary implications. He was the artistic director of the Lenox School of Jazz, a role in which he acted as a superior to white men of high accomplishment in his own field and as a partner to a white woman who herself was exercising power over white men.

Stephanie Barber was never a conventional woman, but in one respect she had followed a conventional gender script: she married her boss. But her union with Philip Barber quickly assumed the shape of a fully co-equal partnership. Stephanie clearly had the upper hand in the day-to-day running of Music Inn, not least because Philip's business responsibilities in New York limited the time he could spend there. Press coverage of the couple focused largely on Stephanie, usually in a way that simultaneously recognized her agency and authority while also containing her within dominant gender structures and images. The headline of an Associated Press syndicated story in July 1955 captured this perfectly: "Blonde Converts Barn to Profit." The article, written by a female reporter, told the story of the Barbers' move to the Berkshires and described their relationship in terms that positioned Stephanie as a physical object and a wife even as it celebrated her success as a businesswoman:

> Stephanie is a sultry blonde who worked as a fashion publicist in New York, married her boss, a good-looking city dweller

Stephanie Barber working in her Music Inn office, 1951. Photograph by Clemens Kalischer.

named Phil Barber, and moved to an estate in the Berkshires which they converted into an establishment named Music Inn. [She] took to country life like a kitten to cream. . . . Phil, a little dazed by the changes wrought in his life by his wife, is filled with nothing but admiration for her. Having taught drama at Yale for six years, he likes having a country theater of his own. But he also likes having an inn-keeping wife who can attract the country's top jazz artists to their little establishment. He likes,

perhaps, the fact that she is able to show a profit on her enterprises, and that despite her talent for hard work and business
acumen she continues to look like a glamour girl.[60]

Shirley Fowler, wife of photographer Warren Fowler, accompanied
her husband to many Music Inn events in the mid-1950s. She loved
"cruising through the crowd" because

> 9 out of 10 times there would be a group of women huddling
> together and going 'What do you suppose Stephanie will have
> on tonight? Is it going to be outrageous? Is it going to be glam-
> orous? How's she going to do her hair? Will she wear a hat
> tonight? I think some people came just to see what Stephanie
> was wearing and didn't give two hoots about the music. . . .
> With Stephanie you never knew from one minute to the next
> and sometimes she'd even change during intermission and
> come back with something different on for the second half of
> the show.[61]

A *Berkshire Eagle* article in August 1958, headlined "Ice-House Barbers Score with Cool Jazz," moved quickly from surveying the couple's dwelling ("soaring two-story living room with balcony, open
stairs, and fireplace") to describing what Stephanie was wearing
("Her costume was striking, but in taste. She wore a smart, black
velvet stole, velvet trousers [not slacks], precariously high heels,
and her blonde hair was smartly gathered to the side"). This was
quite an outfit for a pregnant woman in the middle of August, but
Stephanie made clear that being "in taste" didn't require a Manhattan high-couture approach; a Music Inn do-it-yourself authenticity
approach worked just fine: "I hate maternity dresses. You know, a
wonderful maternity costume can be made from a skirt worn like
an overcape."[62]

Being the one who wore the velvet trousers in her family didn't necessarily mean that Stephanie was better positioned than her husband to work at the uppermost level of the jazz world. But she was keen to do so. Jazz in many ways has produced its own complex social relations and codes of behavior to express and regulate gender. Gender analysis has taught us to recognize that jazz historically has been dominated by men as well as by a masculinist ethos, from the violent gangster milieu of the early music's sporting life environment to the hip, stylized machismo of the jazz-inflected New Frontier. But many jazzmen have brought what are conventionally coded as feminine qualities to the music and its social organization. Further, as Sherrie Tucker and other jazz scholars have demonstrated, there have been many more jazz women—musicians, managers, fans, writers, scholars, photographers, filmmakers—than standard music histories have recognized. Like men, these women have created a fluid continuum of gendered jazz identities, never fully or permanently feminine or masculine.[63] In her groundbreaking study of Charles Mingus, Nichole Rustin-Paschal focuses on women who were crucial to the composer and bassist's career, including his wives, Celia and Sue. Rustin-Paschal stipulates that jazz is a primarily masculine space but then argues provocatively that these women, acting as what she calls "female jazzmen" in their roles as partners and managers, found that space conducive to their own quest for authority, expertise, and freedom *as women*.[64]

Sue Mingus; Charlie Parker's wife, Chan; Dexter Gordon's wife, Maxine; and other white women who married and helped manage the careers of major Black jazzmen present one model of female cross-racial participation in the jazz community. Another is exemplified by Pannonica "Nica" de Koenigswarter, the British-born Jewish jazz patron, writer, and photographer who became known in the 1950s as the "Jazz Baroness." A Rothschild heir, Nica was a major benefactor and friend to the bebop movement. She was so intimately involved in the lives of her favorite musicians that two of jazz's most famous, Charlie Parker and Thelonious Monk, died in her home. Monk, who lived the last ten years of his life in Nica's New Jersey mansion even as his wife, Nellie, continued to labor on his behalf, wrote the well-known composition "Pannonica" in her honor.[65]

Stephanie Barber deftly combined elements from both models. While performing the same kind of essential administrative work as the wife-managers, like Nica, she also brought to the table a certain quotient of cultural capital based on her Manhattan-Berkshires social circle, even as, after establishing the School of Jazz in 1957 and incurring many more expenses than anticipated, she and her husband struggled financially to keep Music Inn afloat. Stephanie Barber's friendships with musicians' wives and with Black female performers like Mary Lou Williams and Mahalia Jackson, who continued to visit the Barbers in years to come, also contributed to her cachet. Musicians recognized the importance of the Barbers' cultural work and the hospitality that came with it, honoring them with compositions, including John Lewis's "Fugue for Music Inn," Dizzy Gillespie's "Wheatleigh Hall," Jimmy Giuffre's "Blues in the Barn," Randy Weston's "Berkshire Blues," and Ran Blake's "Blues for Wheatleigh."

What unites all these women and makes them an important part of jazz culture is that they were all, in the parlance of the day, *cool*. Cool jazz was a marketing term for the relaxed, melodic music that John Lewis and the MJQ, Miles Davis, Gerry Mulligan, Shelly Manne, Chico Hamilton, and others fashioned in the 1950s. But, as Joel Dinerstein shows in *The Origins of Cool in Postwar America* (2017), the term connoted a cultural style and attitude that had taken root in the 1940s when young Black bebop musicians, along with several leading swing performers (notably Lester Young and Billie Holiday from the Count Basie Band) chafed at the minstrelsy-tinged dynamics of the music business, with its image of the musician as a happy-go-lucky servant-entertainer rather than a serious and challenging artist. A new performance persona arrived, catalyzed by wartime demands for racial equality. The cool mask was a survival technique used by Black musicians to ward off the invasive white gaze, a mask of integrity and self-possession to resist Jim Crow indignities and replace the Uncle Tom minstrel mask, the ingenious but outdated survival technique of an earlier generation.

Cool was bebop musicians maintaining dignity in the face of racism and navigating blistering tempos and quicksilver chord changes with regal aplomb. Cool was also Martin Luther King Jr. countering ugly hostility with unflappable poise and an oratory of beautifully flowing cadences. Cool was a style and attitude that resonated strongly across the color line and permeated modern art and thought—in the composed violence and molten sexual allure of Hollywood film noir actors Humphrey Bogart, Alan Ladd, and Robert Mitchum; in Marlon Brando's erotic menace and vulnerability; in Albert Camus's figure of the metaphysical ethical rebel; in the ideal of spiritual balance the Beats pursued through a synthesis of jazz and Zen Buddhism. And though masculinity dominated these overlapping spaces of jazz, '50s rebel cinema, Beat, and existentialism, the cool women—philosopher Simone de Beauvoir; jazz singers Billie Holiday, Anita O'Day, and Abbey Lincoln; actors Juliette Greco, Veronica Lake, Barbara Stanwyck, Lauren Bacall, and Joanne Woodward; the modern jazz baroness, Pannonica de Koenigswarter; the supreme jazz wife, Nellie Monk—were vital threads in this cultural weave.[66]

In gender performance cool disrupts hackneyed notions of men as bellicose and bombastic and women as overemotional and histrionic (the "hot" default positions of each sex) through exhibitions of self-control, nonchalance, forbearance, order, and stealth. Cool holds back, artfully concealing whatever stress and strain goes into its production. But it also gives back, generously rewarding those who wait patiently for what it promises. Cool women are strong and self-possessed, fiercely independent, not to be messed with. They know the score. They are keen and knowing observers. They are not easily read. They hold mystery. They gravitate to the real action, wherever it is, and hold it to its promise.

Stephanie Barber was a member of this tribe. She was a charismatic, jazz-besotted white woman who, unlike the decidedly uncool slumming opera singer in *New Orleans*, engaged Black people and their culture with reverence and intelligence, collaborated with jazz musicians in the creation of a new cultural space—an inn with a barn—and did so, always, with her own inimitable style.

LENOX AND THE SHAPE OF JAZZ TO COME

Jazzwomen were crucial mentors, facilitators, and collaborators in the early career of pianist, composer, and educator Ran Blake. From working for the Barbers when he was a student at the Lenox School of Jazz, he knew Stephanie as both a demanding boss and a dispenser of unexpected kindness. Blake grew close to Thelonious Monk and his family through Nica de Koenigswarter and became a beneficiary of Nica's solicitude, the rare brand of support she reserved for the most special of jazz musicians. He knew Monk's genius as a player and teacher firsthand; he knew too that but for the selfless love and heroic support of Nica and his wife, Nellie ("the queen of the jazz women," Blake calls her), Monk, who battled a bipolar disorder, likely would've been doomed.[1] At Music Inn he saw June Heath, Iola Brubeck, Lorraine Gillespie, Juanita Russell (Giuffre), Marjorie Schuller, and other jazz wives operating not so much as women-be-hind-the-men but as vital collaborators in their husband's artistic labors. Mary Lou Williams took Blake under her wing, asked him to sit in for her at the Cookery and shielded him from the disapproving stare of owner Barney Josephson, loathe to give his stage over to a young unknown. Blake's first recording, *The Newest Sound Around* (1962), a collaboration with singer Jeanne Lee, marked the beginning of a luminous career that has also featured duets with female singers Christine Correa, Sara Serpa, and Dominque Eade.

Blake was the only student who enrolled in the School of Jazz for the four consecutive summers of its operation, 1957 to 1960. He is one of the school's most distinguished alums, a surpassingly original performer and master teacher who remains active in both functions on the eve of his tenth decade. Born in Springfield, Massachusetts, and raised across the border in Connecticut, Blake attended Bard College in upstate New York the same four years that he spent August at the School of Jazz. He helped organize Bard's annual jazz festival and connected with the Bronx-raised Lee, who trailed him by one year in the college. Adam Shatz has written retrospectively of *The Newest Sound Around* that it "captured the sensibility of New York Bohemia as much as John Cassavete's *Shadows* and James Baldwin's novel *Another Country*."[2] The album showcased Lee's arresting contralto and poetic sensibility coupled with Blake's brooding, fractured figures uplifted by gleaming gospel chords. Blake developed a bracing, dark jazz sound graced with blues, film noir, modern classical, and gospel elements. Over the years he's been seen as a jazz eccentric, sweet-spirited but remote, much like Monk but harder to categorize musically. He only rarely plays with rhythm sections but commands an idiosyncratic yet sure sense of time. Blake's film noir passion comes through as a cunning feeling for dramatic pacing. Few jazz performers better exemplify Whitney Balliett's famous description of the music as the "sound of surprise."[3]

"It was quite amazing what the Barbers did. It's a special bit of history," Blake said in a 2024 interview. His parents had shown him a press notice about the historic roundtable in 1956. He couldn't attend but came the next summer for the inaugural year of the school. "My parents met Stephanie. They had never met anybody quite like her," he recalled. "In the daytime she would come down with her hair streaming down her back, wearing some kind of coverall. In

Pianist Ran Blake, during one of his four summers at the Lenox School of Jazz, 1959. Photograph by Clemens Kalischer.

the evening, she could really get decked out with her hair all on top of her head, looking slick carrying a purse that matched her outfit." Blake's parents paid his full tuition the first summer, but in his second year at the school, in 1958, Blake worked off some of his fees by serving as the inn's overnight switchboard operator. He worked alone in the basement of Wheatleigh, where Stephanie "brought me food in the middle of the night." When Stephanie had business in Pittsfield, Blake chauffeured her in the car emblazoned with Music Inn's name on its sidewall.

"I was just fascinated by the two of them. I thought that I should study them," Blake said. He saw the Barbers as master facilitators, keen to introduce people to one another and create an atmosphere where creatively fulfilling relationships could take root and grow. He especially noticed how comfortable they were interacting with Black people. "We were in the Berkshires, not Greenwich Village. You rarely saw intimacy between whites and Blacks in New England. But there were Stephanie and Mary Lou [Williams] hugging each other tightly. And [there were Stephanie's] many, many kindnesses toward Mahalia [Jackson] and [her piano accompanist] Mildred Falls."

Already an unorthodox pianist in his early twenties, Blake didn't fit into the school easily. "There was a lot of criticism about my music. A lot of people put me down, and maybe I played lousily. I think John Lewis liked me moderately. Bob Brookmeyer said I'll never amount to much." He was surprised to find an appreciative mentor in Oscar Peterson, whose keyboard attack couldn't have been more different from Blake's. "I was knocked to death when Oscar liked me. I was his opposite. I had my own technique. It wasn't high velocity like Oscar. I couldn't get over his warmth. He talked me up to Nat Hentoff, and Nat became one of my supporters."

Later, while trying to break into the New York scene, Blake had a side hustle at Atlantic Records, cleaning up, gofering coffee and lunch, and assisting legendary recording engineer and producer Tom Dowd, who'd come up to Music Inn to do live recordings of the MJQ. Peterson gave Blake free lessons in New York, continuing the work they'd started in Lenox. Blake also worked as a waiter at the Jazz Gallery, where, after a letter of introduction from Ralph Ellison, he became Nica's personal waiter—but not before incurring her wrath by putting ice cubes in her Chivas Regal. When he spilled soup in the laps of James Baldwin and Sidney Poitier, Thelonious Monk emitted a gasp from Nica's nearby table. Blake was temporarily banished to the kitchen, then redeemed by Nica, who arranged for deliveries of Reuben sandwiches to his apartment when he fell ill.

Commensal intimacy, the sharing of food and drink and the social congress of the table, is a vital and understudied feature of the jazz life. The Barbers understood this and made sure Music Inn's food and drink were of high quality, the eating and drinking spaces comfortable and inviting. Decades later Blake smacked his lips remembering the

THE POTTING SHED at music inn

D I N N E R M E N U

appetizer	**Tomato juice** **Cranberry juice** **Clam juice** *Dinner includes juice, entree and beverage*	
entrée	**Broiled Sirloin Steak, served with tossed green salad and potatoes**	**$4.00**
	Filet Mignon, broiled to your preference, served with tossed green salad and potatoes	**3.25**
	Turkey Divan, tossed green salad	**1.95**
	Beef Strogonoff, tossed green salad	**1.95**
desserts	**Pecan pie**	**.50**
	Apple pie	**.45**
	Sour cherry pie	**.45**
	Peaches in rum	**.50**
	Peaches in sherry	**.50**
beverage	**Coffee or tea**	
	For our selection of cordials, please ask for the drink list.	
	Massachusetts Old Age Tax 5%	

Dinner menu at the Potting Shed, where guests and locals dined and were entertained by small jazz, folk, and blues groups, late 1950s.

fresh fruit and yogurt served for breakfast and strip steaks with horse-radish for dinner. He worked a few kitchen shifts but couldn't hack chef Claude Levy's disciplinary regime. Levy, he knew, was critical to Music Inn's success. Because the inn's lodging rooms "were quite ordinary, Claude liked to say, 'I make it up to the guests at dinner.'"

Blake forged a special connection with Willis Laurence James, who visited each summer to deliver an evening lecture about jazz's African American roots. "He talked to me about the Black movement, how special Spelman and Morehouse were, how he loved teaching, how he loved coming up [to Music Inn]." In an unscheduled event he repeated over the summers, James shepherded students to the nearby Housatonic River to demonstrate and discuss his concept of the "Negro folk cry." "We'd walk down the banks of the river, and he'd sing so beautifully, so soulfully," Blake recalled; something about the environment and the acoustics both deepened and lifted the sound. In the 1970s Blake recorded an homage to James, titled "Field Cry." Blake's solo piano rings single notes that lead to blues and gospel chords arrayed like a succession of haikus. The tune unfolds as a partially revealed code still clinging to its deepest secrets, limning an ambience by turns guileful and cryptic, consoling and evasive.

An ambitious young jazz pianist of Blake's generation was expected to have a strong command of bebop and, if less than fully comfortable playing modal and free styles, at least to show curiosity in that direction. Blake was musically and culturally curious about everything, so much so it was hard to pinpoint his stylistic and technical center of gravity. With its unique harmonies and qualities of abstraction, space, and mystery unmoored from conventional jazz groove and texture, Blake's sound might have fit better in the classical avant-garde of the late 1950s and early 1960s. Along with vanguardist pianists like Cecil Taylor and Andrew Hill, however, Blake culled a highly personal style out of sonic and intellectual resources embedded within the substrate of jazz language but yet to be fully excavated.

School of Jazz students took jazz history courses with both Marshall Stearns and Gunther Schuller. Blake's aesthetic bears the imprint of Stearns's folkloric and anthropological approach in its absorption of a broad range of musical styles and even more in its orality and aurality, its emphasis on the voice and the ear. This accounts for Blake being perhaps the purest personification of the third-stream concept. Where Schuller, John Lewis, and other conventional third-stream composers employed jazz improvisation and jazz voicings in the context of through-composed pieces, Blake eschewed standard written composition, in effect carrying his compositions in his head and remaking them as he played. Schuller, who recognized Blake's uniqueness and became his key mentor, described his approach this way:

> [Blake's] compositions were never written down, as composers had traditionally done for centuries. I learned that Ran, although he had briefly tried writing his music in full notation, preferred creating his compositions out of his inner ear and putting them together at the piano, in constantly reinvented improvisations. Once the piece was more or less set in his mind, with certain moments or ideas fixed but others less precisely specified, he would then extemporize on that material. It would be recognizable as a particular composition, and yet always evolving each time, reshaped, reinvented, and reimagined.

Before meeting in the classroom at Music Inn in August 1958, Blake and Schuller crossed paths earlier that year at the Atlantic Records offices. Blake was sweeping the floors when Schuller arrived for a meeting with Nesuhi Ertegun, who told Schuller that Blake was a Bard college student, a pianist who "would just like to be around musicians and hang around at our offices." Years later Blake would talk about how meaningful it had been for him to be around the likes of Aretha Franklin, Laverne Baker, and Ruth Brown at Atlantic. When Schuller asked Ertegun if he'd heard Blake play, he said, "Yeah, but boy, it's a *very* strange kind of jazz—if it even is jazz."[4]

"What I found so astonishing about Ran's playing," Schuller later wrote, "is the deep stylistic interpenetration of several musical worlds that Ran's improvisations occupy. I had never heard such a close, seamless fusion, while also allowing both vocabularies to speak from time to time in their own tongues, side by side. It reminded me of a bilingual person effortlessly shuttling back and forth between two languages."[5] In 1973, six years into his presidency of the New England Conservatory, Schuller hired Blake, who eventually chaired the school's Department of Third Stream Studies. Over the ensuing decades, Blake broadened the multiple-stream concept far beyond Schuller's original notion of a jazz-classical alliance. The department eventually morphed into the conservatory's Contemporary Improvisation program, where musicians are encouraged to move beyond traditional boundaries of every kind. Blake's long list of students includes Don Byron, Matthew Shipp, John Medeski, and other figures in contemporary jazz whose music incorporates elements of classical, folk, ethnic, progressive rock, pop, funk, punk, house, and hip-hop and who perform and teach in a wide variety of cultural spaces.

"To Blow You Got to Know"
Ran Blake is not the best known of the School of Jazz's student attendees. That distinction belongs to Ornette Coleman and Don Cherry, the free jazz pioneers who already counted several LPs to their credit when they arrived in Lenox as scholarship students in August 1959, just weeks before their legendary residency at the Five Spot in New York's East Village. Other notable alumni include composer and record producer Arif Mardin, pianist Steve Kuhn, singer Bob Dorough, bassists Chuck Israels and Larry Ridley, trombonist

David Baker, trumpeter Don Ellis, vibraphonist Gary McFarland, tenor saxophonist J. R. Monterose, alto saxophonist and writer Don Heckman, and guitarist Attilla Zoller. Monterose had recorded with Kenny Dorham, Charles Mingus, and Kenny Burrell before coming to Lenox. Kuhn went on from Lenox to work with Kenny Dorham, John Coltrane, Stan Getz, and Steve Swallow, while Israels moved into the bass chair in the Bill Evans Trio after the untimely death of Scott La Faro. Zoller later worked with Oscar Pettiford, Herbie Mann, and Lee Konitz. Ellis recorded as a sideman with Charles Mingus, Eric Dolphy, and his Music Inn mentor, George Russell; led small groups that included Jaki Byard, Paul Bley, Gary Peacock, Ron Carter, and other notables; and became a composer and bandleader known for his experimentation with odd time signatures and third-stream and Indian influences. Over its four years, the school taught a total of 155 students from twenty states, Canada, Brazil, Rhodesia, Austria, Sweden, the Netherlands, India, and Turkey.[6]

Lenox School of Jazz faculty (*standing on top row*) and students (*below*) in front of the Wheatleigh mansion, 1957. Photograph by Warren Fowler.

The school's most substantial legacy is the impact its alumni and faculty have had as jazz educators. Among the students, in addition to Blake's career at the New England Conservatory, David Baker went on to establish the jazz studies program at Indiana University, Larry Ridley directed jazz studies at Rutgers University and Chuck Israels at Western Washington University, while trombonist Herb Gardner worked for many years as a jazz educator in the New York City public schools. Among the faculty Oscar Peterson founded the Advanced School of Contemporary Music in Toronto; Herb Pomeroy, who taught trumpet and led student ensembles in 1959 and 1960, enjoyed a long career at the Berklee School of Music; and violist John Garvey, who taught strings in 1960, established the jazz studies program at the University of Illinois. Because its faculty was a who's who of the idiom's leading players—the MJQ, Dizzy Gillespie, Oscar Peterson, Jimmy Giuffre, Jim Hall, Max Roach, Lee Konitz, George Coleman, Bob Brookmeyer, George Russell, Bill Evans, and Kenny Dorham—the School of Jazz helped establish formal teaching as a regular commitment for even the most acclaimed musicians. Roach and saxophonist Archie Shepp became professors at the University of Massachusetts–Amherst, teaching music and African American studies for many years. Since the 1960s numerous jazz musicians have held visiting artist positions at colleges and universities across the country. Not infrequently, an African American jazz musician in a professorial or visiting artist position was one of the few—if not the only—nonwhite faculty member in a department or college.

The myth that jazz musicians are endowed with natural rhythm and play intuitively by ear and feeling, emotion trumping reason as they empty their hearts and souls, started as a cardinal tenet of the Euro-American primitivist and Francophone Negritude movements that coincided with the blossoming of jazz in the 1920s and 1930s. These movements were crucial to jazz's association with modernism—with the expressive innovations of Pablo Picasso, James Joyce,

Max Roach with students Barry Greenspan (*left*), Larry Ridley (*middle*), and Don Cherry (*right*), 1959. Photograph by Clemens Kalischer.

Gertrude Stein, T. S. Eliot, Ernest Hemingway, and others—and hence to its status as an art form and its appeal to intellectuals. "Primitive" signified feeling, intuition, and expressiveness at a time, in the wake of the horrors of World War I, when Western writers, artists, and intellectuals felt deeply alienated from stale Victorian morality, bloodless industrial technologies, and passionless rationality. An exhausted and desiccated civilization stood in desperate need of revitalization. Jazz—a word that served at the time as a metonym for all forms of high-spirited dance and music and exuberant living—fit the role perfectly. During a period of anxiety over increasing dehumanization, to be in touch with one's body, in tune with one's animal spirit, was to be more human. The figure of the instinctual, improvising dark-skinned jazz musician, bypassing intellection to connect organically with an ineffable soulfulness coursing through the body, became an exhilarating fantasy.[7]

The fantasy endured deep into the twentieth century. In the movie *New Orleans*, the white opera singer's piano accompanist, a German gentleman also smitten with jazz but given to honoring it with far more respect and reverence, shows Louis Armstrong a piece of written music. Obligated by the Hollywood script to personify an unthinking but naturally soulful Black jazzman, Armstrong looks quizzically at the notes of the staff and asks, "Don't these little flags on the fences get in the way of your feelings sometimes?"[8] Radio network orchestras of the 1930s and '40s and television and movie studio orchestras in the 1950s employed large numbers of score-reading jazz musicians. But these well-paying unionized jobs went primarily to white musicians, helping to deepen the perception of a racial division between whites who were trained professionals and Blacks—notwithstanding the music stands and sheet music conspicuously adorning the stages of African American big bands—who simply got in touch with their feelings and wailed.

An inevitable corollary to this myth was the belief that jazz, unlike classical music, could not be taught or, more to the point, should not be taught—that putting it in the classroom would inevitably rob the music of its charisma and authenticity and ignore the self-evident fact that natural ability was the key to jazz excellence. The *Eagle*'s Milton Bass supported the school but warned that "natural genius is still the prime factor in jazz and no amount of practice in technique or exposure to historical precedents is going to provide even a reasonable facsimile."[9] The School of Jazz set out explicitly to counter this view when it advertised itself as "the first effort to present jazz as a creative and vital art form which can be presented and taught as other art forms are taught, in a serious and vital relationship between the student and the creative artist." Gunther Schuller, who worked with John Lewis to select and recruit faculty, heralded the school's importance in countering the cliché that "too much knowledge will inhibit you, man." Schuller particularly lamented the attitude that it was "shamefully 'unhip' to study jazz seriously" at a time when jazz was becoming technically more demanding.[10]

An important if unofficial goal of the school was to function as an agent of the music's middle-class normalization. This became clear when its own administrators, students, and public supporters felt compelled to confront misguided popular perceptions of the jazz musician. "Although the beatniks use jazz as a national anthem, you won't find any of the breed at the School of Jazz," Bass observed. "There may be one or two beards among the students and a few mavericks who feel it their duty to scandalize the bourgeois, but the rest are eager, clean-cut youngsters whose only desire in life is to play that thing. Your daughter is safer there than she would be at summer camp."[11] A short spotlight on Max Roach in the 1958 Berkshire Music Barn program played up his interest in classical music and noted that he'd recently turned down an invitation to have his jazz group appear on a TV benefit program for the purpose of conjuring a musical mood for juvenile delinquency.[12] Some ostensible supporters peddled threadbare tropes in dubious efforts to capture the character of the school. After he visited Music Inn in 1957 and delivered a lecture on jazz and American culture, cultural critic Eric Larrabee wrote in *Harper's* magazine of the school's faculty, "It must be said of all these gentlemen [that] they took their responsibilities very seriously"—as if this should have been surprising. Larrabee found it notable that John Lewis established a strict academic routine with classes starting at 9:00 A.M. sharp, quipping, "It is generally agreed that some faculty members had never before been seen at that hour of the day." To juice up his point, Larrabee cited a report that Dizzy Gillespie, hearing of the morning start time, remarked that at that hour "I can't lift an alarm clock—and my chops, man, I can't even find 'em."[13]

Students summarily rejected such notions of the jazz musician's deviance from mainstream norms while implicitly admitting to having harbored such notions before coming to the school. "The pro-

Modern Jazz Quartet vibraphonist Milt Jackson and student, at Music Inn, 1958.
Photograph by Clemens Kalischer.

fessional jazz musician is a regular, ordinary human being," student
Kent McGarity responded when Marshall Stearns asked his students
to identify the most important lesson they'd learned that summer.
His schoolmate Henry Ettman reported that "the school has given
me what I would consider an accurate picture of the personality of
the jazz musician. With the faculty of excellent jazz musicians, the

student practically lives with these men, getting an accurate view of their personalities. Many of the misconceptions of the jazzmen are cleared up." Francis Thorne deemed it important to have learned that Dizzy Gillespie's cheerful and mischievous stage presence was not an invented persona; he delighted "in watching Mr. Gillespie playing with all the children, roughhousing with Percy Heath, Jr. on the lawn . . . , setting off firecrackers in front of Wheatleigh for the kids and breaking himself up with the children's glee."[14]

More than a few outside observers worried that the advent of a jazz school where students discovered jazz musicians to be "regular, ordinary human being[s]" signaled a loss of the music's vitality. Much of the allure of jazz throughout its history had to do with its radical individualism, its outsider stance, its renegade assault on musty conventions and proprieties. Many of its canonical figures were larger-than-life characters (Satchmo, Billie, Prez, Count, Duke, Bird, Monk, Miles, Mingus), American originals who became subjects of romantic legend and myth. What made jazz special and powerful, for many, was that it was an intrepid music with a heroic narrative full of audacious risk and arduous struggle. How could jazz maintain its verve and vigor if it became another music of the school, the conservatory, the library, and the museum? How could it avoid being consumed by its past and continue to be a living and growing art form? How could creative musicians be free to trust their own instincts, touch their own souls, and express their own personal truths if they were overwhelmed with historical information and critical analysis and forced to advance someone else's idea of what jazz has been and should be? Leonard Feather, a strong supporter of the school, tussled in print with theater critic Douglas Watt, who was convinced that the new development in Lenox "offered evidence that jazz must be a dying art." If "experts have taken over," Watt lamented, it meant that a "music that was distinguished by its spontaneity and gaiety has become [simply] a carefully thought-out exercise." That some of the experts in question happened to be members of the Modern Jazz Quartet did not allay Watt's concern, for in his view the MJQ was "one of the most un-jazzlike units on the scene."[15]

Younger critics who were closely attuned to the struggles and ambitions of the postwar modernists evangelized forcefully on behalf of the school. Nat Hentoff touted the school at every opportunity, articulating why it was important and necessary and pleading for financial support. The School of Jazz was in a tenuous financial situation from the beginning. Faculty members donated their services and worked only for expenses, forfeiting the opportunity for lucrative bookings during the late summer. Even so, the cost of running the school turned out to be much higher than the Barbers had anticipated. While urging record companies and booking agencies to support the school ("they should invest just as Dupont or GM invest in chemistry and engineering departments at colleges"), Hentoff explained that jazz had reached a point in its evolution where it both needed and deserved its own academic infrastructure, since "it will be at least a generation before Julliard and Curtis and Eastman have the sense and sensitivity to our culture to install men like Roach and Peterson as full faculty members." He explained, "A youngster is not likely these days to fall into too many of the jam sessions of the kind that used to be ubiquitous in jazz towns where the tyros tested themselves against the older men and learned greatly in their defeats."[16]

Ralph Gleason made the same point in several of his nationally syndicated newspaper columns. In one he quoted John Lewis: "I never heard from the older musicians such as Coleman Hawkins or Dizzy Gillespie that you can't teach jazz. There are no jam sessions anymore with anybody who can jam. The people who played in those sessions before were already masters. And you can learn from them. There's no value in jamming with someone who can't play anything in the first place. The jam session used to be the school of jazz. There wasn't any other place to learn."[17] Kenny Dorham, who taught trumpet and led ensembles in 1958 and 1959, was more pointed, claiming that the bebop generation had largely abdicated the role of mentoring younger musicians. "When I came to New York as a young boy to play, those fellows wouldn't tell me anything—even Bird with whom I worked for over a year. If I had this kind of chance *then*, I'd have been poundin' at the gates to get in. I hope these kids [at the School of Jazz] realize what they're getting."[18]

Lewis had urged the Barbers to open a jazz school after finding the jazz roundtables in 1956 revelatory and as a result feeling "disturbed that this exchange of such a wide range of jazz knowledge should be so ephemeral." He wanted both well-established musicians and jazz initiates to absorb this knowledge and then take responsibility for "pass[ing] on the traditions, the history, and the theoretical language of jazz music." Only such a comprehensive and evenhanded undertaking, removed from the hurly-burly commercial marketplace and free of sectarianism and endless sophistic arguments about what constituted *real jazz*, could heal the "misunderstanding between the older masters of jazz and the younger jazz innovators."[19]

It was during this period that jazz critic Martin Williams began to formulate the ideas that would result in his canonical study, *The Jazz Tradition* (1970), and his later pet project, *The Smithsonian Collection of Classic Jazz* (1973). Williams's thinking was decisively shaped by his time at Music Inn seeing the Lenox School of Jazz in action. In a *Metronome* column, Williams strongly echoed Lewis: "We are very used to hearing jazz called an art but no real art has ever survived very long whose artists did not have a sense of the tradition in which they were working. . . . Charlie Parker knew he was playing jazz with a new musical language and a new function, but he also knew his Louis Armstrong, Johnny Hodges, Benny Carter, and Lester Young with a deep understanding."[20]

When Williams asked Don Cherry for his impressions after first

Kenny Dorham, John Lewis, and Max Roach (*left to right*) proudly watching the
School of Jazz big band, at Music Inn, 1959. Photograph by Clemens Kalischer.

hearing Louis Armstrong's "West End Blues" in Gunther Schuller's
class, the trumpeter answered, "How could Louis know so much
about how people felt?" Cherry evinced what seemed to Williams
"a kind of personal pride" in Armstrong's beauty. Ornette Coleman
also found revelation in Schuller's class: "Gunther played a thing by
Django [Reinhardt] to illustrate a point about form. To me it was
just incredible pure music, not only form." Coleman also cited Jelly
Roll Morton's Library of Congress recordings as especially moving
and edifying. Gary McFarland told Williams, "I think just being ex-
posed to the music before the Forties was an experience and a lesson,
but I also learned *how* to listen to it and enjoy it." One of the few
female students at the school, Margo Guryan, who studied piano
and composition and later wrote material for the MJQ and singer
Chris Connor and was married for a short time to faculty member

Bob Brookmeyer, testified that she "was utterly amazed at how technically proficient some of the older men were as instrumentalists—Louis Armstrong, Roy Eldridge, Lester Young—and at how harmonically advanced Ellington was." After hearing Ellington's "Braggin' in Brass" in Schuller's class, Don Heckman said he was "proud to learn that such a thing is in the jazz heritage, because it says so much for the jazzman's musicianship, and shows how completely wrong the idea is that only classical music is so exacting."[21]

Most students auditioned for admission to the school by tape. Lewis, the Barbers, and dean of students, Jule Foster, reached out to musician colleagues as well as Hentoff and Williams for help selecting the incoming classes. Their target class size was forty, with balanced distribution across instruments. They achieved this in the school's last three years after miscalculating in 1957, admitting nineteen pianists in a class of thirty-four and thereby making it difficult to put together ensembles. By 1959 over half the students came as recipients of scholarships funded by Atlantic Records, Dizzy Gillespie, George Wein, Norman Granz, Joe Glaser, and the Schaefer Brewing Company. The noteworthiness of Ornette Coleman, Don Cherry, and David Baker disguised the fact that the student body was overwhelmingly white, tilted heavily toward middle-class WASP Ivy League types, and numbered more international students than African Americans. Williams was alone in publicly lamenting this racial disparity, describing the Ivy Leaguers as "dabblers" who were "buying their way into a world they may secretly think they should feel superior to."[22]

One student, Tupper Saussy, complained in the *Jazz Review* about the "poor standard of musicianship of the student body," spinning the tale of a faculty member who "had to have several drinks before his ensemble met because he couldn't deal with its shoddy quality soberly, and by the end of the term was advocating more rigid requirements for admission." Arif Mardin assumed that because he

John Lewis and student Steve Kuhn, at Music Inn, 1959. Kuhn, a recent Harvard
graduate, was a notable exception to the Ivy Leaguers attending the School of Jazz
whom critic Martin Williams derogated as "dabblers." In the next several years,
Kuhn would go on to play first with Kenny Dorham's band and then briefly in John
Coltrane's quartet. Photograph by Clemens Kalischer.

came from Turkey, he'd benefit more than other students from
Marshall Stearns's jazz history course, only to discover that some
of his American classmates "knew almost nothing about jazz before 1952."[23] Princeton student and aspiring bass player John Keyser
was not embarrassed to report that until he came to Lenox he had

never heard of Charlie Parker. Bob Brookmeyer was dismayed to find many students adopting a hipster pose and not taking seriously how much work was required to become a competent jazz musician. "Most of the students at the school were very interested in 'blowing' and obviously, that was what they were there to learn," he wrote. "But to blow you got to know. I think they should have come to the school to know. We weren't there just to rehearse with them, to be their audience, or to hang out with them over a beer or Coke. We were there to show them what we knew had made us successful jazz performers as compared with those who were merely adequate."[24]

After the school session was up and running, mornings were devoted to faculty-led ensemble rehearsals, leading to a capstone student-faculty concert at the end of the three weeks. All students took classes in composition, arranging, theory, and jazz history in the early afternoon, then attended private instrumental lessons in the late afternoon. Evening lectures were given by the faculty in their areas of specialization as well as by visitors such as Eric Larrabee, Willis Laurence James, and Dave Brubeck (on the international jazz audience); Fela Sowande (on African music); Nesuhi Ertegun and George Avakian (on recording jazz); Monte Kay and Pete Kameron (on management and booking); Barry Ulanov (on jazz among the arts); Leonard Feather, Martin Williams, and Milton Bass (on jazz criticism); and Hsio Wen Shih (on acoustics). The Music Barn concert series continued throughout the school session; students attended the concerts for free and often fraternized with the musicians in the days leading up to and following their performances.

Other musicians, writers, and cultural brokers hung around Music Inn, often for a week or so, auditing classes, observing rehearsals, attending concerts, and schmoozing. A striking Kalischer photograph captures visitor Rudi Blesh in conversation with Don Cherry. Earlier, in the jazz roundtables, Blesh pushed his view that real jazz had died in the late 1920s. Blesh amended his position in a postscript written for a second edition of his book *Shining Trumpets* in 1958, praising some small-group bebop as signaling a possible resurrection of the New Orleans ideal. By the end of the decade, largely owing to his time spent at Music Inn gaining exposure to modern jazz, Blesh was advocating the "new thing" of Cherry, Coleman, and several others as a return to small-group polyphony and collective improvisation.[25]

Stephanie Barber's formidable public relations skills, coupled with the support of influential writers such as Feather, Hentoff, Williams, and Gleason, ensured that press coverage of the school was largely positive. Accounts of the school's highlights circulated in both jazz trade publications and general interest magazines. "I have seldom encountered such an exhilarating atmosphere," Eric Larrabee said in his *Harper's* essay. "There is something electric about the meeting of young people who are hungry to learn with teachers who did not know how well they could teach."[26] Student pianist Ron Riddle recalled an ensemble rehearsal in which Dizzy Gillespie stopped the music to explain what was wrong with the chord Riddle had just played. "What followed was an amazingly lucid fifteen-minute lecture-demonstration on the use of diminished chords, altered and unaltered." Not content to simply explain to Riddle why an E-flat–augmented eleventh chord was a better one for the passage they were playing, Gillespie seized the occasion to deliver to all on hand "an enlightening discourse on harmonic theory, with many illustrative examples."[27] Dave Blume, another pianist, lauded Oscar Peterson's ingenious method for helping him strengthen his left hand. Peterson gave him exercises to rehearse first with just his left hand, then to play in unison with both hands. When they got together for subsequent lessons, Blume played the exercises, alternating between his right hand and his left. Peterson listened with his back turned until he was unable to tell which hand Blume was using.[28]

The Lenox School of Jazz had its final season in 1960, buoyed by a late-season $5,000 grant from Michael Bakwin, owner of nearby

Former moldy fig Rudi Blesh (*left*) and avant-gardist Don Cherry (*right*), chatting at Music Inn, 1959. Photograph by Clemens Kalischer.

Avaloch Inn, and featuring trombonist J. J. Johnson and trumpeter Freddie Hubbard as special guests. The Barbers pulled out every stop trying to keep the school afloat, but their decision to purchase the Wheatleigh mansion had strained their financial portfolio more than anticipated. The closing of the school surprised the jazz world, coming so soon after the 1959 session, when Ornette Coleman's and Don Cherry's presence attracted considerable attention. Typical of the public commentary on that season was a wrap-up piece by Jack Maher, including a detailed discussion of the closing concert. While noting instances of sluggish articulation and unsteady section work that he put down to the short rehearsal time, Maher praised the generally high quality of the playing and singled out the original material that was presented—Gary McPartland's ballad "Summer Day," which Maher said, "caught the audience breathless," and Ran Blake's

"Vanguard," a piano solo "whose sense of dynamics, pure sensitivity, and lovely conception" made it "a lovely and beautifully wrought thing." Like others, Maher was captivated by Ornette Coleman. "He seems to be aiming for complete personal and musical freedom, and at his best, he is a striking and moving musician," Maher wrote, before expressing his key reservation: "And yet there were moments when I got the distinct impression that he was making his strange orbital moves purely for the sake of the reaction they would cause in listeners and musicians: sound for the sake of sound rather than for the sake of emotion."[29]

Martin Williams had no reservations about Coleman. Williams had joined with Nat Hentoff in founding the *Jazz Review*, an effort

School of Jazz students Don Cherry (*left*), Ornette Coleman (*center*), and Kent McGarity (*right*) in band rehearsal, 1959. Photograph by Clemens Kalischer.

to elevate jazz criticism to the level of the literary "little magazines," in part by opening their pages to the voices of musicians, most of them fellow Music Inn veterans, including Gunther Schuller, George Russell, Jimmy Giuffre, Bill Russo, Bob Brookmeyer, and Don Heckman. Williams's own most important contribution to the magazine was "A Letter from Lenox, Massachusetts," where he reported on first hearing Coleman. "When he stood up to take a solo on the blues with the big band on the first day of school, I was taken. It was as if he had opened up something in one's soul and opened up the way for jazz to grow. His music makes a new sensibility for one's ears and heart and mind, all the while including the most fundamental things about jazz." He concluded, "what Ornette Coleman is doing on alto will affect the whole character of jazz music profoundly and pervasively."[30] Williams went on to serve briefly as Coleman's manager. Through Hsio Wen Shih, a financial backer of both the *Jazz Review* and the Five Spot, Williams helped Coleman's quartet land their extended engagement at the East Village club that has gone down as a watershed in jazz history.[31]

The Beginning of Beyond

In recent years 1959 has been canonized as a threshold year for jazz. In 2011 the BBC released a documentary film titled *1959: The Year That Changed Jazz*, and courses have been taught on that topic.[32] If the period from 1945 to 1958 brought the emergence and development of modern jazz (bebop, hard bop, progressive), 1959 marked a transition to something beyond modern. John Szwed has pinpointed 1959 as a watershed in which "we first see jazz moving into a state of permanent diversity," a moment when "jazz ceased to follow an evolutionary handbook," and a linear path from the swing paradigm fashioned in New Orleans, Chicago, Kansas City, and New York, which then served as a consensus framework for various modernist tributaries.[33] We are now more than sixty years past this moment, a much longer time span than the entirety of jazz's recorded history up to that point. But look at any jazz textbook published in the past thirty years, and you will notice the vast bulk of the book covering jazz up to the mid-1960s, then straining for a narrative strategy—or even a name for—the jazz that has been produced in the years since.

Any such efforts at periodization are inherently vexed; rarely if ever does the flow of creative production in any art form resolve into clearly delineated segments of time. Yet it is the work—indeed one of the main functions—of critics, historians, and marketers of art forms to fashion historical schema marked by key transitional moments, to bring a sense of order to what is largely a turbulent, disordered unfolding of workaday art-making experience. If a record company like Atlantic, say, in responding to what they hear from musicians and mediators, sets out to market a new sound, the rhetoric they employ will shape the parameters within which all musicians then will be obligated to work. And if Atlantic, with its strong ties to Music Inn, sees a powerful critic like Martin Williams staking his reputation on the claim that Ornette Coleman was the new lodestar of jazz's future, it can feel confident that by naming Coleman's new LP release, *The Shape of Jazz to Come*, it will have cleared open a new space for lively, often contentious jazz creativity and critical discourse.

The musical revolution of the late 1950s and early 1960s fractured the jazz field into a plurality of styles that challenged such received notions of jazz musicianship as centered tonality, a regular beat and tempo, bar divisions, conventional chorus structure, and improvisation based on chord structures. Much was made of bebop's shifting of jazz from entertainment to art, but bebop continued to be a music that listeners turned to for pleasure. After 1959 a widespread feeling set in among critics, listeners, and many musicians that jazz's "new thing" was a willful effort to deny listeners the comforts of recognizable melody and rhythm. Typical—if uniquely piercing—was the British poet and jazz critic Philip Larkin, who found most jazz after Charlie Parker merely ugly, singling out John Coltrane's post-1959 music as being "ugly on purpose."[34] For others there was great beauty in the ostensible ugliness. Among critics LeRoi Jones (later Amiri Baraka) emerged as a beacon for those who heard in the new music a new paradigm of aesthetic value that required new modes of listening and engagement.[35]

The Shape of Jazz to Come is one of several albums from 1959 often cited as evidence of that year's transformative potency. Others include John Coltrane's *Giant Steps*, Dave Brubeck's *Time Out*, and Miles Davis's *Kind of Blue*. Of the four only *Giant Steps* did not have a deep connection to Music Inn. This fact testifies to the outsize impact Music Inn and the School of Jazz had on the history of modern jazz, and yet Lenox has rarely even been mentioned in standard jazz histories. Darius Brubeck, son of Dave Brubeck and a highly accomplished jazz pianist, educator, and historian, draws attention to this lacuna in an essay published in 2002 bearing the title "1959: The Beginning of Beyond." Brubeck, who lived at Music Inn with his family in the summer of 1959, is puzzled why a place that was so obviously integral to that moment in jazz has not been written into the music's historical narrative. "Simply intoning [the] names of teachers and students who were there . . . risks making [the School of Jazz] even more momentous than it was," Brubeck writes. He points to Ornette Coleman ("How long would it have taken for Ornette Coleman to be recognized had he not been there?"); George Russell (whose theoretical treatise *The Lydian Chromatic Concept of Tonal Organization for Improvisation* went into its second edition that year); and the field of jazz education ("It was here [where jazz first became] a formal academic discipline") as evidence of Lenox's role in "modernizing the cultural landscape."[36]

Dave Brubeck's *Time Out* and Miles Davis's *Kind of Blue* were remarkable in moving the 1950s mainstream jazz model forward while also achieving mass popular success. In 1959 both men were already unusually well known for jazz musicians—Brubeck had appeared on the cover of *Time* in 1954 and Davis had secured his place as the *ne plus ultra* of cool masculinity—but both were entering periods of exceptional creative fertility. At a lecture Brubeck gave at Music Inn that summer, he reported on hearing Turkish and Greek folk music while on a State Department tour, being enthralled by the music's unusual time signatures—unusual to jazz, that is—and keen to explore them with his own band. Willis Laurence James was in the audience and asked to come to podium. He proceeded to demonstrate a traditional African American field holler in 5/4 time, his way of endorsing Brubeck's use of that meter in his jazz compositions. James's demonstration specifically honored Brubeck's rhythmic concept for his tune "Take Five," on *Time Out*, which went on to become the biggest-selling single in jazz history.[37] Brubeck continued to experiment with multiple time signatures and grooves on his next album, *Time Further Out*, which was written at Music Inn. Steven Feld, an ethnomusicologist who spent five years in Ghana researching his book *Jazz Cosmopolitanism in Accra* (2012), has reported that the musicians he met and played with embraced Brubeck's work from this period as authentic African jazz.[38]

Miles Davis's masterpiece *Kind of Blue*, the bestselling album in jazz history and the starting point for many jazz initiates, distills an exquisitely hip melancholy out of each of its songs' shapely melodies. Davis's main pianist on the session, Bill Evans, would go on to become one of modern jazz's most affecting players, his chamber-like trio work striking in its gentle poignancy and tenderness at a time when much of the music became more aggressive to suit the increasingly roiling political climate. Evans was an acolyte of his fellow Lenox School of Jazz faculty member George Russell, a composer and musical theorist who had introduced to jazz a new concept of tonal organization. Starting in the late 1940s, Russell composed large ensemble works, including "Cubano Be, Cubano Bop" for Dizzy Gillespie's

Dave Brubeck delivering a lecture, audited by Gunther Schuller (*left*), John Lewis (*center*), and John Garvey (*right*), at Music Inn, 1959. Photograph by Clemens Kalischer.

orchestra. He was part of a clique, including Miles Davis, John Lewis, saxophonist Gerry Mulligan, and composer-arranger Gil Evans, who plotted jazz's future from Evans's midtown Manhattan basement. Lewis invited Russell to teach composition and theory in Lenox.

Bebop tunes begin with a theme that introduces a set of chords for the soloists, who in turn improvise using the governing chord progression. The method had reached a kind of ecstatic peak in Coltrane's performance on "Giant Steps," where the tenor saxophonist bobsleds with breathless technical virtuosity through the tune's dense chordal maze. Russell's powerful innovation was to use musical modes rather than chord progressions, leaving more space for soloists to craft melodies not beholden to a stable tonal center. Ancient Greek music was based on seven major and minor modes; Russell showed how several of them could enhance the expressive language of jazz. The Dorian mode, a minor scale that meshes with the familiar sound of the blues, lent itself to a hypnotic, haunting poignancy, a register hard to achieve in bebop, which relied overwhelmingly on the bright melodies and standard chord changes of popular tunes. Miles Davis and Bill Evans used the mode to stunning effect on "So What," the first track on *Kind of Blue*.

In the 1960s Davis led a quintet whose pianist, Herbie Hancock, and saxophonist, Wayne Shorter, would in turn become key composers of modal jazz. John Coltrane, who played on *Kind of Blue*, adopted the modal approach with his classic quartet of the early 1960s on arresting tunes like "Impressions" and "India." His 1965 album, *A Love Supreme*, synthesized modal and free jazz while also moving the music into the new expressive territory of spiritual awakening and purity ritual. By turns devotional and ecstatic, tender and frenzied, the album exerted widespread totemic influence from the Black arts movement to rock groups like the Byrds and the Doors and the guitar effusions of Jimi Hendrix and Carlos Santana.

A week before the release of *Kind of Blue* in August 1959, Miles Davis was scheduled to be in Lenox for a concert at the Music Barn. Davis had cultivated a reputation for being angry, stubborn, and fiercely protective of his privacy. He had earned the Barbers' enmity by canceling a scheduled concert in 1957 at the last minute.[39] Excitement ran high for the 1959 concert because Bill Evans had a reel-to-reel tape of the *Kind of Blue* master and had played it for George Russell and others at the school. Alas, the concert had to be canceled when Davis, evidently exhausted from the grueling national tour he and his band had just completed, failed to show up. Davis's saxophonist, Cannonball Adderley, perhaps feeling guilty about the cancellation, drove up to Lenox from New York by himself and spent hours talking and socializing with School of Jazz faculty and students.[40]

One of the indelible memories of the summer of 1959 was the jam sessions in which Ornette Coleman and Jimmy Giuffre spurred each other on to more and more expressive freedom. Giuffre immediately grasped Coleman's genius and, in a case of the student teaching the teacher, eagerly absorbed his influence. Giuffre had received a lot of attention in the mid-1950s, much of it generated by an issue of the *Saturday Review* in 1957 that pictured him on the cover and featured a story and interview by Nat Hentoff. At the time Giuffre was crafting an approach with clear third-stream influences and a cool personal signature. Giuffre explained to Hentoff that he was drawing on a "slow-motion counterpoint technique used by Bach, Beethoven, and Shostakovich" that he found effective for creating "a certain feeling of suspension, or distance." In his first drummer-less trio with guitarist Jim Hall and bassist Ralph Pena, Giuffre said, "While the clarinet is playing eighth notes, the bass may be playing whole notes and the guitar could be in between. They're all coordinated so that you can hear every note each man plays." His hope was that listeners could follow all the lines "because in my writing, the harmonies are the results of the lines rather than the lines being fitted to the harmonies."[41]

Gunther Schuller told the story of a late afternoon when Ornette Coleman, Don Cherry, and several other students gathered in the Potting Shed to experiment with freer harmonies and melodies than they were able to play within the parameters of the school's formal curriculum. Schuller had seen Coleman and Cherry gently persuading Giuffre to move in their direction with his horn playing, which they admired but thought could benefit from some loosening up. Schuller happened to arrive just as Giuffre showed up with his saxophone and joined the jam session. "Jimmy had decided [that] instead of playing in his usual cool, folksy, modal style, [he would now try] to emulate Ornette's atonal, fragmented, wailing, gliding, swooping style."

As Jimmy's playing became more frantic he gradually slid to the floor from his initial standing position, rolling around on the stone floor in a kind of hysterical paroxysm, as if he'd been bitten by a tarantula. His feet were up in the air, gyrating in frenzied, twitching movements, while he was blowing like mad into his tenor, holding it high up in the air above his head, producing the most God-awful cacophony of cracked notes and screaming, screeching, honking sounds. . . . I couldn't tell whether he was enjoying himself, or whether he was under the spell of some satanic ritual, becoming completely unhinged.[42]

Giuffre later told Schuller he'd had a cathartic experience, "a kind of release of something." Viewed in retrospect, however, what Giuffre took from Coleman was less an impetus to change the way he played clarinet and saxophone than a more general license toward greater freedom ("Ornette has cut the strings") and a group sound design that veered from the jazz mainstream approach.[43] His new trio with pianist Paul Bley and bassist Steve Swallow featured contrapuntal interplay and free improvisation glued together with oscillating pulses and bursts of rhythmic energy, a chamber music version of free jazz different from the muscular, sometimes ferocious one played by John Coltrane, Eric Dolphy, Archie Shepp, Albert Ayler, and Pharoah Sanders. The divergence was not simply one of white and Black styles of free jazz but also of gender and place. Giuffre appeared in the "October Revolution in Jazz," a free jazz festival organized by trumpeter Bill Dixon in New York in 1964. But as the New York jazz scene channeled and amplified the increasingly fractious and masculinist racial politics of the mid to late 1960s, Giuffre found it more difficult than the Black musicians, with whom he shared a gentle manner and serene, introspective personality, to continue working in the city.

WITH HIS WIFE, Juanita, who earlier was married to George Russell, Giuffre bought property in the Berkshires and spent more and more time there. He taught for fifteen years at the New England Con-

School of Jazz faculty party, 1959. In the front are Jimmy Giuffre (*left*) and Milt Jackson (*right*), and in the back are Juanita Russell (*left*), Peri Cousins (*center*), and Bill Evans (*right*). Photograph by Clemens Kalischer.

servatory, where his students included drummer George Schuller, who later played in a Giuffre repertory band, and trumpeter Dave Douglas. Giuffre's music resonates with a highly personal voice distilled from his Texas childhood, his period as a leader of the West Coast cool movement, and his many years ambivalently positioned between the pastoral Berkshires and the New York avant-garde—an astute, serene, and supple sound fringed with a gentle edge of abstraction.

Ornette Coleman was also from Texas. His sound combined deep southern blues with a part-scholarly, part-bohemian iconoclasm. He galvanized (or annoyed) listeners with the keening sound of his alto saxophone and the striking range and originality of his tonal palette. Coleman seemed to recover an ancient soulfulness in long skeins of haunting melody that sounded utterly personal, nothing jazz had sounded like before, and yet, because of its uncanny rural blues overtones, strangely familiar.

Ornette Coleman and Don Cherry came to Lenox from Los Angeles, where earlier they'd cut two albums for Contemporary Records. For the first, *Something Else!!!!* (1958), Coleman, who at the time was working as an elevator operator, assembled the group of musicians (Don Cherry, bassist Charlie Haden, and drummers Billy Higgins and Ed Blackwell) who would later be part of his celebrated quartet of the early 1960s. For the second, *Tomorrow Is the Question! The New Music of Ornette Coleman* (1959), Coleman used Red Mitchell and Percy Heath on bass. Heath came back to New York raving about Coleman, prompting John Lewis and Nesuhi Ertegun to strategize how best to lure him and his quartet to New York and to make Atlantic his recording home. The Atlantic Records scholarships Coleman and Cherry were awarded to attend the School of Jazz were part of the strategy.

Schuller recalled what happened when Coleman arrived in Lenox:

> It was no surprise to me that Ornette was not particularly welcomed at the school. As a twenty-eight-year-old professional, he was considered a bit of an intruder. Initially there were feelings of envy among the students generated by all the attention and praise he was receiving in the jazz press; and of course, very few of them could relate at all to what they regarded as Ornette's out-of-tune, erratic, fragmented, makes-no-sense kind of playing. . . . There was much snickering behind his back, which Ornette ignored with remarkable philosophical aplomb.[44]

Later, when Coleman got to New York for his quartet's ballyhooed engagement at the Five Spot, Bob Brookmeyer sat at the bar night after night coming to terms with Coleman's startlingly fresh sound and concept. But at Music Inn Brookmeyer had been the most prominent of Coleman's detractors, leaving his faculty post midseason in part because of his discomfort with Coleman's presence at the school.[45]

Much of the snickering Schuller refers to dwelled on the question of whether Coleman could read and write music. Later, with Coleman's release of several third-stream–inspired LPs including *Skies of America* (1972), a scored-through composition Coleman created for his quartet and the London Symphony Orchestra, the question grew more complicated and interesting.[46] But already in August 1959, when Brookmeyer and others at Music Inn asked the question, it intensified a debate that had begun in the 1956 musicians' roundtable of what really constituted composition in jazz, in particular whether standard notational practice in Western classical music was the right or best model for defining what it means to write and read music in a jazz context. Herb Pomeroy, who led the School of Jazz big band that performed at the season's concert finale, has testified that he and others had to come up with workarounds to bring Coleman up to speed on the written material—essentially, letting him learn his parts by ear, which he then elevated significantly with his brilliant playing. Given this, one of Clemens Kalischer's most intriguing Music Inn photographs complicates the question even further. In it we see Bill Russo leading several students in the singing of Bach chorales. Coleman wears one of his trademark flat-collar dark cable sweaters. He stands between two callow blazer-clad white students, avidly involved, reading from the Bach score.

Whatever tools Coleman did or did not have in his kit, the sound of his horn shocked everyone who heard it. Gunther Schuller and Martin Williams were sitting in the Barn, on the Saturday at the end of the school's first week, listening to a student jam session. Coleman came and sat in front of them. After twenty minutes Coleman rose from his seat and took the stage with his fellow students. "What suddenly burst out of Ornette's horn," Schuller later recalled, "was one

School of Jazz faculty member Bill Russo (*left*), leading students including Ornette Coleman (*holding score*) and Kent McGarity (*right*) in the singing of Bach chorales, at Music Inn, 1959. Photograph by Clemens Kalischer.

of those moments in music that you never forget. It was one of his patented blazing, swirling runs, the notes flying by so fast you didn't hear them as individual pitches, more like some gigantic cluster or a dense cloud of sounds. It was Ornette signaling—not arrogantly or angrily, just dramatically—hey, listen up." Coleman wore out three rhythm sections before finishing, alternating between blistering skeins of jagged sound and what Schuller describes as "lighthearted arabesques as only he could contrive." Along the way, as Coleman built up one chorus after another, he began to reference the styles of his saxophone predecessors (Johnny Hodges, Charlie Parker, Benny Carter, Earl Bostic, Zoot Sims, and others), "tracing that long beautiful history, modifying his sound as needed, darkening, brightening, choosing lines and figures that harkened back to those earlier times without losing his own identity. It was an amazing tour de force."[47]

The Future of Form

Another notable album recorded in 1959 was Gunther Schuller's *Conversations*. The title refers to the interplay Schuller curates between a classical string quartet and the Modern Jazz Quartet. It was the first recording of one of Schuller's own third-stream compositions, a full two years after he coined a term for the genre and began proselytizing it through his writing and his presence as a mediator in and between the jazz and classical worlds. Atlantic recorded this album and five subsequent Schuller ones under the supervision of Nesuhi Ertegun and at the behest of John Lewis, who believed so strongly in the music that he covered the recording costs out of his own account with the record company.[48] *Conversations* did not enjoy anything like the kind of heavy publicity, wide reception, and enduring legacy as *The Shape of Jazz to Come*, *Time Out*, or *Kind of Blue*. It is very much a document of its own time and place. It enacts third-stream methodology through a series of exchanges between the two units, each drawing on their own idiomatic approaches to improvisation, the MJQ's in the manner of standard jazz practice, the string quartet's in the new postwar development in European classical modernism known as aleatoric music, with the players using chance procedures to provide frameworks for their extemporizations. Up to that point, Schuller's compositional aesthetic had spanned neoclassicism and the Second Viennese School's twelve-tone method. Now he was moving into a lane parallel to those occupied by such stalwarts of late modernism and postmodernism as John Cage, Karlheinz Stockhausen, and Iannis Xenakis.

In retrospect Schuller's impact in this period came less from his own music than from his writings about other performers and the jazz field as a whole. His first published piece, "The Future of Form in Jazz," appearing in the *Saturday Review* in 1957, surveys the work of musicians seeking alternatives to the standard format of an opening and closing theme wrapped around a set of solos based

Gunther Schuller and John Garvey working with string players, at Music Inn, 1959.
Photograph by Clemens Kalischer.

on the same chord changes but otherwise not necessarily related
to each other. Music Inn–connected figures feature prominently in
the essay: Charles Mingus, John Lewis, Jimmy Giuffre, Teo Macero,
Teddy Charles, and, especially, George Russell. Schuller carefully
analyzes Russell's composition "Lydian M-1," a leading example of
what the composer called "the war on the chord" being waged by
fellow post-bebop jazz vanguardists. Schuller warns against an im-
portation into jazz of classical forms like the sonata and the fugue,
asserting that jazz "is strong and rich enough to find within its own

domain forms much more indigenous to its own essential nature."
Were Charlie Parker still alive, Schuller claims, he would have been
searching for a "more complex context" in which to embed his
unique style.[49]

Schuller's support of Russell was important at a time when few
jazz critics had warmed to him. His 1956 LP, *The Jazz Workshop*, a
collection of his compositions using modality, African-influenced
rhythms, and changing tempos, confounded the *New Yorker*'s Whitney Balliett, who said, "It comes dangerously close to a highly skilled
travesty of jazz that might have been cooked up, in anger and con-
descension, by someone who despised the music."[50] When two
Lenox students, David Baker and Don Ellis, became members of the
George Russell Sextet, Schuller heralded the development as one of
the school's glories and predicted that the group would expand jazz
form and language by overthrowing "the tyranny of the ¼ meter,"
absorbing the influence of Anton Webern, Karlheinz Stockhausen,
and John Cage, and crafting "atonal collective improvisation."[51] The
sextet made a string of recordings in the early 1960s, including *Jazz
in the Space Age* (1960), *Stratusphunk* (1960), and *The Outer View* (1962),
that waxed futuristic even while carrying out Russell's theories of
the ancient foundations of organized sound. Russell's experiments
in new meters and complex textures, coupled with his openness to
electronic instrumentation, presaged the jazz-rock fusion of the late
1960s and '70s. Russell was another of his School of Jazz faculty colleagues that Schuller hired at the New England Conservatory.

Schuller's attention to complexity of form and formalist analysis was even stronger in a piece he published in 1958—the very first
feature essay in the inaugural volume of Nat Hentoff and Martin
Williams's *Jazz Review*. Sonny Rollins had come to Music Inn that
summer, performed at the Music Barn, and recorded an Atlantic
album with the Modern Jazz Quartet that came with liner notes written by Schuller. That fall Schuller's "Sonny Rollins and the Challenge

Composer George Russell teaching a class in the Potting Shed, at Music Inn, 1958.
Photograph by Clemens Kalischer.

of Thematic Improvisation" appeared in the *Jazz Review*. In what
was widely heralded as a seminal work of formalist jazz analysis,
Schuller argues that Rollins's improvised solo on his 1956 recording
of "Blue Seven" signaled that jazz had reached a new threshold of
"intellectual enlightenment." He exalts Rollins's skill as a "thematic"
improvisor, one who, in developing motivic elements of a composed
theme, proves that jazz has overcome its "humble beginnings" by
favoring "the power of reason and comprehension" over "purely in-
tuitive emotional outpouring."[52] Martin Williams, by later including
"Blue Seven" in *The Smithsonian Collection of Classic Jazz* and largely
adopting Schuller's interpretation of the record's significance, canonized not just Rollins's performance but also Schuller's theoretical
perspective and conceptual framework.

We can easily see how Schuller's approach to "Blue Seven" not only aligned with his own third-stream concept but also synchronized with Music Inn's mission to overcome barriers between jazz and classical music and to advance racial equality. Schuller knew Black jazz musicians as personal friends and respected their intelligence; in attributing reason rather than emotion to Rollins's skill as an improvisor, he was evoking a high-minded liberal sensitivity to latter-day primitivist assumptions about African American musicians. But he was also inadvertently enshrining a value system in which the methods and putative intellectual superiority of European classical music are held to represent a universal standard that jazz musicians must meet if their music were to achieve its promise as an art form.

Soon after Schuller's article appeared, Rollins took a sabbatical to reassess his life and career. "I read all the magazines when they were writing about me," he later said. "I began to worry about things I shouldn't have. People said that I did a certain kind of thing, and I began to believe them, and by the time I figured out how I did it, I was unable to achieve the effect anymore."[53] There was speculation but never a confirmation from Rollins that Schuller's widely discussed article had imposed an especially heavy burden. During his two-year exile from the public stage, Rollins practiced on his horn late at night on the Williamsburg Bridge high above the East River between Manhattan and Brooklyn. It is tempting to think of Sonny Rollins alone on the bridge, reworking his sound, as an existential act of creative independence, freeing himself from institutional and ideological demands (including those represented by Music Inn and its associated networks), rescuing and refurbishing jazz's narrative of the heroic outsider.

Musicologist Benjamin Givan persuasively argues that Schuller was wrong about "Blue Seven": Rollins did not approach his solo as an exercise in thematic development—the theme itself, as well as the rest of the performance, was completely improvised. Givan suggests that Schuller's third-stream orientation, combined with his integrationist politics, led him to misinterpret Rollins's performance and, in general, to downplay differences between jazz and classical music. Givan's critique is sharply illuminating. But it runs the danger of essentializing jazz and classical music by enshrining improvisation and composition as wholly separate and mutually exclusive activities. By extension it also implies a division between "white" and "Black" that could lead us to miss how Schuller's own classical compositions, for instance, might have been influenced by his study of African music or how certain African musicians have absorbed the music of the European avant-garde.[54]

Schuller's emphasis on complexity and intellectuality as absolute markers of aesthetic value was wholly of a piece with its historical moment, a symptom of the era's mandates to raise jazz's level of cultural legitimacy as well as society's level of respect for African American art and artists. In retrospect, after decades of political and intellectual work aimed at unraveling racialized structures of perception and power, it is not hard to see the limitations and even—as with the Rollins example—unintentionally adverse consequences of Schuller's analysis. It is also a supreme lesson in the power of ideology in fixing ideas about what progress really is. In his School of Jazz teaching and his subsequent writing, Schuller had few if any peers in terms of the depth and critical virtuosity of his engagement with the entire history of jazz. In so many respects, his educational and critical work uniquely embodied and singularly advanced John Lewis's hope that the School of Jazz would put an end to the traditionalist-modernist sectarian war and produce an open-minded, ecumenical jazz culture equally respectful of the old and the new. Schuller is the man who introduced Louis Armstrong to Don Cherry and Jelly Roll Morton to Ornette Coleman. But the logic of his jazz criticism implied that musicians like Cherry, Coleman, Mingus, Giuffre, Russell, Lewis, and others were shepherding jazz to a higher level

Sonny Rollins, Percy Heath, and John Lewis performing in the Music Barn, 1958.
Photograph by Clemens Kalischer.

of achievement than their predecessors, if only because the atmosphere in which they worked encouraged them to bring "the power of reason and comprehension" to bear on their art. It is hard not to conclude that the primary institutional site of this atmosphere was the Lenox School of Jazz.

Even if Schuller was right in supposing that Charlie Parker would have sought out a "more complex context" for his playing, would this necessarily have resulted in better music than that which Parker had already produced? Is it not possible that a more complex context could have worked against Parker, distracting him from his core strengths? In technical terms the twelve-bar blues is the simplest of forms, the one every jazz player is expected to master. Does that mean that when jazz musicians choose to play that form, they are consciously deciding to deliver suboptimal music?

Earlier in the decade, before Schuller arrived, pianist and Julliard teacher John Mehegan was one of the figures who brought a patina of academic authority to Music Inn. He was a dyed-in-the-wool modernist, an admirer of Lennie Tristano and Bill Evans, and an advocate for enhanced technical knowledge among jazz musicians. Yet, in 1959, in *DownBeat*'s *Silver Anniversary Edition*, in an article titled "The Case for Swinging," he issued a jeremiad that might as well have been advertised as a takedown of the School of Jazz, along with other sectors of jazz's late 1950s cultural ambit: "If we continue to smother [jazz] with a superstructure of complexity and intellectuality it cannot possibly support, we will eventually destroy it. This applies specifically to the cabalists, the metaphysicians, the formalists, the pretenders, the beatniks, the Zen Buddhists and the been-zootists."[55] Mehegan's jape was but the tip of an iceberg that gathered considerable heft in the next several years, as charges of anti-jazz apostasy rained down on the third stream, Ornette Coleman, John Coltrane, Cecil Taylor, and others. That iceberg has grown exponentially over the past sixty years, the jazz conversation bringing one salty indictment after another of musicians accused of abandoning jazz's putative essential quality—swing—in favor of this or that better-than-jazz affectation. Straight and taut is the line stretching from John Mehegan's egging of the "been-zootists" in the 1950s to Stanley Crouch's firestorms in the 1990s against anyone put off by Wynton Marsalis and Lincon Center Jazz's traditional swing autocracy.

Closer to home, Milton Bass weighed in a couple of years later with his own arraignment of Gunther Schuller, John Lewis, Jimmy Giuffre, Ornette Coleman, and others, labeling their music "Non-jazz Jazz" in an armchair state-of-the-field piece for the *Atlantic*. Bass complains about jazz musicians who "are not really satisfied unless they have a hundred symphonic musicians behind them." Exhibit A: Jimmy Giuffre's *Piece for Clarinet and Orchestra*, "about as earnest a disaster as can be imagined." He then impugns a group he calls "jazz seekers"—Ornette Coleman, Sonny Rollins, Cecil Taylor, Don

Ellis, and Paul Bley—who "have been making their sound either by running up and down the scales at breakneck speed while changing chords, according to the phases of the moon, or by grabbing individual notes and beating them to death." Bass concludes that just as jazz has become "a subject for learned discussion, [m]ost of the expressions of happiness have been squeezed out of it."[56]

What was happening—not for the first or last time—was a shift not just in jazz music but also in jazz *musicking*, a change in the material and ideological conditions in which the music was made and consumed—above all, a change in the practice of *listening*. The new music demanded a different kind of listening than the older music: a different attunement and sensitivity, a different relationship to sound, different kinds of mental and physical engagement, different expectations. Mehegan and Bass spoke for a sizeable majority of the jazz audience in saying they were not willing to make these changes, to embrace these differences. For others the new sounds rattling in their ears were perfectly calibrated to feelings and desires unleashed by the momentous political turmoil and aesthetic adventurism of the time. Yet others charted a middle course. "To the average listener," Darius Brubeck writes, "the problem with much of free jazz had less to do with not being 'based on the chord' than with the strident and deliberately 'unmusical' sounds often associated with it. Nevertheless, in the long run, the mainstream benefited from avant-garde explorations of an enlarged sound-world, e.g. how instruments are played, which sounds are musical and how sound is organized."[57]

No other bricks-and-mortar institution, no other physical space, no other place better registered the pulsing changes in jazz music and jazz musicking over the course of the 1950s and into the New Frontier future than Music Inn. It was there, off Hawthorne Street in Lenox, where the jazz mainstream and the jazz tradition crystallized not just as concepts or ideas but as courses of study and methods of sonic practice. And in 1959 it was there, more sharply and robustly than anywhere else, where the shape of jazz to come was meditated on, mapped out, argued over, imagined, and felt.

Future Shock

By the early 1960s, rock and roll had replaced the jazz swing-bebop-cool mainstream as the dominant force in modern American popular culture. Jazz and rock shared the same DNA, but as modern jazz developed into more and more of a cerebral listening music, the blues and gospel legacy of stomping, hand-clapping, pleasure-centered music and dance fell to Ray Charles, Muddy Waters, B. B. King, Etta James, Elvis Presley, Little Richard, Chuck Berry, and other artists in the rhythm and blues and rock and roll orbit. The 1960s British Invasion blues-based rock and its various US imitations, producer Phil Spector's "wall of sound," Motown pop, Memphis soul, and the first stirrings of hard rock gained massive cross-racial popularity among the exploding baby boomer demographic, leaving jazz with an aging and diminishing audience. In 1960 the look of music-world hipness was the cover of a Blue Note LP with a stylish image of Black jazz musicians working hard at their craft. By 1970 that image seemed like an archival remnant suddenly supplanted by celebrity photographs of pale-faced, androgynous, libertine rock superstars. Atlantic Records became a powerhouse of 1960s soul music and caught the wave of late 1960s hard rock; by the end of the decade, the label's identity as a premier jazz label had been supplanted by its alliance with Stax Records, the Memphis-based soul label, and its investments in British acts like Cream and Led Zeppelin.[58]

With the racially integrated School of Jazz faculty and Music Barn concerts and roundtables that included blues, folk, gospel, and African and Caribbean performers, the implicit ideology at Music Inn was liberal and multicultural. This was quite progressive for the 1950s, but it was far removed from the pulse of contemporary Black popular culture. Black music had always defied conventional genre boundaries, and the exaltation of jazz as an elite and singular music—the implicit position of Music Inn and other legitimizing institutions—had always been in dynamic tension with Black culture's strong impulse toward inclusive populism. John Coltrane, Ornette Coleman, Eric Dolphy, Albert Ayler, and other avant-garde jazz musicians started their careers in rhythm and blues bands, while many of the musicians who played on other popular rhythm and blues and soul recordings of the 1960s had started their careers as jazz musicians. The idea of jazz as part of a unified Black music aesthetic and ethos—what Amiri Baraka later famously called "the changing same"—resonated in soul jazz, a Black roots–infused style of the 1950s and '60s marked by tuneful blues voicings, song titles displaying the speech inflections of Black vernacular speech, and a general ambience redolent of the down-home rhythms and spirit of the sanctified church. Horace Silver, Bobby Timmons, and others associated with this style were never part of the Music Inn scene or curriculum.[59]

While Music Inn alumni took their place in the 1960s jazz avant-garde, newer forms of more popular jazz, featuring lean grooves, gospel-rich chords, and a hip urban vibe, became the ambient sound of Black neighborhoods in cities across the country. Jazz-label recordings like Herbie Hancock's "Watermelon Man" (and its Latin cover by Mongo Santamaria), Lee Morgan's "The Sidewinder," Ramsey Lewis's "The 'In' Crowd," and Cannonball Adderley's "Mercy, Mercy, Mercy" rose to the top of the rhythm and blues charts. Keyboardist Jimmy Smith pioneered the use of the Hammond B3 organ in a trio with drums and saxophone or guitar, a soul jazz offshoot that became a standard live format in urban neighborhood bars. Saxophonists Pharoah Sanders, Joe Henderson, and Gary Bartz popularized John Coltrane's spiritualism in a new Afrocentric style, combining ethereal sonorities drawn from free jazz with danceable grooves augmented by African percussion. In the early 1970s, Herbie Hancock's albums found a mass cross-racial audience in both the older soul jazz cohort and among younger college students. Wielding a Fender Rhodes electric piano, synthesizers, and clavinet and modeling a Sly Stone–influenced Afro-futurist look, Hancock drew on African percussion and deep grooves to fashion a new subgenre: jazz funk.

These and other new directions in 1960s and '70s jazz can be traced at least in part to the aesthetic experimentation that prevailed at Music Inn in the late 1950s. George Russell and Ornette Coleman would continue to make harmonic innovations and embrace rhythmic and timbral features adjacent to—but for some antithetical to—the jazz mainstream. Russell's use of the electric bass in his post mid-1960s bands later ran afoul of the purity strictures of the 1980s and '90s neoclassical movement, complicating Jazz at Lincoln Center's plans to commemorate his career.[60] Coleman developed an idiosyncratic musical philosophy and method of composition and improvisation he called "harmolodics." While cloaked in obscure theoretical language redolent of 1950s high modernism, the music Coleman produced under that banner won considerable support from musicians, critics, and audiences otherwise primarily associated with funk, hard rock, and even punk.[61] This might seem to be a long way from Coleman's playing on Gunther Schuller's *Jazz Abstractions* LP (1960) or even his own concert works such as *Forms and Sounds for Wind Quartet* (1965) or *Inventions of Symphonic Poems* (1967). But Schuller himself thought Coleman had been practicing harmolodics well before hatching a theory of that name, including at Music Inn, where the polytonal and heterophonic nature of his playing was strikingly evident, thrilling some listeners and puzzling others.[62]

The pianist and writer Ethan Iverson has speculated that Coleman, "faced with people like Schuller and everybody else at Lenox who could read and notate the most complicated music as easily as Ornette could create it, felt compelled to come up with his own alternative system [harmolodics] that he could teach and talk about."[63] If so, we can include Coleman with other Lenox School of Jazz faculty

Ornette Coleman on Music Inn grounds, 1959. Photograph by Clemens Kalischer.

and students (George Russell, Gunther Schuller, Ran Blake, David Baker, Larry Ridley, and others) whose post-Lenox careers helped ensure that the shape of jazz to come would include the kind of educational practices and varieties of informal discourse that had taken place at Music Inn throughout the 1950s.

CONCLUSION: THE PLACE TO BE

After shuttering the Lenox School of Jazz at the end of August 1960, Philip and Stephanie Barber made a go of it as proprietors of Wheatleigh, turning the mansion into an upscale hotel and restaurant. Philip also turned back to the theater. His play, *I Elizabeth Otis, Being of Sound Mind*, was staged in the United States and the United Kingdom in the late 1960s, and in 1970 he cofounded and served as the first artistic director of the Manhattan Theater Club. The Barbers continued to move genially through overlapping social worlds, bolstering their reputation as first-rate guests and not-to-be-missed hosts. Ran Blake fondly remembers dinners at the Barbers' home throughout the 1960s and 1970s, where he ate and drank very well and met VIPs from the worlds of music, art, business, and politics. The Barbers sold Wheatleigh in 1976, the same year Philip became president of the nearby Becket Arts Center. In the years to come, Stephanie gave more time to her singing career, became an active board member of Berkshires cultural institutions, sold real estate, and doubled down on her practice of seizing every occasion for the theatrical presentation of a fabulous hat. Philip Barber died in 1981, Stephanie in 2003.

Since the 1960s, and especially from the 1980s on, the Berkshires has grown in reputation as a premier space of cultivated leisure, a favorite destination for urbanites and suburbanites in search of thriving cultural and performing arts institutions nestled in a bucolic, small-town, woods-and-lakes environment. As in many other similar areas across the United States, economic development schemes and real estate market shifts that follow such popularity pose a threat to the very on-the-ground conditions that generated that popularity in the first place. The site of Music Inn is now occupied by White Pines, an upscale condominium complex whose marketing employs the same kind of pastoral rhetoric the Barbers did when they started out, but to very different ends. Whereas once the Berkshires caught the pulse first of postwar modern jazz and then of the post-1960 counterculture—owing especially to Music Inn's programming of blues-based rock and reggae under David Rothstein in the 1970s—population shifts in recent decades have turned the area into a string of retirement communities. Increasingly, these retirees are boomers who came of age from the late 1950s to the early 1970s and can be counted on to fill seats for music from that period staged at local and regional venues. While Tanglewood remains the bedrock of the Berkshires' summer cultural tourist economy, for years it has faced a steady diminution of the classical music audience. One of its key survival strategies has been to make jazz and folk rock—a yearly concert by local resident James Taylor draws Tanglewood's largest audiences—a regular part of its programming.

Demographically and culturally, the Berkshires remains overwhelmingly white. As in other similar communities across the country, however, the declining white birthrate has made the local economy dependent on an influx of recent immigrant families, mainly from Latin America. Following another national trendline, the Berkshires has played catch-up in recognizing and memorializing its African American history. A spate of excellent library, historical-society, and civic-organization initiatives have helped recover local African American histories, often using words like *invisible* and *hidden* to frame their efforts.[1] The language illustrates how public-facing histories of specific places, whether neighborhoods or nations, tend to foreground the perspective of the powerful, even when ostensibly focused on the experience of the marginalized. The marginalized are never invisible to themselves, and an important part of their agency is an ability to peer with sharp acuity into the lives of the more powerful. W. E. B. Du Bois understood this very well. "We who are dark can see America in a way that white Americans cannot," he wrote in 1926.[2]

Du Bois himself became largely invisible in the Berkshires during the years he reigned as a singular figure in African American letters, politics, and intellectual life—only to achieve sharp visibility as an object of controversy and scorn triggered by efforts to memorialize him in his hometown of Great Barrington. By comparison Music Inn's first decade, the jazz and folk period of the Barbers, Alan Lomax, Pete Seeger, Randy Weston, Marshall Stearns, the Modern Jazz Quartet, and others, has fared far better in local memory—notwithstanding the fact that the inn's early 1950s association with the blacklist made it vulnerable to the same Red Scare forces that defamed Du Bois as "anti-American."[3] Admittedly, this comparison is strained: Music Inn was a performing arts institution and leisure site that didn't go out of its way to advertise its ideological slant; Du Bois was an individual of fierce political conviction who directly challenged the Cold War political establishment. Still, there is no gainsaying the significance of the efforts made by the Barbers, Marshall Stearns, John Lewis, and others to resist the dominant racial patterns of American life; to stage performances of a wide variety of American, African, and Afro-Caribbean vernacular music; and to pioneer an approach to jazz education that enabled students to study with the idiom's leading players, composers, and theorists while grappling with the music's history and sociocultural significance.

We began our history of the first ten years of Music Inn with

David Baker (*left*) and Gunther Schuller (*right*), at Music Inn, 1959. Photograph by Clemens Kalischer.

New York Times jazz writer John S. Wilson heralding the venue as a new place on the jazz map, "totally different" from New Orleans but similar in significance as a "seedbed" of the music. Wilson was channeling the dominant jazz discourse of the 1950s, a period when the music's artistic legitimization and mainstream normalization ran hand in hand with civil rights–era racial integrationism and African American bourgeoisification. I've argued that the location of Music

Inn in the Berkshires made it an especially powerful agent of these cultural and political forces—in part because of the cultural capital that accrued to the inn owing to its proximity to Tanglewood and iconic spaces of American literary culture; in part because of the area's uncanny combination of Gilded Age old money, traditional New England Yankee whiteness, and elite Jewish and African American cultural aspiration and achievement; and in part because of the area's function as a conduit between rural pastoralism, small-town life, and urban cosmopolitanism. Further, Music Inn's mash-up of blues, folk, African and Afro-Caribbean music, and jazz styles; its synthesis of scholarship and sociality; and its jumble of folkloric and modernist ideologies underscored the singularity of this cultural geography.

"Musicians create and listeners are drawn to certain sounds, forms, and grooves because of the identities they celebrate or the ideas and emotions they convey or evoke *at a particular place and time,*" writes jazz scholar David Ake. Music Inn captured a particular moment in jazz history, a certain constellation of ideas and aspirations: Randy Weston's Afrocentrism, Marshall Stearns's folkloricism, John Lewis's cosmopolitanism, Gunther Schuller's modernism, George Russell's modalism, Ran Blake's eclecticism, Ornette Coleman and Don Cherry's avant-gardism, and more. These ideas would continue to shape jazz for decades to come. But just as the sounds, forms, and grooves of Music Inn changed after the Barbers moved on, so too did the inn's particular place-based approach to jazz give way to other developments in the music's ecosystem.

Throughout the 1960s and into the 1970s, most significantly, African American musicians went about creating new spaces where they could exercise greater control over their own creativity and connect it to grassroots community-building efforts in urban neighborhoods. Much of this activity converged with the activist efforts of politically engaged artists and intellectuals who positioned jazz as a bulwark of the interdisciplinary Black arts movement. A great deal of the most compelling jazz of the period found its origins in Black arts institutions whose atmosphere was thick with colliding energies from the arts (music, dance, theater, painting, poetry), social activism, and Black consciousness. The Black arts ethos most notably manifested itself in the Association for the Advancement of Creative Musicians in Chicago, which birthed the Art Ensemble of Chicago; the Black Arts Group in Saint Louis, spawning ground for the World Saxophone Quartet; and the Union of God's Musicians and Artists Ascension, the Watts Writers Workshop, and other organizations in Los Angeles, where Stanley Crouch, Jayne Cortez, Arthur Blythe, David Murray, Butch Morris. and other vital contributors to the downtown New York scene in the 1970s first worked in a cross-arts, collaborative community setting.[4]

Music Inn's model and the Black arts movement were not mutually exclusive; in fact, there was significant continuity between them, most notably in Billy Taylor's and Max Roach's presence at the University of Massachusetts, where their scholarship and teaching introduced an approach to studying jazz (and other idioms, including European classical music) that centered what Taylor called an "Afro-American value system." That value system emphasizes the social messages embodied in the music and foregrounds music's function as a form of communal bonding, ritual, and social interaction. Jazz, in this formulation, is not just a collection of sounds but a way of living in the world. Rather than conceiving of jazz history as an evolution of styles driven by purely aesthetic concerns, Taylor argued that "the Afro-American value system was the determining factor of what elements remained in the music or were discarded. Did the music make you want to dance, party, get drunk, make love? Did it express frustration, anger, joy, sadness? Afro-American music had to have a purpose, had to say something to the person; or it was altered or discarded."[5]

Jazz performance education, so important a part of Music Inn's legacy through the pioneering efforts of Taylor and others, has now been a mega-industry for decades. The March 2023 issue of *DownBeat* features a section on jazz summer camps with twenty-seven pages of camp listings and another twenty-two pages of advertising. *DownBeat* and other successful jazz magazines owe their financial stability to the advertising dollars generated from such special sections as well as regular accounts with instrument manufacturers, sheet-music publishers, and other education-adjacent businesses. It is not an exaggeration to say that since the 1970s, jazz education has been the economic and cultural pillar of the music, literally keeping it alive. Virtually every professional jazz musician has some variety of formal jazz education in their background. Even the most acclaimed jazz stars take on guest artist residencies at colleges and universities if they are not already regular faculty members.

One indicator of the importance of institution-based jazz performance education is the fact that some of the leading jazz scholars working today—David Ake, Tracy McMullen, Ken Prouty, and Kimberly Hannon Teal among them—have turned their attention to this phenomenon as an object of study.[6] The central questions addressed in this scholarship are the same ones that surfaced in response to the opening of the Lenox School of Jazz in 1957: Does the institutionalization of jazz education separate the music from its traditional communities of origin, especially African American ones? Does it devalue tried-and-true practices of informal mentoring within the jazz musician network? Does it thereby rob the music of its authenticity? Does it emphasize theory and technique at the expense of spontaneity, experimentation, and risk? Does it impose a white Eurocentric value system on a Black music? These are the very binaries (Black/ white, European/African, formal/informal, institutional/noninstitutional, authentic/contrived, inside/outside) that Music Inn sought to deconstruct. That jazz discourse continues to be structured by such binaries more than half a century later testifies not to Music

Inn's failure as a model of jazz education but rather to its prescience and its enduring relevance.

Debates about jazz education—and jazz culture more generally—are implicitly debates about the *place* of jazz. When jazz scholar and musician Paul Berliner took up the issue in his magisterial study, *Thinking in Jazz: The Infinite Art of Improvisation* (1994), he argued that the "jazz community" provided its own "educational system" in the form of "record shops, music stores, musicians' union halls, social clubs for the promotion of jazz, musicians' homes, booking agencies, practice studios, recording studios, nightclubs, all provid[ing] places where musicians interact with one another."[7] Conspicuously absent from Berliner's list of jazz community spaces was the college and university. Fifteen years later, when David Ake addressed the issue, he observed that "by nearly any measure, college-based programs have not only replaced the proverbial street as the primary training grounds for young jazz musicians, but they've also replaced urban nightclubs as the primary professional homes for hundreds of jazz performers and composers."[8] With its barn, meadow, and other pastoral features, Music Inn defined itself in opposition to urban nightclubs, and its three-week jazz summer-school concept hatched by John Lewis was put into practice by Gunther Schuller, David Baker, Larry Ridley, John Garvey, Ran Blake, Jimmy Giuffre, Chuck Israels, and others who were instrumental in founding and developing college- and conservatory-based jazz programs after they left Lenox. As such, it is hard to overstate the historical importance of Music Inn as what Teal calls a "jazz place."[9]

I've aimed to show how the story of Music Inn folds into long-standing place-based cultural histories, including the Marshall Stearns–led jazz roundtables' search for deeper understanding of the music's African, Afro-Caribbean, and African American roots and character, using the tools of folklore, anthropology, and ethnomusicology. This heavy emphasis on the African diaspora ran alongside the European-

School of Jazz student Nico Buninck helping fellow student Larry Ridley carry his acoustic bass across the Music Inn lawn, 1959. Photograph by Clemens Kalischer.

inflected cosmopolitanism of John Lewis, Gunther Schuller, and others, creating a truly multicultural and transnational jazz frame-work—perhaps best exemplified in the work of Randy Weston—that both complicated and enriched the idea of jazz as an *American* music. The composition of the School of Jazz's student body showed that jazz was both American and international. It would become decid-edly more so during and after the 1960s in ways that demonstrated Music Inn's importance. In Europe several flourishing jazz scenes extended the avant-garde developments that took shape in Lenox and gathered momentum in the 1960s through their affiliation with the Black arts movement and various sects of the counterculture.[10] Viewed through a transnational lens, jazz by the 1980s had splintered into many different sects, but a basic division obtained between a US-based neoclassical movement associated with Wynton Marsalis and a younger generation of musicians stressing the music's African American provenance, and an avant-garde, strongest in Europe and Canada, fiercely committed to pushing the boundaries of sound.

As Mike Heffley shows in *Northern Sun, Southern Moon: Europe's Reinvention of Jazz* (2005), European jazz musicians like Peter Brotzmann, Derek Bailey, Evan Parker, and Willem Breuker both emulated and diverged from American jazz culture during the apogee of Black cultural nationalism, embracing the ethos of free improvisation associated with John Coltrane, Ornette Coleman, Albert Ayler, and others but also embarking on an effort to cultivate a separate jazz aesthetic informed by a non-American cultural ethos. Both the neoclassical and the avant-garde movements could find inspiration from what had happened at Music Inn in the 1950s.

To say that jazz is international is to say that it is *more* local, not less. Jazz's internationality makes the specificity of place—where the music is produced and consumed, under what material and ideological conditions—even more important to consider. Every live music performance is a cultural event shaped by the physical spaces in which the music is played and heard and the unique meanings those spaces carry as sites of social interaction. A musical performance is imbued with the history of the place where it happens; it is part of a flow of sensual experience, of sound making and listening, of bodies in motion, of accumulated thought and feeling, of touch, reflection, and memory. Musicians can never play the same music more than once; they may play the same set list, start and finish the songs in the same way, and maybe even repeat note for note what they played

Leon James executing a jump on the Music Inn grounds, 1951. Photograph by Clemens Kalischer.

last night or last week. But each performance is still different and unique—and not just because of the audience's size and energy level and the musicians' state of mind and body. It's different and unique because it takes place on a certain stage, in a certain building, in a certain town, in the presence of certain social vibrations, at a certain time, and under conditions shaped by how the players and the audience travel to and from the performance, what they bring, and what they take.

The concept of musicking expands our understanding of what music is, and in doing so it obliges us to engage all our senses. I hope the photographs adorning this book have helped readers to see themselves as part of Music Inn's musicking.[11] These photographs are significant not just as graphic illustrations of Music Inn; they subtly and adroitly shift our visual focus from jazz as a collection of individual personalities to jazz as *scene*, jazz as *community*, jazz as *place*.[12] They illustrate jazz modernity as a fusion of time, people, and place. They create a record of musicking at its most routine and ordinary and at its most poignant, beautiful, and transcendent. Through these photographs, as much as anything that's been written or said here or elsewhere, we much better understand why Music Inn—the Barn, the Potting Shed, the sun-dappled lawns, the tree shade, the walking paths, and all the other spaces of the Berkshires property that Philip and Stephanie Barber cultivated with their hard work, care, and vision—was the place to be in the 1950s.

ACKNOWLEDGMENTS

One fateful day in 1991, when I was an American Studies graduate student conducting research at the Institute of Jazz Studies at Rutgers University–Newark, I came upon a photograph of bluesman John Lee Hooker attending one of Marshall Stearns's jazz roundtables four decades earlier. I was utterly mesmerized by the photo—even before finding out that it was taken in Lenox, Massachusetts, my hometown. That discovery first tickled my spine, then stirred my imagination: could this be an opportunity to uncover a piece of history both personally meaningful and strongly aligned with the themes and methods of my chosen academic field? If I hadn't already been deep into a project on jazz criticism, Music Inn likely would have become the focus of my doctoral dissertation and first book.

As it happened, I found a place for the Hooker photo and a brief discussion of Music Inn in the jazz criticism book, which led to a warm friendship with the photographer, Clemens Kalischer. During my visits with Clemens at Image Gallery in Stockbridge, his place of work and business since the 1960s, we began to envision a publication coupling my text with a gallery of his Music Inn photographs. Doug Mitchell, my editor at the time, was enthralled by the photographs. He'd heard about Music Inn as a young jazz enthusiast growing up in western Massachusetts, and he delighted in my stories about seeing Randy Weston perform in Lenox and regale his audience with affectionate memories of his summers in the Berkshires. By the time a book contract came through, I'd become friendly with Jimmy Giuffre and George Russell, stalwarts of the 1950s avant-garde whose memories of their time at Music Inn deepened my sense of its importance in jazz history and its allure as a story about the Berkshires. Meanwhile, other efforts to memorialize the Stephanie and Philip Barber period at Music Inn—a magazine feature by critic Seth Rogovoy; a gala event paying tribute to Stephanie; a documentary directed by filmmaker Ben Barenholtz, researched by George Schuller, and narrated by Benjamin Barber; and a book on the Lenox School of Jazz by musicologist Jeremy Yudkin—showed that I wasn't alone in my interest and taught me much I didn't know. Any thoughts I had about ceding the field to these superb projects were quashed by Clemens, who was convinced I had a unique and valuable angle on the story.

Nevertheless, for a variety of reasons I made the difficult decision to move this project to the back burner to free up time and headspace to work on another book I had in the hopper. Shortly after that book was published and I was ready to move forward on this one, Doug Mitchell passed away—a sad occasion, to be sure, but thankfully one that came after he'd been properly feted by his publishing world colleagues and the many authors who'd enjoyed the gift of his discerning mind, whimsical humor, epicurean acumen, and one-of-a-kind conviviality. Finding another editor keen to take on a photo-heavy publication proved very challenging. The project might have died but for the intercession of several people, starting with my wife, Emily Bernard, who recognizes a worthy book project when she sees it, knew how much this one meant to me, and persistently renewed my belief in it.

It was Emily, in fact, who was responsible for my initial meeting with Clemens Kalischer. Walking down Main Street in Stockbridge one late December day, we noticed Image Gallery's sidewalk marquee and, inside it, the John Lee Hooker photograph. This seemed providential. I had yet to decide to use the photo in my jazz criticism book, so I hadn't started the process of securing permission for it. Emily, a scholar and writer, had work to do and peeled off to the Stockbridge Library, but she insisted I go into the gallery to see what I could find out. That's when I met Clemens. Over the next several hours he showed me some of the hundreds of photos he'd taken at Music Inn a half century earlier. Over the next decade I came to know the most remarkable man I've ever met.

Lenox native Kate Coulehan was the last of Clemens's assistants at Image Gallery, where she tended to his invaluable archive with meticulous care and listened to his absorbing stories with rapt attention. Her detailed knowledge of his Music Inn photographs became an indispensable resource for me. I'm not being magnanimous when I say that this book is Kate's as much as mine; this is simply the truth, and Kate has become a wonderful friend and valued confidante through the ups and downs of its making. So too has George Schuller, who knows more about Music Inn in the 1950s than anyone alive. This book would not exist but for his exceptional generosity in sharing his research, reading my drafts, fielding my endless questions, and rescuing me from my colossal ineptitude in all things digital. When this book took shape and it became clear that a handful of photos not taken by Clemens would be needed to illustrate important parts of my narrative, he put me in touch with Scott Fowler, Hilary Barber, Seth Gopin, and Kati Meister, who were prompt and generous in granting permission for my use of the Warren Fowler, Frank McCarthy, Leonard Rosenberg, and Carol Reiff photographs that appear in these pages. I can only hope George's selfless efforts will in some way advance his own vital, ongoing work on the memory of Music Inn, the Modern Jazz Quartet, and the extraordinary life and career of his father, Gunther Schuller.

When I finally met Tanya Kalischer after a long correspondence, I encountered a woman of radiant spirit and astute intellect whose work as an educator pays honor to the monumental legacy of her father, who died in 2018, and her mother Angela, a dancer, actor, and beloved teacher who passed in 2021. Tanya's timely support and her patience in helping me craft a small part of her father's story abetted the completion of this book, and her friendship has enriched my life. Only a scrupulously researched and sensitively assembled book or film focused solely on Clemens and Angela can possibly do justice to the full scope of their life and work. Let us hope to see such a project come to fruition in the future.

The Lenox Library has held special meaning for me since my youth, when I regularly perused its stacks for intriguing titles then nestled into one of its cozy nooks to dig into what I'd found. It means even more now, these many years later, after a great deal of the granular detail in this book emerged from my time spent in a backroom poring over materials held in the library's Philip and Stephanie Barber Music Inn Collection. That this effort was facilitated by Amy Lafave, a fellow Lenox Memorial High School alum and old family friend, brought special pleasure to the endeavor. Amy is not just a consummate librarian but also an expert in Lenox history and folklore. Her suggestions and insights sharpened my research, and her spirit warms these pages.

While I'm deeply indebted to the aforementioned for such virtues as this book may possess, they bear no responsibility for its flaws. That goes as well for other friends and colleagues whose encouragement and advice nourished and guided my efforts along the way. Jeremy Yudkin gifted me and everyone else interested in Music Inn and the Barbers the fruits of his careful research and writing and kindly cheered me on when I told him what I was up to. Benjamin Cawthra and Alan Ainsworth helped me better understand the significance of Kalischer's work and modeled how to use visual evidence to craft multilayered jazz history. Sam Stephenson, whose work has set the standard for this kind of project, offered his gracious support at a critical time. On the conference circuit, and especially at convivial jazz studies gatherings in Amsterdam, Birmingham, Dublin, and Graz, colleagues offered valuable feedback and encouragement after presentations of my ongoing research and during informal coffee-break chats. I hope not to forget anyone in this roll call of brilliant and benevolent scholars when I thank Tracy McMullen, Nichole Rustin, Dee Spencer, Walter van de Leur, Tony Whyton, Nick Gebhardt, Christa Bruckner-Haring, Loes Rusch, Damian Evans, Gabriel Solis, Wolfram Knauer, Krin Gabbard, Bruce Raeburn, Dana Gooley, Andrew Berish, Christopher Coady, Mark Lomanno, and Darius Brubeck.

During a recent conference in Graz, Darius and his wife, Catherine, sat down with me to look over a bunch of Kalischer photographs, including ones of his family. Our conversation and Darius's recollections of his summers at Music Inn in the late 1950s were both informative and invigorating. So too was the afternoon Ran Blake hosted me in his home and waxed eloquent about working and studying at Music Inn and the impact this had in launching his lustrous career. I'm indebted to Dominique Eade for helping to bring about that meeting.

Here's the place to thank Elizabeth Surles and Vincent Pelote of the Institute of Jazz Studies for facilitating my continued research in their archive, the *ne plus ultra* of jazz scholarship. For years, the splendid jazz researcher Michael Fitzgerald ran an excellent Lenox School of Jazz website, and I'm indebted to him for bringing to my attention some IJS documents that I'd missed. Thanks as well to my dear friends Jim Hall, Joseph Sciorra, and Pat Sullivan for backing this project from the beginning and renewing their support through the years. Jim, supreme mensch that he is, has always had my back. Joseph helped me sharpen my thinking about folklore. Pat arranged for me to share my research with her students and colleagues in the University of South Carolina history department and at a local cultural institution, Historic Columbia. The combination of these two audiences (professional historians, on the one hand, and a diverse public audience interested in the arts and issues of race, on the other) bolstered my sense of the story's potential crossover appeal and helped me calibrate my approach accordingly. A sign that I might be on the right track came when the estimable Honor Moore graciously read some of the material and gave me a thumbs up.

I'm forever grateful to Irene Fuster and her late husband Robert, my family's long-time Lenox neighbors, for including me in several social gatherings with their cherished friends Jimmy and Juanita Giuffre and George and Alice Norbury Russell. Can you imagine anything more hospitable than plying your neighbor with single malt scotch while he hijacks Christmas Eve dinner by grilling one of the guests about his Lydian Chromatic Concept of Tonal Organization? I'm similarly indebted to Stan Rosen, formerly an executive with the National Music Foundation, in which capacity he expertly organized the Stephanie Barber tribute in 1998, where my conversations with Dave Brubeck, Percy Heath, Randy Weston, and other Music Inn alums yielded a deeper appreciation of just how much this place meant to them. It was a great pleasure collaborating on that event with Ed Bride, a dedicated arts consultant who later became the founder of Berkshires Jazz, Inc., and president of the New England Jazz Alliance—non-profits that help sustain the music and build its audience in the region.

I owe special thanks to the esteemed music scholar Anna Harwell Celenza not just for reading one of my provisional drafts with painstaking care and dazzling insight, but also for leading me to my publisher. Only because I took up Anna's suggestion to reach out to Brandeis University Press do I now have occasion to write these words. Mere hours after I emailed a letter of inquiry to BUP, I found myself on the phone with the press's director, Sue Ramin. Seasoned and savvy publishing professional that she is, Sue had already been on the trail of Clemens Kalischer and was keen to feature some of his photographs embedded within a larger cultural history. Some back-and-forth with Sue as well as BUP's editorial director Sylvia Fuks Fried very quickly generated a shared vision for the book. These conversations unfolded with an easy rapport that should make every fellow author deeply envious.

So too did my communication and collaboration with BUP's Ashley Burns and Maxine Rosenfeld, production editor Hannah Krasikov, copyeditor Susan Silver, indexer Jessica Freeman, print production manager Angie Dombroski, and designer Lisa Diercks.

Several colleagues at the University of Vermont have earned my lasting gratitude for their impactful support of this project. Howe Library staff were lightning fast in processing my inter-library loan requests. Much of the final round of my research took place while I chaired the Department of English, and my administrative assistants Holly Brevent, Beth Wilbur, and Lynn Cawthra adroitly handled bureaucratic matters that facilitated my book-related work and made my day job not just tolerable but often rewarding and sometimes even joyful. Faculty colleagues Jane Kent and Bill McDowell submitted what must have been persuasive recommendations on my behalf that helped deliver a sabbatical and an internal campus award (the Research Enhancement in the Arts, Creative Disciplines, and Humanities grant) that together afforded precious time to complete my writing as well as funding to cover photograph permission fees. I'm indebted as well to the UVM Humanities Center for a production subvention grant. I'm also thankful to the College of Arts and Sciences and its dean, Bill Falls, for an earlier Faculty Research Award and other forms of support through the years. I'm not sure I can ever repay my colleague Hilary Neroni for her many acts of kindness, not least spending several hours contending with my stupendously un-photogenic face for the author's photo.

My final and most important expression of gratitude must go to my twin daughters, Giulia and Isabella. My full reimmersion in this project coincided with their first year of high school and its completion with their first year of college. Along the way came a plague, a so-called racial reckoning, an insurrection, the ascension of post-truth media and politics, and various grave threats to global stability. Through it all these smart, soulful, very funny girls have grown into industrious and resilient young women, whose parents fairly burst with pride and joy. Back when they were kindergarteners and I still had control of the car stereo, our rides home from their afterschool program featured the Modern Jazz Quartet, Ornette Coleman, and Randy Weston mixed in with Aretha Franklin, Dionne Warwick, Bob Dylan, Chaka Khan, Angie

Stone, Joni Mitchell, Blondie, Steely Dan, Prince, and others. One afternoon we were walking to the car when either Giulia or Isabella (I forget which), wanting to butter me up, announced with great ceremony, "Daddy, tonight I'll eat all of my vegetables, and I'll drink only milk, not chocolate milk." Her sister, not to be out-virtue-signaled, righteously effused, "And let's listen to jazz, the kind with no singing!" That night we feasted on Ornette and extra helpings of kale.

Many were the times these last few years when I was glued to the computer screen tinkering with a sentence while the girls were texting me or screaming down from their bedrooms, "What's for dinner?" As I write this sentence, darkness has fallen on a cold January late afternoon, and I expect to hear those three words from Giulia and Isabella any minute now. I'll be disappointed if I don't. There's been enough sentence tinkering for the day, and the question they ask is the right one. It always has been.

NOTES

Introduction: Jazz on the Hillside

1. Wilson, liner notes to *Modern Jazz Quartet*.

2. Gross, "Jazz's New 'Commercial Beat,'" 32.

3. Marek, "Dive to the Dean," 120.

4. Holmes, "Golden Age / Time Present," 100–101.

5. Lipsitz, *How Racism Takes Place*, 1–72.

6. This phrase has become a commonplace of Berkshires' tourist marketing rhetoric. For one example, see Elfenbein, *Insiders' Guide*, back cover.

7. Berish, *Lonesome Roads*, 4.

8. Berish, *Lonesome Roads*, 23.

9. Many scholars have written about the 1950s as an especially important period in jazz's legitimization as an art form. See, for example, Lopes, *Jazz Art World*.

10. O'Meally, *Living with Music*, 50–64.

11. R. Williams, *Politics of Modernism*, 174–75.

12. Denning, *Cultural Front*, xiii–xvi. These artists coalesced into the US wing of the Popular Front, an alliance forged between radicals and New Deal liberals in the mid-1930s in response to the rise of German Nazism and other fascist movements in Europe. Denning carefully demonstrates that the Popular Front was part of a larger formation of leftist culture—what he calls the cultural front—in which the Communist Party was not nearly as important and powerful as J. Edgar Hoover's FBI, House Un-American Activities Committee, and other Red Scare witch-hunters believed. See Denning, *Cultural Front*, 309–47; Stowe, *Swing Changes*, 60–72; and Gennari, *Blowin' Hot and Cool*, 34–36, 43–53, for discussions of the relation between jazz, the Popular Front, and the American Left.

13. The "new jazz studies" is well represented in two anthologies: O'Meally et al, *Uptown Conversations*; and Gebhardt et al., *Routledge Companion*.

14. Rogovoy, "Tribute Recalls."

15. Excessive licensing fees demanded by the corporate owners of the rights to the music used in the film forestalled the distribution of *Music Inn*.

16. Yudkin, *School of Jazz*.

17. Small, *Musicking*, 2.

18. Teal, *Jazz Places*, 6–7.

19. I'm alluding here to John Kouwenhoven's famous 1956 essay "What's American about America?," which makes a fascinating argument about jazz's Americanness.

20. Teal, *Jazz Places*, 1.

21. As Benjamin Cawthra argues in *Blue Notes*, photographs of jazz musicians have been crucial in shaping Black freedom and modern racial liberalism, providing images of dignity, humanity, and grace that powerfully countered images of Black inferiority and servility that dominated US popular culture from blackface minstrelsy to Hollywood's amiable

"darkies." They have made jazz synonymous with hipness, cool, and charisma—in short, "American culture at its most alluring." The visual personalities of legendary jazz musicians—the elegant Duke Ellington, the spellbinding Billie Holiday, the insouciant Benny Goodman, the ebullient Dizzy Gillespie, the mysterious Miles Davis, the studious Dave Brubeck, the commanding Sonny Rollins, the meditative John Coltrane—collectively constitute nothing less than the cultural DNA of urbane American modernity. On the history of jazz photography in the United States, see also Ainsworth, *Sight Readings.*

22. Warren Fowler was a staff photographer for the *Berkshire Eagle* during these years, and from 1955 to 1957 he served as the semi-official photographer for Music Inn itself. Leonard Rosenberg, who shot photographs at Music Inn's inaugural event in 1950, was from the family that owned Shadowood, an inn on Hawthorne Street just a couple miles from Music Inn (coincidentally, Lena Rosenberg, who ran the inn, provided lodging for Clemens Kalischer in a cabin on the property when he first arrived in the Berkshires). Jay Maisel (aged ninety-three as of this writing) is a blue-chip New York–based commercial photographer who counts the cover of Miles Davis's *Kind of Blue* LP as one of his many significant achievements. His outdoor photograph of the MJQ and Jimmy Giuffre seems to have been the only one he shot in Lenox. Carole Reiff, who was on hand for the 1956 musicians' roundtables, was a noted jazz photographer whose work was collected in *Nights in Birdland.* Other photographers shot at Music Inn during this period, including Lisette Model, a Jewish Austrian émigré who was part of the Photo League circle.

The Town and the City

1. Yudkin, *Lenox School of Jazz*, 21–25; Owens, *Berkshire Cottages*, 193–94; Nonko, "Size Mattered"; "Days Gone By."

2. B. Barber, "Remarks." Benjamin Barber (1939–2017) was a prominent political scientist best known for his 1996 bestseller *Jihad vs. McWorld: How Tribalism and Globalism Are Shaping the World.* He spent his teenage summers working at Music Inn and served as narrator for the 2007 documentary film *Music Inn.*

3. "Philip W. Barber"; Skipper, *Meredith Willson.*

4. P. Barber, *Scene Technician's Handbook.*

5. Flanagan, *Arena*, 193.

6. "WPA Federal Theatre Project."

7. Smith, "*Macbeth* in Harlem."

8. Denning, *Cultural Front*, 285–95. The Works Progress Administration shut down *The Cradle Will Rock* shortly before it was scheduled to debut on Broadway in 1937. It was performed in 1938 in the first season of the Mercury Theater, the production company started by Orson Welles and John Houseman.

9. US Congress, Special House Committee on Un-American Activities, "Investigations of Un-American Propaganda Activities in the US," Hearings of the 75th Cong., 3rd sess., December 7, 1938, 4, cited in Ross, "Role of Blacks," 43.

10. During the war Barber served as an administrator at Hart Mountain Camp in Cody,

Wyoming, one of the locations where Japanese Americans were interned. Not much is known about the particulars of Barber's work in this position, one that obviously carried a very different political valence than his previous leadership role in the FTP. Benjamin Barber posited a continuity between his father's prewar New York theater and wartime government experiences, saying that Philip had come to "abhor the idea of a world defined by race" (B. Barber, "Remarks").

11. "Folk Music Concerts"; "Philip W. Barber"; Happel, "Ice-House Barbers"; "Christian Dior."

12. Gentile, "Danced the Night Away"; Happel, "Ice-House Barbers"; "Articulate Innkeeper"; "History."

13. Veblen, *Leisure Class*. Gilded Age Lenox was a perfect illustration of Veblen's theory. We can only speculate on how he would have made sense of the post–World War II social order and the role within it of phenomena such as middle-class cultural tourism.

14. Barber and Barber, "Music Barn," 3.

15. "Days Gone By"; Barber and Barber, "About Music Inn."

16. Bailyn, *Voyagers to the West*; Bellamy, *Duke of Stockbridge*; Middlekauff, *Glorious Cause*; Richards, *Shay's Rebellion*.

17. Owens, "Connections."

18. Chakrabarti and Bologna, "G.E. Left Behind"; Clark, *Roots of Rural Capitalism*; Dobrowolski, "Mills"; Drew and Chapman, "William Stanley."

19. Mansfield, "Literary Life"; Delbanco, *Melville*; Wineapple, *Hawthorne*; H. Lee, *Edith Wharton*; Goldstein, *Statue*.

20. B. King, "Visits in Our Valley."

21. Owens, *Berkshire Cottages*.

22. Fox, *Jews of Summer*.

23. Here I draw on anecdotes from conversations with local elders who lived and worked in the Berkshires in the 1950s. Similar anecdotes circulated widely when I grew up there in the 1960s and '70s. They comport with my personal experience working in restaurants, inns, and a gas station in the 1975–84 period.

24. Soloman, *American Mirror*.

25. Durwood, "Transformation in the Berkshires." Durwood's *Times* article was one of several that appeared in New York and Boston newspapers in the late 1950s, responding to the opening of the New York State Thruway and Massachusetts Turnpike. (See also "Mass Turnpike" and Durgin, "Today.") Each article emphasized the Berkshires' natural beauty and enchanting small-town ambience while celebrating the new transportation option as a boon to the area's cultural tourism industry. Over the ensuing decades, this combination of pastoralism and commercialism would become a palpable tension, as many worried that increased patronage of Berkshire cultural institutions would bring changes in the local real estate market and the character of the population, along with an automobile culture (car traffic, motels, fast food restaurants, chain stores, plazas, etc.) that would spoil the pas-

toral landscape and undercut local civic culture and social relations. This classic American paradox—American studies pioneer Leo Marx calls it "the machine in the garden" in his canonical study of American technology, environment, and art—was playing out all over the country in the age of postwar suburbanization (Marx, *Machine in the Garden*).

26. Berthold, "Tidy Whiteness."

27. Schoenberg, "In Pittsfield."

28. Wind, "Jews in the Berkshires"; Hoberman, *How Strange It Seems*.

29. D. Lewis, *W. E. B. Du Bois*; "W. E. B. Du Bois Center."

30. Bellow, "James Weldon Johnson."

31. Haskins, *James Van Der Zee*, 22–42, 146–92; Willis-Braithwaite and Birt, *VanDerZee*, 26–74.

32. Rampersad, *Ralph Ellison*, 442.

33. De Lone and De Lone, "John Dewey Is Alive"; Chartock, "Windsor Mountain School," 124–32. In 1963 Heinz Bondy helped start A Better Chance (ABC), a program that identified high-achieving minority students and facilitated their admission to New England private schools. Among the beneficiaries of the program was Deval Patrick, from the South Side of Chicago, who graduated from Milton Academy in 1975 and years later served as Massachusetts governor.

34. Pitt, "Hans K. Maeder," sec. 1, p. 46.

35. Bay, *Traveling Black*; Lipsitz, *How Racism Takes Place*, 66. I'm especially indebted for my thinking about this issue to Lipsitz's chapter "Black Spatial Imaginary" (51–70).

36. Tucker, *Swing Shift*, 145. Tucker draws on her interviews with members of mixed-race "all girl" jazz bands in the 1940s. An excellent example of the larger history is found in the PBS/BBC documentary film *Rock and Roll*, episode 4, in a section covering the tours undertaken by Motown musicians in the early 1960s.

37. Berish, *Lonesome Roads*, 13.

38. Dinerstein, *Swinging the Machine*, 64.

39. Murray, *Stomping the Blues*, 117–26. Samuel Floyd Jr. connects the train trope in the blues to the figure of the chariot in the spirituals, in songs like "Swing Low, Sweet Chariot" (214–17).

40. This is beautifully illustrated and discussed by Little Richard in episode 1 of Espar and Levi, *Rock and Roll*.

41. At least since the 1930s, efforts to tell the story of jazz have relied heavily on movement and geography as a key organizing principle and theme. Many jazz textbooks are sequenced into chapters devoted to New Orleans jazz, Chicago jazz, Kansas City jazz, and so on, even if they make little or no attempt to reflect on the issue of jazz and place. Berish's *Lonesome Roads* is a study of place, mobility, and race in jazz of the 1930s and '40s, conducted by an excellent musicologist. Dinerstein's *Jazz* is a shrewdly conceived introductory text focusing on cities as incubators of the music, written by a leading American studies scholar.

42. A recent example is Levy, *Saxophone Colossus*.

43. For an understanding of how migration became a common narrative theme in African American literature, music, and art, see Griffin, *"Who Set You Flowin'?"*

44. Teal, *Jazz Places*, 15–41; Gold, *Sittin' In.*

45. Perchard, "Mid-century Modern Jazz"; Farmer, *Playboy Swings.*

46. Lipsitz, *How Racism Takes Place*, 25–50; Lipsitz, *Possessive Investment in Whiteness*, 1–23; Freund, *Colored Property.*

47. The expansive literature on this topic includes accounts found in jazz autobiographies and biographies; see, for example, Holiday, *Lady Sings the Blues*; Bernhardt, *I Remember*; Gillespie, *To Be or Not*; Davis, *Miles*, 129–33, 148–52, 171–74; Levy, *Saxophone Colossus*, 87–88, 158–59, 187–95; and Kelley, *Thelonious Monk*, 138–43, 151–52, 267–68.

48. Davis, *Miles*, 238–40.

49. "Retrospective of Music Inn." This comes from the video of an interview that Seth Rogovoy conducted with Billy Taylor and screened at the outset of this event.

50. Weston, *African Rhythms*, 22, 16–17, 37, 43.

51. Weston, *African Rhythms*, 26–27, 39–40.

52. Weston, *African Rhythms*, 43–44.

53. F. Douglass, *Narrative of the Life*, 16–17.

54. Weston, *African Rhythms*, 44–45.

55. Mills, *Racial Contract*, 42, cited by Lipsitz, *How Racism Takes Place*, 28.

56. Weston, *African Rhythms*, 47–49.

57. Weston, *African Rhythms*, 48–49.

58. Weston, *African Rhythms*, 53–54.

59. Weston, *African Rhythms*, 45.

60. Rogovoy, "Life and Times," 34.

61. Quoted by Yudkin, *Lenox School of Jazz*, 32.

62. Rampersad, *Ralph Ellison*, 443.

63. Baum, "Harlem on Whose Mind."

64. Notably, see Boone, *Nimble Arc.* An exception to my point is the solo exhibition of Van Der Zee's work that the Lenox Library mounted in 1970. An important factor contributing to the absence of Van Der Zee's official memorialization is that the home he grew up in on Hubbard Street was razed when the Massachusetts Department of Transportation built a Route 7 bypass around the historic center of town.

65. A. Bass, *Those about Him.* Bass's main source is the *Berkshire Eagle*, which through the years meticulously covered the controversy in its news reporting and editorialized in favor of honoring Du Bois.

66. Blumenthal, *Berkshire Blues*; Weston, *African Rhythms*, 207. Weston writes that Ellington's new recording company was to be called Piano Records, and Duke's initial lineup was to be Bobby Short, Earl Hines, Abdullah Ibrahim, and himself. In the event the recording venture didn't take and Ellington abandoned it—but not before recording *Berkshire Blues*, which later was sold to Arista.

67. Weston, *African Rhythms*, 59–62, 206–11.

68. Gitler, "Randy Weston," 17, 36.

69. Jazz critic Stanley Crouch writes, "Randy Weston has the biggest sound of any jazz pianist since Ellington and Monk as well as the richest and most inventive beat" (*African Rhythms*, 206).

70. On African Americans and African anticolonialism, see Von Eschen, *Race against Empire;* Monson, *Freedom Sounds*; and Gaines, *American Africans in Ghana*.

71. Weston, *African Rhythms*, 82–101; Feather, "Weston's Keynote," 52.

72. Blumenthal, *Berkshire Blues*; Monson, *Freedom Sounds*, 147–51.

73. Rogovoy, "Life and Times," 36.

74. Russonello, "Randy Weston."

75. For a discussion of the ideological dimensions of Cold War jazz diplomacy, see Von Eschen, *Satchmo Blows Up*; and Gennari, *Blowin' Hot and Cool*, 150–55.

76. On the politics and dynamic cultural flow of jazz from Africa to America and back, see Kelley, *Africa Speaks*; and Monson, *Freedom Sounds*. In *Jazz Diaspora* Bruce Johnson makes the provocative argument that "jazz was not 'invented' and then exported; it was invented in the process of being disseminated" (3).

77. Blumenthal, *Berkshire Blues*.

Marshall Stearns, McCarthyism, and the Jazz Roundtables

1. Goddard, "Night Groundhog" ("horned-rimmed"), 25; M. Bass, "Lively Arts," September 9, 1956 ("Toynbee"), 12; "Jazz Hoot" ("disparate beats"), 7.

2. On Stearns generally, see Dunkel, "Marshall Winslow Stearns"; Dunkel, "Stories of Jazz," 313–50; and Gennari, *Blowin' Hot and Cool*, 144–55.

3. Burford, "Mahalia Jackson," 438.

4. Gehman, "Jazz Scholar"; Lucas, "Jazz Goes to College."

5. Following Stearns's death, the Institute of Jazz Studies moved to the Newark campus of Rutgers University, where it has functioned ever since as a leading center for jazz research.

6. Lubin, *New Orleans*.

7. Stearns, "Jim Crow at College"; Dunkel, "Stories of Jazz," 315–18.

8. Stearns, "Reds Can't Comprehend Jazz"; Stearns, "Is Jazz Good Propaganda?"

9. Dunkel, "Stories of Jazz," 318.

10. In the wealth of recent scholarship about this movement, for the purposes of this discussion I especially recommend Anderson, *Deep River*.

11. See, especially, Filene, *Romancing the Folk*, 47–75.

12. Szwed, *Alan Lomax*, 66.

13. Cited by Cantwell, *When We Were Good*, 73.

14. Stearns's series ran in *DownBeat* from 1936 to 1938. The most important piece for my purposes was the one published in the June 1936 issue, "Jazz Was Born."

15. James Maher, "Chronology"; Dunkel, "Stories of Jazz," 20–22.

16. Stearns, "UHCA."

17. Gennari, *Blowin' Hot and Cool*, 19–43, 75–77, 115.

18. Stearns, "UHCA."

19. Years earlier Kittredge had played a crucial role in John Lomax's career. Lomax was born in a Mississippi farming village and, as a toddler, traveled with his family in a covered wagon to central Texas, where he grew up chopping cotton, tending cattle and horses, and hanging out with ranch cowhands "who could ride and rope and shoot and sing." In 1907 he moved from Texas to Cambridge for graduate studies he hoped would bestow scholarly validation on his work of collecting cowboy songs and frontier ballads. Lomax's cohort at Harvard included T. S. Eliot and Van Wyck Brooks, who were destined for preeminence in American literature and criticism, but Kittredge was more interested in Lomax, seeing the cowboy song as a recent, indigenously American vernacular form and the foundation for the development of a full archive of regional American folk songs. Kittredge would support Lomax's endeavors over the next three decades. He arranged several presentations at the prestigious Modern Language Association conference, sponsored concerts at Harvard, and wrote the foreword to *American Ballads and Folk Songs*, John's book with his son Alan, an anthology of their folk song discoveries as well as those of Carl Sandberg, Willa Cather, Robert Frost, and others, published to great fanfare in 1934.

20. Lowes, "George Lyman Kittredge"; James Maher, "Chronology"; Abrahams, "Mr. Lomax." Like many American scholars of his generation, Kittredge had done graduate-level training in Germany, where oral forms like the ballad and the folktale held great esteem ever since the Romantic philosopher and poet Johann Gottfried von Herder and the Brothers Grimm hailed them as the authentic expression of the German common people, the purest form of the country's national literature and culture, the distinctive German voice.

21. Szwed, *Alan Lomax*, 66

22. Stearns's primary liaison to the American studies community was Tremaine McDowell, who chaired the University of Minnesota's Program in American Studies in the 1950s. The two men consulted about syllabi for Stearns's New School course "The Role of Jazz in American Culture" and McDowell's seminar "American Life." Stearns tried hard to get McDowell to attend the 1953 jazz roundtable, but McDowell's schedule did not permit it. Stearns did succeed at recruiting McDowell to serve on the Institute of Jazz Studies' advisory board (McDowell, letter to Stearns, May 29, 1953).

23. Stearns, *Story of Jazz*, 27.

24. Stearns, Columbia Lecture Bureau leaflet.

25. Stearns, Columbia Lecture Bureau leaflet, 24.

26. Schrecker, *Age of McCarthyism*, 244.

27. Cantwell, *When We Were Good*, 112.

28. Cantwell, *When We Were Good*, 119, 122. For a fuller elaboration of Lomax, Seeger, and Guthrie as figures in the folk movement, see pages 81–189; and Filene, *Romancing the Folk*, 9–75. The definitive work on Lomax is Szwed, *Alan Lomax*.

29. Cantwell, *When We Were Good*, 313–35.

30. Michael Denning observes that White, McGhee, and Terry "have been overshadowed by Guthrie, Leadbelly, and Pete Seeger in most accounts of the cultural front's folk music movement. This is not only an injustice to White, Terry, and McGhee, the most accomplished musicians of the movement, [but] it has also distorted the history of the left-wing 'folk revival.'" White folk music collectors and white groups like the Almanac Singers and the Weavers, Denning asserts, "have often received more attention than the vernacular musicians they labored to promote" (*Cultural Front*, 359). Music Inn can be credited for its efforts to correct this injustice.

31. S. Barber, "Chanson de Stephanie," 5.

32. Pete Seeger to Stephanie Barber, August 19, 1998 (copy in possession of author).

33. Szwed, *Alan Lomax*, 144–45.

34. Szwed, *Alan Lomax*, 148–50

35. A. Lomax, *Mister Jelly Roll*, xii.

36. Szwed. *Alan Lomax*, 235–306.

37. The terms *perfect scale* and *tempered scale* were the ones used by Stearns, so I've used them here. But one is hard-pressed to find the terms used in this way in mainstream musicology.

38. Noble, letter to Stearns, September 10, 1950. G. Kingsley Noble was an anthropologist then working at Northwestern University as Herskovits's colleague. Herskovits was unable to accept Stearns's invitation to attend the first roundtable and sent Noble as his emissary. I'm quoting here from a six-page summary of the roundtable that Noble attached to his letter.

39. Drew, "Jazz at Tanglewood," 6.

40. John Mehegan, a Julliard School of Music piano teacher who was fluent in all styles from barrelhouse to bop, was an important presence at one of the 1951 sessions and then throughout the decade.

41. Burford, "Mahalia Jackson," 444; see also James, "Romance."

42. Stearns, "Toward a Definition," 3, 4.

43. Stearns, *Story of Jazz*, 282.

44. M. Jackson, "I Can't Stop Singing," 20–21.

45. See McKible, *Circulating Jim Crow*.

46. Goreau, *Just Mahalia*, 35.

47. Burford, "Mahalia Jackson," 471.

48. Stearns, *Story of Jazz*, 7.

49. Hayakawa, "Popular Songs."

50. Blesh, *Shining Trumpets*, 176, 285–91, 337.

51. M. Bass, "Lively Arts," July 5, 1951.

52. "Fourth Jazz Roundtable."

53. Gunn, "Major and Minor."

54. "Retrospective of Music Inn."

55. I've drawn on the following sources for my discussion of Kalischer's biography: "Interview with Clemens Kalischer"; Christianson, "Photographer Clemens Kalischer"; Roberts, "Clemens Kalischer"; Unger, "Invisible Man"; and J. Waterman, "From Father to Son." The best source on Varian Fry and the Emergency Rescue Committee is Isenberg, *Hero of Our Own*. Fry had left Marseilles before the Kalischers arrived there.

56. See Klein and Evans, *Radical Camera*, for the history of the Photo League.

57. Kalischer's "straight photography" approach and gentle humanism separated him aesthetically and psychologically from several of the photographers of the 1940s and '50s who became famous through the recent advent of the photo book. *Naked City* (1945), the work of Weegee (Arthur Fellig), originally shot for New York daily newspapers, focused on the chaotic underside of the city in a hard-boiled, flashy tabloid style of grotesque and distorted figures. Robert Frank's *The Americans* (1959) cast a trenchantly observant eye on dark corners of American life, rife with racial conflict, paranoid politics, boredom, and conformism. Frank fashioned a fluid, spontaneous style of off-kilter angles, blurred motion, and atmospheric dissonance. See Livingston, *New York School*; and Orvell, *American Photography*, for overviews of American photography in this period.

58. Jacobs, letter to Stearns, May 24, 1951.

59. See Von Eschen, *Satchmo Blows Up*.

The Barn, the Eagle, and the "Negro Gentleman"

1. "Series of Jazz Concerts"; "Tanglewood Gets Jazz Barn."

2. "Jazz to Vie"; "Lenox to Have"; "Long Hair."

3. "Family Reunion."

4. "Series of Jazz Concerts."

5. "Fourth Musical Dimension."

6. Waksman, *Live Music*, 347.

7. "Music Inn."

8. Stearns, *Story of Jazz*, 305, 307.

9. Stearns, *Story of Jazz*, 305, 307.

10. Waksman, *Live Music*, 372.

11. Gennari, *Blowin' Hot and Cool*, 226–28, 237–49.

12. Balliett, "Jazz at Newport," 25.

13. Gehman, "Newport News."

14. Hentoff, *Jazz Life*, 101–2.

15. "Exit the Ombudsman."

16. "Eagle Tradition."

17. Dobrowolski, "Longtime Eagle Journalist."

18. In September 1958 Bass joined Leonard Feather, Martin Williams, and Dom Cerulli for a Music Inn panel discussion on the state of jazz criticism. He came away with sympathy for jazz critics and disappointment in the musicians, who he believed were in the habit of attacking the critics unreasonably. "It all boils down to the fact that [jazz musicians] tolerate

criticism when it is favorable, and go stark, raving berserk when it is unfavorable," he wrote. "Not one of the musicians who questioned the panel had any knowledge or interest in the relationship of the critic to the reading public. Each one could only see the critic according to his own needs and prejudices" ("Lively Arts," September 4, 1958).

19. James Maher, "Chronology," 2.

20. The *Albany Times Union*, *Schenectady Gazette*, *Holyoke Transcript Telegraph*, and *Springfield Republican*, all with offices within an hour's drive from Lenox, also covered Music Inn events, if not with the regularity of the *Eagle*. The Sunday edition of the *Republican* ran several impressive rotogravure photo spreads of the inn and paid special attention when programs featured Springfield native Joe Morello, the drummer in Dave Brubeck's quartet, and vibraphonist and pianist Teddy Charles, from nearby Chicopee Falls.

21. M. Bass, "Lively Arts," August 23, 1959.

22. "Ahmad Jamal Enraptures."

23. M. Bass, "Lively Arts," July 19, 1955.

24. M. Bass, "Lively Arts," August 16, 1957; August 6, 1956.

25. M. Bass, "Lively Arts," August 6, 1956; July 8, 1957.

26. M. Bass, "Lively Arts," July 23, 1959.

27. As Stephanie Barber told the story years later, Thelonious Monk had been rude and seemed dissatisfied during the days of his arranged visit in 1955 but then came to her and asked if could stay an additional night, which he did. In another episode Miles Davis was scheduled to perform a concert at eight o'clock but didn't show up until midnight. Davis had no intention to stay any longer than he had to. From the available evidence, Monk and Davis were the only musicians whom she didn't warm to. "Everyone told me they were geniuses," she recalled. "I didn't see it" (S. Barber, "Chanson de Stephanie").

28. M. Bass, "Lively Arts," July 19, 1955.

29. M. Bass, "Lively Arts," July 19, 1955.

30. M. Bass, "Lively Arts," July 8, 1957.

31. M. Bass, "Lively Arts," August 20, 1957.

32. M. Bass, "Lively Arts," July 15, 1957.

33. M. Bass, "Lively Arts," August 25, 1958.

34. M. Bass, "Lively Arts," September 13, 1956.

35. M. Bass, "Lively Arts," September 13, 1956.

36. Wilson, "Jazz Workshop."

37. "Swinging over the Hills," 17, 18.

38. "Composer in Jazz," 20.

39. "Composer in Jazz," 22.

40. Hentoff, "Historic Concert."

41. Kelley, *Thelonious Monk*, xiv, 26.

42. Floyd, *Power*, 35–86; Gabbard, *Better Git It*, 25–31; Ramsey, *Who Hears Here*, 14–90, 219–40; Southern, *Music*, 105–310.

43. *Max Roach*.

44. Schuller, *Life*; Ratliff, "Pleasant Swim."

45. The performance was recorded in Germany in 1960 as the Atlantic LP *The Modern Jazz Quartet and Orchestra*.

46. Goldberg, *Jazz Masters*, 127.

47. Coady, *John Lewis*, 4.

48. Baraka, *Blues People*, 211. For contextualization and analysis of Baraka's writing in this period, see Gennari, *Blowin' Hot and Cool*, 264–89.

49. M. Bass, "Music Barn Ends Summer."

50. Hentoff, "Jazz and the Intellectuals," 111.

51. Kerouac, *On the Road*, 179–80.

52. Brinkley, "Jack Kerouac's America." For a thorough and nuanced analysis of Kerouac in relation to jazz, see Dinerstein, *Origins*, 239–70.

53. Hentoff, *Jazz Life*, 140.

54. Hentoff, *Jazz Life*, 171.

55. The classic sociological text on the African American middle class is Frazier, *Black Bourgeoisie*. A recent and very good historical treatment of the topic is E. Taylor, *Original Black Elite*.

56. Szwed, "Really."

57. Coady, *John Lewis*, 11.

58. Goldberg, *Jazz Masters*, 113.

59. Brookmeyer, "Testimonial."

60. Rae, "Blonde Converts Barn."

61. Shirley Fowler, interview with George Schuller, March 7, 2004, Lenox, MA. My thanks to George Schuller for making this interview available to me. Fowler had more to say about Stephanie Barber's hats: "She was very judicious about her hat wearing though because as you noticed many of her hats had enormous big brims and only during intermissions or between things would she walk around the inside area of the seating area with the hat on because she didn't want to obstruct anyone's view of the stage or the musicians. So she would either leave when the band started or walk to the back of the hall and take her hat off. She didn't want to bother anyone's view. So she was wonderful."

62. Happel, "Ice-House."

63. See Tucker, *Swing Shift*; and Tucker and Rustin, *Big Ears*.

64. Rustin-Paschal, *Kind of Man*, 95–155.

65. See Rothschild, *Baroness*.

66. See Dinerstein, *Origins*, especially 165–86, 403–38; Tucker and Rustin, *Big Ears*, 235–66.

Lenox and the Shape of Jazz to Come

1. This and other Blake quotations in this section are from Ran Blake, interview with the author, May 24, 2024, Brookline, MA.

2. Shatz, "Invitation from Jeanne Lee," 14.

3. Balliett, *Sound of Surprise.*

4. Schuller, *Life*, 475.

5. Schuller, *Life*, 476.

6. Fitzgerald, "School of Jazz." A small number of female students enrolled at the school: Vera Auer, Jean Bernheim, Lucille Butterman, Norma Feur, Margo Guryan, and Mona Neves.

7. See Gioia, *Imperfect Art*; and Lane, *Machine-Age Imperialism.*

8. Lubin, *New Orleans.*

9. M. Bass, "Lively Arts," June 25, 1959.

10. Schuller and Heckman, "Two Views," 14. The Lenox School of Jazz was not, in fact, the first effort to teach jazz. The issue turns on how one chooses to define jazz education, jazz teaching, and jazz learning. As I discuss further in the conclusion, as scholars continue to debate this issue, they tend to draw a distinction between jazz teaching and learning within the jazz community and jazz education programs located outside of that community (a term that itself deserves scrutiny) such as in colleges, universities, and conservatories. Preceding the Lenox School of Jazz were jazz programs at the University of North Texas (1946) and the Berklee School of Music (1954). Both specialized in training students for employment in big bands. That the Lenox School of Jazz received so much attention as a seminal effort owes in large part to the reputations of its faculty members as leading players, composers, and theorists, as well as to its attention to jazz history and the music's sociocultural context.

11. M. Bass, "Lively Arts," June 25, 1959.

12. "Something of Max Roach."

13. Larrabee, "Jumping Julliard," 38.

14. Fitzgerald, "Student Comments and Testimonials."

15. Watt, quoted in Feather, "Battle of Jazz."

16. Hentoff, "Jazz Scholarships," 8.

17. Gleason, "Summer Jazz School."

18. Quoted in Brookmeyer and Giuffre, "School of Jazz," 17.

19. Lewis, "Testimonial."

20. M. Williams, "School of Jazz," 23.

21. M. Williams, "School of Jazz," 24.

22. M. Williams, *Jazz Masters*, 33.

23. Saussy and Mardin, "School of Jazz," 18, 19.

24. Brookmeyer and Giuffre, "School of Jazz," 18.

25. Blesh, *Shining Trumpets*, 342–81.

26. Larrabee, "Jumping Julliard," 39.

27. Riddle, quoted by Fitzgerald, "Student Comments."

28. "School of Jazz," 23.

29. Jack Maher, "School of Jazz," 15.

30. M. Williams, *Jazz Masters*, 34.

31. See D. Lee, *Five Spot*.

32. See, for example, "1959."

33. Szwed, *Jazz 101*, 209–22.

34. Larkin, *All That Jazz*, 20.

35. See Baraka, *Black Music*; and Gennari, *Blowin' Hot and Cool*, 279–89.

36. Brubeck, "1959," 188, 178.

37. I have heard several different versions of this story. The one I have told here is based on information given to me by George Schuller (phone conversation with the author, July 26, 2020).

38. Feld, "Whose Borders, What Beyond?"

39. A story has circulated that Davis redeemed himself by showing up at Music Inn close to midnight, hanging out under the summer moon with a group of faculty and students, and even playing his trumpet. George Schuller tells me he has searched high and low for confirmation of the story but has not found it.

40. Ted Casher and Herb Pomeroy, interview with George Schuller, August 7, 2003, Gloucester, MA. My thanks to George Schuller for making this interview available to me.

41. Hentoff, "Jimmy Giuffre."

42. Schuller, *Life*, 484.

43. Schuller, *Life*, 492.

44. Schuller, *Life*, 489.

45. Yudkin, *Lenox School of Jazz*, 89.

46. See Iverson, "Ornette 1," for a thoughtful discussion of the issue.

47. Schuller, *Life*, 490.

48. Schuller, *Life*, 473.

49. Schuller, *Musings*, 18–25.

50. Balliett, *Collected Works*, 24.

51. Schuller and Heckman, "Two Views," 17.

52. Schuller, *Musings*, 86–97.

53. Goldberg, *Jazz Masters*, 102.

54. Givan, "Gunther Schuller."

55. Mehegan, "Case for Swinging," 44. The rest of Mehegan's piece is an analytical tour de force. If one is inclined to agree with Mehegan that the recent work of Charles Mingus, Teddy Charles, Teo Macero, and Cecil Taylor had been "ill-fated" and that jazz simply should not entertain atonality, a more persuasive prosecution of the case is hard to find.

56. M. Bass, "Non-jazz Jazz," 130.

57. Brubeck, "1959," 198.

58. The primary and secondary literature on Atlantic Records has focused more on Ahmet Ertegun's and Jerry Wexler's triumphs with rhythm and blues, soul, and rock than on Nesuhi Ertegun's vitally important work as a jazz producer. This is dispositive of the

point I'm making here about the shift from jazz to other genres in the 1960s in terms of mass popularity. The Modern Jazz Quartet continued to record for Atlantic until 1975, but they were no longer the label's bread and butter as they'd been in the 1950s.

59. Baraka, *Black Music*, 180–212.

60. See Harrison, "George Russell."

61. See, for example, Vincent, *Funk*, 147.

62. See Ronald Radano's lucid discussion of Coleman's embrace of the "language and ideas of musical modernism," including his footnoted reference to Schuller, who "suggested that harmolodics is based on the superimposition of the same musical phrase (or phrase relatives) in varying keys, producing a kind of polytonality and heterophony" (*New Musical Figurations*, 109–10n97).

63. Iverson, "Ornette 1."

Conclusion: The Place to Be

1. See Blechman, "Black Berkshires"; and "Invisible Community." Notably, the southern Berkshires, especially Du Bois's hometown of Great Barrington, has become known for its thriving Jewish community, marked by an increase in synagogue attendance as well as secular Jewish-inflected recreational activity, food, music, and other arts. Seth Rogovoy, the former *Berkshire Eagle* music critic and *Berkshire Magazine* editor whose writing on Music Inn sparked much of the local interest in its history, has become both a civic leader in the Great Barrington Jewish community and a nationally acclaimed writer and editor of Jewish-themed cultural journalism, with books on klezmer music and Bob Dylan as a Jewish "prophet mystic poet." See Axelrod, "Jewish Traveler." Seth Rogovoy's blog, *Rogovoy Report*, is an extraordinarily rich and informative Jewish cultural space.

2. Du Bois, "Criteria of Negro Art," 291.

3. See Lanham, "Du Bois Was 'Un-American.'"

4. See Isoardi, *Dark Tree*; G. Lewis, *Power*; and Looker, "Point From."

5. B. Taylor, *Jazz Piano*, 86.

6. Ake, *Jazz Matters*; McMullen, "Lessons of Jazz"; Prouty, *Learning Jazz*; Teal, *Jazz Places*.

7. Berliner, *Thinking in Jazz*, 55.

8. Ake, *Jazz Matters*, 103.

9. Teal, *Jazz Places*.

10. Heffley, *Northern Sun*.

11. Cawthra, *Blue Notes*. See also Ainsworth, *Sight Readings*.

12. Travis Jackson brilliantly theorizes the concept of the jazz scene and brings it to life in the case of New York City in *Blowin' the Blues Away*.

BIBLIOGRAPHY

1959: The Year That Changed Jazz. London: British Broadcasting Company, 2011.

"1959: The Year That Changed Jazz." San Francisco Jazz Center. November 2022. www.sfjazz .org.

Abrahams, Roger D. "Mr. Lomax Meets Professor Kittredge." *Journal of Folklore Research* 37, nos. 2–3 (May–December 2000): 99–118.

"Ahmad Jamal Enraptures Audience at Music Barn." *Holyoke Transcript Telegram*, July 29, 1959.

Ainsworth, Alan John. *Sight Readings: Photographers and American Jazz, 1900–1960*. London: Intellect, 2022.

Ake, David. *Jazz Matters: Sound, Place, and Time since Bebop*. Berkeley: University of California Press, 2010.

Anderson, Paul Allen. *Deep River: Music and Memory in Harlem Renaissance Thought*. Durham: Duke University Press, 2001.

"Articulate Innkeeper Discusses Her Fashion Philosophy." *Berkshire Eagle*, June 6, 1958.

Axelrod, Toby. "The Jewish Traveler: The Berkshires." *Hadassah Magazine*, June–July 2005. www.hadassahmagazine.org.

Bailyn, Bernard. *Voyagers to the West: A Passage in the Peopling of America on the Eve of the Revolution*. New York: Knopf, 1986.

Balliett, Whitney. *Collected Works: A Journal of Jazz, 1954–2001*. New York: St. Martin's Press, 2002.

———. "Jazz at Newport: 1956." *Saturday Review*, July 28, 1956, 25.

———. *The Sound of Surprise: 46 Pieces on Jazz*. New York: Dutton, 1959.

Baraka, Amiri. *Black Music*. New York: Morrow, 1967.

Baraka, Amiri (Leroi Jones). *Blues People: Negro Music in White America*. New York: Morrow, 1963.

Barber, Benjamin. "Remarks." Stephanie Barber and Music Inn tribute event. August 22, 1998. Philip and Stephanie Barber Music Inn Collection. Lenox Library, Lenox, MA.

Barber, Philip. *The Scene Technician's Handbook*. New York: Whitlock, 1928.

Barber, Philip, and Stephanie Barber. "About Music Inn." Typescript document. Philip and Stephanie Barber Music Inn Collection. Lenox Library, Lenox, MA.

———. "Music Barn, 1950–1958." Berkshire Music Barn program. 1958. Philip and Stephanie Barber Music Inn Collection. Lenox Library, Lenox, MA.

Barber, Stephanie. "Chanson de Stephanie." Unpublished transcript of interview with Jule Foster. August 18, 1995. Philip and Stephanie Barber Music Inn Collection. Lenox Library, Lenox, MA.

Barenholtz, Ben dir. *Music Inn*. Projectile Arts, 2005.

Bass, Amy. *Those about Him Remained Silent: The Battle over W. E. B. Du Bois*. Minneapolis: University of Minnesota Press, 2009.

Bass, Milton. "Ahmad Jamal Trio." *Berkshire Eagle*, July 27, 1959.

———. "Dave Brubeck Quartet Plays to 900 at Music Barn." *Berkshire Eagle*, July 9, 1956.

———. "Dorsey Brothers Orchestra Plays at Lenox Music Barn." *Berkshire Eagle*, July 30, 1956.

———. "Lively Arts." *Berkshire Eagle*, July 5, 1951; July 19, 1955; August 6, 1956; September 9, 1956; September 13, 1956; July 15, 1957; August 16, 1957; August 20, 1957; September 4, 1958; June 25, 1959; July 3, 1959; August 23, 1959.

———. "Music Barn Concerts." *Berkshire Eagle*, August 25, 1958.

———. "Music Barn Ends Summer." *Berkshire Eagle*, September 4, 1956.

———. "Non-jazz Jazz." *Atlantic*, October 1962, 130–32.

———. "Teddy Charles Quartet Plays at Music Barn." *Berkshire Eagle*, August 1, 1955.

Baum, Kelly, Maricelle Robles, and Sylvia Yount. "'Harlem on Whose Mind?' The Met and Civil Rights." Accessed January 13, 2024. www.metmuseum.org.

Bay, Mia. *Traveling Black: A Story of Race and Resistance*. Cambridge: Harvard University Press, 2021.

Bellamy, Edward. *The Duke of Stockbridge: A Romance of Shay's Rebellion*. 1890. Reprint, Cambridge, MA: Belknap, 1962.

Bellow, Heather. "The Home of James Weldon Johnson: Legacy of the Harlem Renaissance Reborn." *Berkshire Edge*, June 19, 2015. https://theberkshireedge.com.

Berish, Andrew S. *Lonesome Roads and Streets of Dreams: Place, Mobility, and Race in Jazz of the 1930s and '40s*. Chicago: University of Chicago Press, 2012.

Berliner, Paul. *Thinking in Jazz: The Infinite Art of Improvisation*. Chicago: University of Chicago Press, 1994.

Bernhardt, Clyde E. B. *I Remember . . . Eighty Years of Black Entertainment, Big Bands, and the Blues*. With Sheldon Harris. Philadelphia: University of Pennsylvania Press, 1986.

Berthold, Dana. "Tidy Whiteness: A Genealogy of Race, Purity, and Hygiene." *Ethics and the Environment* 15, no. 1 (Spring 2010): 1–26.

Blake, Ran. *The Primacy of the Ear*. With Jason Rogers. Boston: Third Stream Associates, 2010.

Blechman, Andrew B. "Black Berkshires: A Hidden and Not-So-Hidden Legacy." *Berkshire Edge*, November 27, 2020. https://theberkshireedge.com.

Blesh, Rudi. *Shining Trumpets: A History of Jazz*. New York: Da Capo, 1958. First published 1946 by Knopf (New York).

Blumenthal, Bob. Liner notes to Randy Weston. *Berkshire Blues*. Black Lion 760205, 1995. Originally released in 1965.

Boone, Emilie. *A Nimble Arc: James Van Der Zee and Photography*. Durham: Duke University Press, 2023.

Brinkley, Douglas. "Jack Kerouac's America." Lecture. University of Texas, Austin. April 24, 2008. www.youtube.com.

Brookmeyer, Bob. "Testimonial." Stephanie Barber and Music Inn tribute event. August 22, 1998. Personal letter in possession of the author.

Brookmeyer, Bob, and Jimmy Giuffre. "The School of Jazz: Faculty Views." *Jazz Review*, January 1959, 16, 18.

Brubeck, Darius. "1959: The Beginning of Beyond." In *The Cambridge Companion to Jazz*, edited by Mervyn Cook and David Horn, 176–201. Cambridge: Cambridge University Press, 2002.

Burford, Mark. "Mahalia Jackson Meets the Wise Men: Defining Jazz at the Music Inn." *Musical Quarterly* 97, no. 3 (Fall 2014): 429–86.

Cantwell, Robert. *When We Were Good: The Folk Revival.* Cambridge, MA: Harvard University Press, 1996.

Casey, Edward S. "How to Get from Space to Place in a Fairly Short Stretch of Time." In *Senses of Place*, edited by Steven Feld and Keith H. Basso, 1–52. Santa Fe, NM: School for Advanced Research, 1996.

Cawthra, Benjamin. *Blue Notes in Black and White: Photography and Jazz.* Chicago: University of Chicago Press, 2013.

Chakrabarti, Meghna, and Jamie Bologna. "GE Left behind a Complex Legacy in Pittsfield." WBUR. June 29, 2016. www.wbur.org.

Chartock, Roselle Kline. *Windsor Mountain School: A Beloved Berkshire Institution.* Cheltenham, UK: History, 2014.

"Christian Dior: The New Look." Metropolitan Museum of Art. Accessed March 21, 2024. https://artsandculture.google.com.

Christianson, Scott. "Photographer Clemens Kalischer Survived Holocaust but Struggles to Adapt." *Forward*, April 30, 2013. https://forward.com.

Clark, Cristopher. *The Roots of Rural Capitalism, Western Massachusetts, 1780–1860.* Ithaca: Cornell University Press, 1990.

Coady, Christopher. *John Lewis and the Challenge of "Real" Black Music.* Ann Arbor: University of Michigan Press, 2016.

Coleman, Ornette. *The Shape of Jazz to Come.* Atlantic 1317, 1959.

"The Composer in Jazz: More Time for Deep Thought." *Jazz Today*, December 1957, 19–23.

Courlander, Harold. *The Drum and the Hoe: Life and Lore of the Haitian People.* Berkeley: University of California Press, 1960.

The Dave Brubeck Quartet. *Time Further Out.* Columbia 8490, 1961.

———. *Time Out.* Columbia 1397, 1959.

Davis, Miles. *Kind of Blue.* Columbia 8163, 1959.

———. *Miles: The Autobiography.* With Quincy Troupe. New York: Simon and Schuster, 1989.

"Days Gone By: Images of Wheatleigh from the *Eagle*'s Archives." *Berkshire Eagle*, November 29, 2021. www.berkshireeagle.com.

Delbanco, Andrew. *Melville, His World and Work.* New York: Knopf, 2005.

De Lone, Richard H., and Susan T. De Lone. "John Dewey Is Alive and Well in New England." *Saturday Review*, November 21, 1970, 69–71.

Denning, Michael. *The Cultural Front.* London: Verso, 1996.

Dinerstein, Joel. *Jazz: A Quick Immersion.* New York: Tibidabo, 2020.

———. *The Origins of Postwar Cool.* Chicago: University of Chicago Press, 2017.

———. *Swinging the Machine: Modernity, Technology, and African American Culture between the World Wars.* Amherst: University of Massachusetts Press, 2003.

Dobrowolski, Tony. "Longtime Eagle Journalist Milton Bass Dies at Age 91." *Berkshire Eagle,* October 16, 2014. www.berkshireeagle.com.

Douglass, Frederick. *Narrative of the Life of Frederick Douglass.* 1845. Reprint, New York: Dover, 1995.

Douglass, Margaret. "Berkshire Boast: A Partisan of a Famous Massachusetts Resort County Finds it Unexcelled." *New York Times,* June 8, 1958, sec. 5, p. 33.

Drew, Bernard A., and Gerard Chapman. "William Stanley Lighted a Town and Powered an Industry." *Berkshire History* 6, no.1 (Fall 1985): 1–30. https://berkshirehistory.org.

Drew, Peter. "Jazz at Tanglewood." *Record Changer,* October 1950.

Du Bois, W. E. B. "Criteria of Negro Art." *Crisis* 32 (October 1926): 290–97.

Dunkel, Mario. "Marshall Winslow Stearns and the Politics of Jazz Historiography." *American Music* 30, no. 4 (2012): 468–504.

———. "The Stories of Jazz: Narrating a Musical Tradition." *Jazz Forschung/Research* 48 (2016): 1–391.

Durgin, Cyrus. "Today the Berkshire Music Festival Is for All the People from All Over." *Boston Globe.* Philip and Stephanie Barber Music Inn Collection. Lenox Library, Lenox, MA.

Durwood, James. "Transformation in the Berkshires." *New York Times,* June 6, 1959.

"The Eagle Tradition." *Time,* January 15, 1972.

Eflenbein, Gae. *Insiders' Guide to the Berkshires.* Lanham, MD: Rowman and Littlefield, 2004.

Espar, David, dir. *Rock and Roll.* Episode 4, "Respect." Boston: WGBH Educational Foundation/BBC, 1995.

Espar, David, and Robert Levi, dirs. *Rock and Roll.* Episode 1, "Renegades." Boston: WGBH Educational Foundation/BBC, 1995.

"Exit the Ombudsman." *Time,* August 28, 1972.

"Family Reunion." *Boston Daily Globe,* April 29, 1955.

Farmer, Patty. *Playboy Swings: How Hugh Hefner and Playboy Changed the Face of Music.* New York: Beaufort Books, 2015.

Feather, Leonard. "Battle of Jazz: Eggheads and Yahoos," *HiFi Music at Home,* August 1958.

———. "Weston's Keynote Is in the Sounds of Africa." *Los Angeles Times,* October 13, 1985, 52.

Feld, Steven. *Jazz Cosmopolitanism in Accra: Five Musical Years in Ghana.* Durham: Duke University Press, 2012.

———. "Whose Borders, What Beyond?" Keynote address at Jazz beyond Borders conference, University of Amsterdam, September 4, 2014.

Filene, Benjamin. *Romancing the Folk: Public Memory and American Roots Music*. Chapel Hill: University of North Carolina Press, 2000.

Fitzgerald, Michael. "The Lenox School of Jazz." Jazz Discography. Accessed June 12, 2020. www.jazzdiscography.com.

———. "School of Jazz Student Listing (Where Are They Now?)." Jazz Discography. Accessed June 12, 2020. www.jazzdiscogography.com.

———. "Student Comments and Testimonials." Jazz Discography. Accessed June 12, 2024. www.jazzdiscography.com.

Flanagan, Hallie. *Arena: The Story of the Federal Theatre*. 1940. Reprint, New York: Limelight, 1969.

Floyd, Samuel A., Jr. *The Power of Black Music: Interpreting Its History from Africa to the United States*. New York: Oxford University Press, 1995.

"A Fourth Musical Dimension." *Berkshire Eagle*, April 27, 1955, 16.

Fox, Sandra. *The Jews of Summer: Summer Camp and Jewish Culture in Postwar America*. Palo Alto: Stanford University Press, 2023.

Frazier, E. Franklin. *Black Bourgeoisie*. New York: Free Press, 1957.

Freund, David M. P. *Colored Property: State Policy and White Racial Politics in Suburban America*. Chicago: University of Chicago Press, 2007.

Gabbard, Krin. *Better Git It in Your Soul: An Interpretive Biography of Charles Mingus*. Berkeley: University of California Press, 2016.

Gaines, Kevin. *American Africans in Ghana: Black Expatriates and the Civil Rights Era*. Chapel Hill: University of North Carolina Press, 2006.

Gebhardt, Nicholas, Nichole Rustin-Paschal, and Tony Whyton, eds. *The Routledge Companion to Jazz Studies*. New York: Routledge, 2019.

Gehman, Richard. "The Jazz Scholar." *New York Herald-Tribune*, May 9, 1954, sec. 7, p. 13.

———. "The Newport News' of 1957." *Saturday Review*, July 28, 1957.

Gennari, John. *Blowin' Hot and Cool: Jazz and Its Critics*. Chicago: University of Chicago Press, 2006.

Gentile, Derek. "'She Danced the Night Away': Music Inn Co-founder Stephanie Barber Dies." *Berkshire Eagle*, August 27, 2003, 1, 4.

Gilder, Cornelia Brooke. *Hawthorne's Lenox: The Tanglewood Circle*. With Julia Conklin Peters. Cheltenham, UK: History, 2008.

Gillespie, Dizzy. *To Be or Not to Bop*. With Al Fraser. New York: Da Capo, 1979.

Gioia, Ted. *The Imperfect Art: Reflections on Jazz and Modern Culture*. New York: Oxford University Press, 1988.

Gitler, Ira. "Randy Weston." *DownBeat*, February 27, 1964.

Givan, Benjamin. "Gunther Schuller and the Challenge of Sonny Rollins: Stylistic Content, Intentionality, and Jazz Analysis." *Journal of the American Musicological Society* 67 no. 1 (2014): 167–237.

Gleason, Ralph. "Summer Jazz School Scheduled." Syndicated column. Philip and Stephanie Barber Music Inn Collection. Lenox Library, Lenox, MA.

Goddard, Frank Anthony Peter Vincent. "The Night Groundhog Was the King of the Gate." *Village Voice*, November 26, 1954, 25.

Gold, Jeff. *Sittin' In: Jazz Clubs of the 1940s and 1950s*. New York: HarperCollins, 2020.

Goldberg, Joe. *Jazz Masters of the '50s*. 1968. Reprint, New York: Da Capo, 1983.

Goldstein, Ernest. *The Statue: Abraham Lincoln; A Masterpiece by Daniel Chester French*. Minneapolis: Lerner, 1997.

Gordon, Eric A. *Mark the Music: The Life and Work of Marc Blitzstein*. New York: St. Martin's Press, 1987.

Goreau, Laurrain. *Just Mahalia, Baby*. 1975. Reprint, New York: Firebird/Penguin, 1998.

Griffin, Farah Jasmine. *"Who Set You Flowin'?" The African American Migration Narrative*. New York: Oxford University Press, 1996.

Gross, Mike. "Jazz's New 'Commercial Beat.'" *Variety*, January 7, 1959, 32.

Gunn, Glenn Dillard. "'Major and Minor': Roundtable Concerning 'Definitions in Jazz' Is a Tangle Added to Tanglewood's Activities." *Washington Times-Herald*, September 2, 1951.

Hammond, John. "Jazz Moves Outdoors into the Country Air." *New York Herald-Tribune*, August 7, 1955, 1, 15.

Happel, Richard. "Ice-House Barbers Score with Cool Jazz." *Berkshire Eagle*, August 8, 1958, 4A.

Haskins, Jim. *James Van Der Zee: The Picture Takin' Man*. New York: Dodd, Mead, 1979.

Hayakawa, Samuel Ichiye. "Popular Songs vs. the Facts of Life." *ETC: A Review of General Semantics* 12, no. 2 (Winter 1955): 83–95.

Heffley, Mike. *Northern Sun, Southern Moon: Europe's Reinvention of Jazz*. New Haven: Yale University Press, 2005.

Hentoff, Nat. "Jazz and the Intellectuals: Somebody Goofed." *Chicago Review* 9, no. 3 (Fall 1955): 111–15.

———. *The Jazz Life*. 1961. Reprint, New York: Da Capo, 1978.

———. "Jazz Scholarships, Anyone?" *Metronome*, December 1957, 8.

———. "Jimmy Giuffre: Blues in Counterpoint." *Saturday Review*, July 13, 1957.

———. Liner notes to *Historic Concert at Music Inn*. Atlantic 1298, 1958.

Herskovits, Melville J. *The Myth of the Negro Past*. New York: Harper and Sons, 1941.

Herskovits, Melville J., and Franz Boas. *The Science of Man in the Making*. New York: Scribner's Sons, 1953.

"History." *Music Inn: A Documentary Film*. Accessed March 22, 2024. www.musicinnfilm.net.

Hoberman, Michael. *How Strange It Seems: The Cultural Life of Jews Living in Small-Town New England*. Amherst: University of Massachusetts Press, 2008.

Holiday, Billie. *Lady Sings the Blues*. With William Dufty. New York: Avon, 1956.

Holmes, John Clellon. "The Golden Age/Time Present." *Esquire*, January 1959.

Howe, Mark Anthony DeWolfe. *The Tale of Tanglewood: Scene of the Berkshire Music Festivals*. New York: Vanguard, 1946.

"An Interview with Clemens Kalischer." Jewish Historical Society of Western Massachusetts. Accessed May 1, 2024. www.youtube.com.

"The Invisible Community: African Americans in Berkshire County (1830–2012)." Berkshire County Historical Society. Accessed June 28, 2024. https://berkshirehistory.org.

Isenberg, Sheila. *A Hero of Our Own: The Story of Varian Fry.* New York: Random House, 2001.

Isoardi, Steven. *The Dark Tree: Jazz and the Community Arts in Los Angeles.* Berkeley: University of California Press, 2006.

Iverson, Ethan. "Ornette 1: Forms and Sounds." Do the Math. Accessed January 20, 2025. https://ethaniverson.com.

Jackson, Mahalia. "'I Can't Stop Singing.'" *Saturday Evening Post,* December 5, 1959, 19–21, 98.

Jackson, Richard S., Jr., and Cornelia Brooke Gilder. *Houses of the Berkshires, 1870–1930.* New York: Acanthus, 2006.

Jackson, Travis A. *Blowin' the Blues Away: Performance and Meaning on the New York Jazz Scene.* Berkeley: University of California Press, 2012.

Jacobs, Marvin. Letter to Marshall W. Stearns. May 24, 1951. Folder 20. Box 9. Marshall Stearns Papers. Institute of Jazz Studies, Newark, NJ.

James, Willis Laurence. "The Romance of the Negro Folk Cry in America." *Phylon* 16, no. 1 (1955): 15–30.

"The Jazz Hoot." *New Yorker,* April 1, 1950, 7.

"Jazz to Vie with Symphony at Lenox." *Montpelier, Vt. Argus,* April 28, 1955.

Johnson, Bruce. *Jazz Diaspora: Music and Globalisation.* New York: Routledge, 2020.

Kelley, Robin D. G. *Africa Speaks, America Answers: Modern Jazz in Revolutionary Times.* Cambridge: Harvard University Press, 2012.

———. *Thelonious Monk: The Life and Times of an American Original.* New York: Free Press, 2010.

Kemble, Frances Anne. *Journal of a Residence on a Georgian Plantation, 1838–1839.* 1863. Reprint, Athens: University of Georgia Press, 1984.

Kerouac, Jack. *On the Road.* New York: Viking, 1957.

King, Charles. *Gods of the Upper Air: How a Circle of Renegade Anthropologists Reinvented Race, Sex, and Gender in the Twentieth Century.* New York: Anchor, 2020.

King, Brian F. "Visits in Our Valley." *Springfield (MA) Sunday Republican,* May 31, 1959.

Klein, Mason, and Catherine Evans. *The Radical Camera: New York's Photo League, 1936–1951.* New Haven: Yale University Press, 2011.

Kouwenhoven, John Atlee. "What's American about America?" *Harper's,* July 1956.

Lane, Jeremy. *Jazz and Machine-Age Imperialism: Music, 'Race,' and Intellectuals in France, 1918–1945.* Ann Arbor: University of Michigan Press, 2013.

Lanham, Andrew. "When W. E. B. Du Bois Was 'Un-American.'" *Boston Review,* January 13, 2017. www.bostonreview.net.

Larkin, Philip. *All That Jazz: A Record Diary, 1961–1971.* New York: Farrar, Straus and Giroux, 1985.

Larrabee, Eric. "Jumping Julliard." *Harper's,* November 1957.

Lee, David Neil. *The Battle of the Five Spot: Ornette Coleman and the New York Jazz Field.* Hamilton, Ontario: Wolsak and Wynn, 2006.

Lee, Hermione. *Edith Wharton*. London: Vintage, 2008.

Lee, Jeanne, and Ran Blake. *The Newest Sound Around*. RCA Victor LSP-2500, 1962.

"Lenox to Have Musical Extremes." *Lawrence (MA) Eagle*, April 29, 1955.

Levy, Aidan. *Saxophone Colossus: The Life and Music of Sonny Rollins*. New York: Hachette Books, 2022.

Lewis, David Levering. *W. E. B. Du Bois: A Biography, 1868–1963*. New York: Holt, 2009.

Lewis, George. *A Power Stronger Than Itself: The AACM and American Experimental Music*. Chicago: University of Chicago Press, 2008.

Lewis, John. "Testimonial." Stephanie Barber and Music Inn tribute event. August 22, 1998. Personal letter in possession of the author.

Lipsitz, George. *How Racism Takes Place*. Philadelphia: Temple University Press, 2011.

———. *The Possessive Investment in Whiteness: How White People Profit from Identity Politics*. Philadelphia: Temple University Press, 2006.

Livingston, Jane. *The New York School Photographs, 1936–1963*. New York: Stewart, Tabori and Chang, 1992.

Lomax, Alan. *Mister Jelly Roll: The Fortunes of Jelly Roll Morton, New Orleans Creole and "Inventor of Jazz."* New York: Grosset and Dunlap, 1950.

Lomax, John A. *Cowboy Songs and Other Frontier Ballads*. New York: Macmillan, 1910.

Lomax, John A., and Alan Lomax, eds. *American Ballads and Folk Songs*. New York: Macmillan, 1934.

"Long Hair, Boogie Woogie to Mingle in Bay State." *Newport (RI) News*, April 28, 1955.

Looker, Benjamin. *"Point from Which Creation Begins": The Black Arts Group of St. Louis*. St. Louis: Missouri Historical Society, 2004.

Lopes, Paul. *The Rise of a Jazz Art World*. Cambridge: Cambridge University Press, 2002.

Lowes, John Livingston. "George Lyman Kittredge: February 28, 1860–July 23, 1941." *American Scholar* 10, no. 4 (Autumn 1941): 469–71.

Lubin, Arthur, dir. *New Orleans*. Majestic Productions / United Artists, 1947.

Lucas, Robert. "Jazz Goes to College." *Negro Digest*, August 1951, 45–49.

Maher, Jack. "The School of Jazz: Amazing Talent Marks Third Year." *Metronome*, October 1959, 14–15.

Maher, James T. "Chronology of Marshall Winslow Stearns." Unpublished manuscript. Philip and Stephanie Barber Music Inn Collection. Lenox Library, Lenox, MA.

Mansfield, Luther Stearns. "Literary Life in Nineteenth-Century Berkshire County." *Berkshire History* 2, no. 1 (Spring 1976). Accessed January 10, 2024. https://berkshirehistory.org.

Marek, George. "From the Dive to the Dean, Jazz Becomes Respectable." *Good Housekeeping*, June 1956, 120–24.

Marx, Leo. *The Machine in the Garden: Technology and the Pastoral Ideal in America*. New York: Oxford University Press, 1964.

Massey, Doreen. *Space, Place, and Gender*. Minneapolis: University of Minnesota Press, 1994.

"Mass Turnpike Brings the Berkshires to Boston's Back Yard." *Boston Sunday Herald*, June 16, 1957, sec. 3, p. 4.

Max Roach with the Boston Percussion Ensemble. EmArcy, MG36144, 1958.

May, Elaine Tyler. "'The Radical Roots of American Studies': Presidential Address of the American Studies Association, November 9, 1995." *American Quarterly* 48, no. 2 (June 1996): 179–200.

McDowell, Tremaine. Letter to Marshall Stearns. May 29, 1953. Folder 22. Box 9. Marshall Stearns Papers. Institute of Jazz Studies, Newark, NJ.

McKible, Adam. *Circulating Jim Crow: The* Saturday Evening Post *and the War against Black Modernity.* New York: Columbia University Press, 2024.

McMullen, Tracy. "The Lessons of Jazz: What We Teach When We Teach Jazz in College." In *Artistic Research in Jazz: Positions, Theories, Methods,* edited by Michael Kahr, 85–97. Oxfordshire, UK: Routledge/Taylor and Francis, 2022.

Mehegan, John. "The Case for Swinging." *DownBeat,* August 20, 1958, 43–44.

Middlekauff, Robert. *The Glorious Cause: The American Revolution, 1763–1789.* Oxford History of the United States. London: Oxford University Press, 2005.

Mills, Charles W. *The Racial Contract.* Ithaca: Cornell University Press, 1997.

"Mills: The Strength of Early Industry." *Berkshire Eagle,* March 30, 2014. www.berkshireeagle .com.

The Modern Jazz Quartet and Orchestra. Atlantic 1359, 1960.

Monson, Ingrid. *Freedom Sounds: Civil Rights Call Out to Jazz and Africa.* London: Oxford University Press, 2007.

Murray, Albert. *Stomping the Blues.* 1976. Reprint, New York: Da Capo, 2000.

"Music Inn: They Come to Play." *Business Week,* September 19, 1953, 108–10.

Nettl, Bruno. "Richard Waterman (1914–1971): In Memoriam." *Anuario Interamericano de Investigacion Musical* 7 (1971): 125–27.

Niccoli, Ria A. "Stearns Conducts Jazz Panel Series." *DownBeat,* September 7, 1951, 18.

Noble, G. Kingsley. Letter to Marshall Stearns. September 10, 1950. Folder 22. Box 9. Marshall Stearns Papers. Institute of Jazz Studies, Newark, NJ.

Nonko, Emily. "Size Mattered: Upper East Side Mansions of the Gilded Age Retain Their Cachet." *Observer,* April 6, 2016. https://observer.com.

O'Meally, Robert G., ed. *The Jazz Cadence of American Culture.* New York: Columbia University Press, 1998.

———, ed. *Living with Music: Ralph Ellison's Jazz Writings.* New York: Modern Library, 2001.

O'Meally, Robert G., Brent Hayes Edwards, and Farah Jasmine Griffin, eds. *Uptown Conversations: The New Jazz Studies.* New York: Columbia University Press, 2004.

Orvell, Miles. *American Photography.* New York: Oxford University Press, 2003.

Owens, Carole. *The Berkshire Cottages, A Vanishing Era.* Englewood Cliffs, NJ: Cottage, 1984.

———. "Connections: Elizabeth Sedgwick's Lenox 'Culture Factory.'" *Berkshire Eagle,* December 1, 2015.

Perchard, Tom. "Mid-century Modern Jazz: Music and Design in the Postwar Home." *Popular Music* 36, no. 1 (2017): 55–74.

"Philip W. Barber, 78, a Writer, Dramatist and Teacher at Yale." *New York Times*, May 27, 1981, A22.

Pitt, David E. "Hans K. Maeder, Stockbridge Founder, Dies at 78." *New York Times*, September 11, 1988, sec. 1, p. 46.

Prouty, Ken. *Learning Jazz: Jazz Education, History, and Public Pedagogy.* Jackson: University Press of Mississippi, 2023.

Radano, Ronald. *New Musical Figurations: Anthony Braxton's Cultural Critique.* Chicago: University of Chicago Press, 1994.

Rae, Dorothy. "Blonde Converts Barn to Profit." Associated Press. July 22, 1955.

Rampersad, Arnold. *Ralph Ellison: A Biography.* New York: Knopf, 2007.

Ramsey, Guthrie P., Jr. *Who Hears Here? On Black Music, Pasts and Present.* Berkeley: University of California Press, 2022.

Ratliff, Ben. "A Pleasant Swim with the Man Who Named the Third Stream." *New York Times*, March 20, 2001, E1.

Reiff, Carole. *Nights in Birdland: Jazz Photographs, 1954–1960.* New York: Fireside, 1987.

"Report on the Fourth Jazz Roundtable at Music Inn, Lenox, Mass." *Second Line* 3, nos. 11–12 (November–December 1952): 3–4.

"Retrospective of Music Inn." Panel discussion moderated by Seth Rogovoy. October 14, 2006. Berkshire Museum, Pittsfield, MA.

Richards, Leonard L. *Shay's Rebellion: The American Revolution's Final Battle.* Philadelphia: University of Pennsylvania Press, 2002.

Riddle, Ron. "A Look Back at Lenox." *Jazz*, October 1958, 29–32.

Roberts, Sam. "Clemens Kalischer, 97, Refugee Photographer of Humanity." *New York Times*, June 15, 2018.

Rogovoy, Seth. "The Life and Times of Music Inn." *Berkshire Magazine* 14, no. 2 (Summer 1995): 32–41.

———. *Rogovoy Report* (blog). Accessed January 26, 2025. https://rogovoyreport.com.

———. "Tribute Recalls When Jazz Ruled at Music Inn." *Berkshire Eagle*, August 24, 1998, B1, B3.

Rothschild, Hannah. *The Baroness: The Search for Nica, the Rebellious Rothschild.* New York: Knopf, 2013.

Ross, Ronald. "The Role of Blacks in the Federal Theatre, 1935–1939." *Journal of Negro History* 39, no. 1 (January 1974): 38–50.

Rudy, Jill Terry. "Transforming Audiences for Oral Tradition: Child, Kittredge, Thompson, and Connections of Folklore and English Studies." *College English* 66, no. 5 (May 2004): 524–44.

Russonello, Giovanni. "Randy Weston, Pianist Who Traced Roots of Jazz to Africa, Dies at 92." *New York Times*, September 1, 2018.

Rustin-Paschal, Nichole. *The Kind of Man I Am: Jazzmasculinity and the World of Charles Mingus, Jr.* Middletown, CT: Wesleyan University Press, 2017.

Saussy, Tupper, and M. Arif Mardin. "The School of Jazz: Student Views." *Jazz Review*, January 1959, 17–19.

"The School of Jazz at Music Inn." *DownBeat*, October 3, 1957, 23–24.

Schrecker, Ellen. *The Age of McCarthyism: A Brief History with Documents*. New York: Palgrave, 2002.

Schuller, Gunther. *Early Jazz: Its Roots and Musical Development*. New York: Oxford University Press, 1968.

———. *A Life in Pursuit of Music and Beauty*. Rochester: University of Rochester Press, 2011.

———. *Musings: The Musical Worlds of Gunther Schuller*. New York: Oxford University Press, 1986.

———. *The Swing Era: The Development of Jazz, 1930–1945*. New York: Oxford University Press, 1989.

Schuller, Gunther, and Don Heckman. "Two Views on the School of Jazz." *Jazz Review*, November 1960.

"Series of Jazz Concerts Planned at Tanglewood." *Worcester (MA) Telegram*, April 28, 1955.

Shatz, Adam. "An Invitation from Jeanne Lee." *New York Review of Books*, June 11, 2020, 14–17.

Shoenberg, Shira. "In Pittsfield, General Electric Plant Closures Leave Bitter Memories." MassLive. January 19, 2016. www.masslive.com.

Skipper, John C. *Meredith Willson: The Unsinkable Music Man*. New York: Da Capo, 2000.

Small, Christopher. *Musicking: The Meanings of Performing and Listening*. Middletown, CT: Wesleyan University Press, 1998.

"Smart of Mind and Smart of Dress." *Berkshire Eagle*, August 13, 1955.

Smith, Wendy. "Macbeth in Harlem." In *The Harlem Reader: A Celebration of New York's Most Famous Neighborhood*, edited by Herb Boyd, 114–26. New York: Three Rivers, 2003.

The Smithsonian Collection of Classic Jazz. Compiled by Martin Williams. Washington, DC: Smithsonian Collection, 1972.

Soloman, Deborah. *American Mirror: The Life and Art of Norman Rockwell*. New York: Farrar, Straus and Giroux, 2013.

"Something of Max Roach." Berkshire Music Barn program. 1958. Philip and Stephanie Barber Music Inn Collection. Lenox Library, Lenox, MA.

Southern, Eileen. *The Music of Black Americans: A History*. New York: Norton, 1971.

Stearns, Marshall W. Columbia Lecture Bureau leaflet. 1955. Folder 25. Box 9. Marshall Stearns Papers. Institute of Jazz Studies, Newark, NJ.

———. "The Conquest of Jazz." *Saturday Review*, January 14, 1956, 24–27.

———. "Is Jazz Good Propaganda? The Dizzy Gillespie Tour." *Saturday Review,* July 14, 1956, 28–31.

———. "Jazz Was Born in New Orleans Around 1900." *DownBeat*, June 1936, 4.

———. "Jim Crow at College." *Tomorrow* 6, no. 6 (February 1947): 5–10.

———. "Reds Can't Comprehend Jazz, So Put It Down." *DownBeat*, March 23, 1951, 19.

———. "Roundtable on Jazz." *New York Times*, August 24, 1952.

———. *The Story of Jazz*. New York: Oxford University Press, 1956.

———. "Toward a Definition of Jazz." *Record Changer* 10, no. 3 (1951): 3–5, 12.

———. "The UHCA: Its Purpose, Progress to Date, Future Plans." *Tempo*, April 1936, 3.

Stearns, Marshall W., and Jean Stearns. *Jazz Dance: The Story of American Vernacular Dance*. New York: Macmillan, 1966.

Stowe, David. *Swing Changes: Big-Band Jazz in New Deal America*. Cambridge: Harvard University Press, 1994.

"Swinging over the Hills: Experts Discuss Rhythm Sections." *Jazz Today*, July 1957, 16–18.

Szatmary, David P. *Shay's Rebellion: The Making of an Agrarian Insurrection*. Amherst: University of Massachusetts Press, 1980.

Szwed, John. *Alan Lomax: The Man Who Recorded the World*. New York: Viking, 2010.

———. *Jazz 101: A Complete Guide to Learning and Loving Jazz*. New York: Hyperion, 2000.

———. "Really the (Typed Out) Blues: Jazz Fiction in Search of Dr. Faustus." *Village Voice*, July 2, 1979, 72.

"Tanglewood Gets Jazz Barn Almost Next to Symphony." *Boston Herald*, April 28, 1955.

Taubman, Howard. "Country Jazz." *New York Times*, August 7, 1955.

Taylor, Billy. *Jazz Piano: History and Development*. Dubuque, IA: Brown, 1982.

Taylor, Elizabeth Dowling. *The Original Black Elite: Daniel Murray and the Story of a Forgotten Era*. New York: Amistad/HarperCollins, 2018.

Teal, Kimberly Hannon. *Jazz Places: How Performance Spaces Shape Jazz History*. Oakland: University of California Press, 2021.

"Three Folk Music Concerts to Open in Lenox Saturday." *Berkshire Eagle*, June 28,1950.

Tucker, Sherrie. *Swing Shift: "All-Girl" Bands of the 1940s*. Durham: Duke University Press, 2000.

Tucker, Sherrie, and Nichole T. Rustin. *Big Ears: Listening for Gender in Jazz Studies*. Durham: Duke University Press, 2008.

Unger, Miles. "Invisible Man: The Photographs of Clemens Kalischer." In *Clemens Kalischer*, edited by Norbert Bunge and Denis Brudna, 6–12. Berlin: Cantz, 2002.

Veblen, Thorstein. *The Theory of the Leisure Class: An Economic Study of Institutions*. New York: Macmillan, 1899.

Von Eschen, Penny. *Race against Empire: Black Americans and Anticolonialism, 1937–1957*. Ithaca: Cornell University Press, 1997.

———. *Satchmo Blows Up the World: Jazz Ambassadors Play the Cold War*. Cambridge: Harvard University Press, 2004.

Waksman, Steve. *Live Music in America: A History from Jenny Lind to Beyoncé*. New York: Oxford University Press, 2022.

Waterman, Jill. "From Father to Son: Tracing the Roots of Clemens Kalischer's Humanist Vision." B and H. June 20, 2021. www.bhphotovideo.com.

Waterman, Richard. "Hot Rhythm in Negro Music." *Journal of the American Musicological Society* 1 (1948): 24–37.

"W. E. B. Du Bois Center." University of Massachusetts. Accessed January 12, 2024. http://duboiscenter.library.umass.edu.

Weston, Randy. *African Rhythms: The Autobiography of Randy Weston*. With Willard Jenkins. Durham: Duke University Press, 2010.

Williams, Martin. *Jazz Masters in Transition, 1957–1968*. New York: Da Capo, 1970.

———. *The Jazz Tradition*. New York: Oxford University Press, 1970.

———. "The School of Jazz and the Acquisition of Things Past." *Metronome*, February 1961, 23–24.

Williams, Raymond. *The Politics of Modernism: Against the New Conformists*. London: Verso, 1989.

Willis-Braithwaite, Deborah, and Roger C. Birt. *VanDerZee, Photographer, 1886–1983*. New York: Abrams, 1993.

Wilson, John S. "Jazz Workshop to Grow Next Year." *New York Times*, September 9, 1956.

———. Liner notes to *The Modern Jazz Quartet at Music Inn*. Atlantic 1247, 1956.

Wind, Barbara. "Jews in the Berkshires." *Jewish Link*. September 6, 2018. https://jewishlink.news.

Wineapple, Brenda. *Hawthorne: A Life*. New York: Knopf, 2003.

Wood, David H. *Lenox Massachusetts Shire Town*. Published by the Town, 1969.

"The WPA Federal Theatre Project, 1935–1939." Library of Congress. Accessed March 21, 2024. www.loc.gov.

Yudkin, Jeremy. *The Lenox School of Jazz: A Vital Chapter in the History of American Music and Race Relations*. South Egremont, MA: Farshaw, 2006.

ILLUSTRATION CREDITS

Page 124: Photograph by Warren Fowler. Courtesy of Scott Fowler.

Page 131: Photograph by Clemens Kalischer. Courtesy of the Estate of Clemens Kalischer.

Page 132: Photograph by Warren Fowler. Courtesy of Scott Fowler.

Page 137: Photograph by Carol Reiff. Courtesy of the Carole Reiff Photo Archive.

Page 141: Photograph by Clemens Kalischer. Courtesy of the Estate of Clemens Kalischer.

Page 143: Photographer unknown. Reproduced in *Music Inn: A Documentary Film*, dir. Ben Barenholtz (2007). Courtesy of the Institute of Jazz Studies.

Page 144: Photograph by Clemens Kalischer. Courtesy of the Estate of Clemens Kalischer.

Page 147: Photograph by Clemens Kalischer. Courtesy of the Estate of Clemens Kalischer.

Page 149: Photograph by Clemens Kalischer. Courtesy of the Estate of Clemens Kalischer.

Page 150: Photograph by Clemens Kalischer. Courtesy of the Estate of Clemens Kalischer.

Page 156: Photograph by Warren Fowler. Courtesy of Scott Fowler.

Page 160: Photograph by Clemens Kalischer. Courtesy of the Estate of Clemens Kalischer.

Page 163: Photograph by Clemens Kalischer. Courtesy of the Estate of Clemens Kalischer.

Page 171: Photograph by Clemens Kalischer. Courtesy of the Estate of Clemens Kalischer.

Page 173: Courtesy of the Estate of Stephanie Barber.

Page 177: Photograph by Warren Fowler. Courtesy of Scott Fowler.

Page 179: Photograph by Clemens Kalischer. Courtesy of the Estate of Clemens Kalischer.

Page 182: Photograph by Clemens Kalischer. Courtesy of the Estate of Clemens Kalischer.

Page 186: Photograph by Clemens Kalischer. Courtesy of the Estate of Clemens Kalischer.

Page 188: Photograph by Clemens Kalischer. Courtesy of the Estate of Clemens Kalischer.

Page 191: Photograph by Clemens Kalischer. Courtesy of the Estate of Clemens Kalischer.

Page 192: Photograph by Clemens Kalischer. Courtesy of the Estate of Clemens Kalischer.

Page 197: Photograph by Clemens Kalischer. Courtesy of the Estate of Clemens Kalischer.

Page 201: Photograph by Clemens Kalischer. Courtesy of the Estate of Clemens Kalischer.

Page 204: Photograph by Clemens Kalischer. Courtesy of the Estate of Clemens Kalischer.

Page 206: Photograph by Clemens Kalischer. Courtesy of the Estate of Clemens Kalischer.

Page 208: Photograph by Clemens Kalischer. Courtesy of the Estate of Clemens Kalischer.

Page 211: Photograph by Clemens Kalischer. Courtesy of the Estate of Clemens Kalischer.

Page 217: Photograph by Clemens Kalischer Courtesy of the Estate of Clemens Kalischer.

Page 221: Photograph by Clemens Kalischer. Courtesy of the Estate of Clemens Kalischer.

Page 226: Photograph by Clemens Kalischer. Courtesy of the Estate of Clemens Kalischer.

Page 228: Photograph by Clemens Kalischer. Courtesy of the Estate of Clemens Kalischer.

INDEX

Page entries in *italics* refer to photographs.